GEORGENE SUMMERS

MAYHEM, MONEY, AND MURDER
TRUE STORY

Copyright 2022 by Georgene Summers

Library of Congress

ISBN:

All rights reserved. This book or parts thereof may not be reproduced in any form without the written permission of the author, except for the inclusion of brief quotations in a review.

CONTENTS

Paradise and Purgatory 5
Purgatory 101 11
Descent into Hell 17
A Conspiracy of Angels 25
The Big Lie 35
Where Angels Fear to Tread 49
The Poison Apple 63
Prisoner of Darkness 67
Promises and Piecrusts 75
Broken Promises 87
Moonlight and Madness 97
Diamonds and Drugs 127
The Pain of Silence 143
Midnight and Fantasies 151
Queen of the Night 165
Another Day, Another Cliff! 193
Don't Stop the Music 213
A Solitary Journey into Myself 219
THE SOLITARY JOURNEY 225
The Reinvention of Captain Marvel 313
Captain Marvel Strikes Again 329
From Out of the Ashes 337

PARADISE AND PURGATORY

Who am I? I am the antithesis of who I thought my mother *was*. A warrior, adventurer, risk-taker, lover of life, a fearless being jumping off cliffs without a net. I am what so many others dream to be. My life has been a series of wild, sometimes reckless, exciting trips into the unknown. An adventurer who knows no boundaries and doesn't take *no* for an answer. I am someone who believes I can do it, even if I never tried before, and above all, I say yes to all challenges. I have been bullied, applauded, hated, loved, lusted after, befriended, and lonely. I have been teased, made fun of, called names, and driven to tears. I have dealt up close and personal with some very dark and dangerous people during my nightclub days in Manhattan and have lived to talk about it. I was drawn headfirst into a heinous act of murder and mayhem, with my only son right in the middle of it, on trial for his life, and yet I have come out on top. Whether I was staring down a lion that was on the hood of my car in the Ngorongoro Crater in Tanzania, mingling with celebrities like Andy Warhol and Grace Jones at my nightclub in Manhattan, crashing a wedding in Thailand, sitting on a cow dung bench in a Maasai hut in a boma in Kenya, dancing on a tabletop in Mykonos, climbing to the top of Victoria Falls, or riding on the back of a bull elephant in Zambia, I have lived. So, get ready for the ride of your life, and enjoy a part of my life in the fast lane with some of my fascinating and dangerous cohorts.

✦ ✦ ✦

I certainly wouldn't characterize the object of that particular night's sexual adventure as dangerous or even fascinating, but there I was anyway, naked in an unfamiliar bed staring up at the ceiling as if I thought it would suddenly come alive. I continued to stare at the pointed white bits of stucco that appeared to be dripping down and wondered what I was doing here with this strange man.

We had met the night before at a bar in Beverly Hills. I suppose it was a testament to my newfound boldness and the idea that, at last, I could throw any inhibitions out the window and do whatever the hell I wanted to do. There were no judgments to be had any longer. The Devil himself or herself could be damned. I was free, and I was over twenty-one, no strings, no stress theoretically, and no struggles, or so I thought.

His name was Ron something or other, and he was tall, skinny, and not particularly good-looking. But he had been attentive to me over a couple of cosmopolitans, using terms like we and us when describing our future together, and at that moment, his utterances filled a void I didn't even realize was there. The sex was rote, almost mechanical, not much better than if I had utilized Edward Scissorhands, my dildo-shaped vibrator with the rabbit ears, and almost as indifferent. The only difference was that Mr. Scissorhands always made me climax, reducing me to a screaming mass, while rote Ron failed miserably at the task.

Conversation with Ron was not unlike communication I had many times over with E. Scissorhands. His responses were inaudible, and his emotions lacked feeling. Battery-operated sex toys are also like that. Having spent many a night in the company of one or two of them, I was well acquainted with their method of operation, their failures and successes, and always made sure to have enough batteries on hand.

While their communication skills usually left a lot to be desired, from the standpoint of making me climax and scream loud enough to break the sound barrier, they never failed. With Ron, however, I was reduced to fantasizing to achieve what appeared to be an orgasm, which Edward Scissorhands always accomplished much easier, faster, and without any need for fantasies.

There was something sincere and honest about Edward that I failed to see in Ron. He was of course a human given to fumbling with the buttons on his shirt and my dress. At least Edward didn't fumble; he simply put his latex covering on my clit and brought me to tears of delight, whereas the human being was far too constrained to put his tongue on my throbbing pussy. I remained wet and hungry for satisfaction until the morning, when I interrogated my sanity and my decisions, and went home to Edward.

It wasn't often that I found myself naked in bed with a stranger. Although, over the past few months, I had decided to take a slightly more male viewpoint of sex and give myself permission to have sex just for sex's sake. I wanted to have someone slide their dick deep inside of me and make me come without feeling that I needed to be in a lifelong, committed relationship.

That night with Ron was to be remembered forever, not for one of great passion or incredible love, but rather the night that I lost my head for what I thought was the last time, and for my grandmother. At that moment, I truly thought it would be the last time I would lose my head. It wasn't, but my foolishness would serve to punish me all my remaining days. Some months earlier I decided that I no longer wanted to be enamored with my sexual partners but rather would just walk away when it was over in my mind. It was, to say the least, freeing, or so I thought.

I had failed at lasting emotional attachments since my divorce and felt pretty good about the entire arm's-length experience. That was until Ron and the demise of my only known grandmother.

Of course, I never told my parents where I had been or what I had been up to. What else was I to do? *In truth, I had been fornicating with a stranger while my father was frantically trying to locate me, using every method but GPS, which fortunately for me wasn't around then.*

My grandmother was dying, and I was having sex with a stranger that I had met the night before. The guilt I would suffer from that one foolish error in judgment haunted me for decades.

My sexual escapades, coupled with a newfound freedom to sleep with whoever, whenever I wanted, came to a crescendo during a trip to Europe in the mid-1980s. I had just escaped from my second marriage and thought I had found the fountain of youth.

I felt younger than springtime and looked better than I had at seventeen when I was in high school in Los Angeles. I was determined to take advantage of the occasion of my youth. So, I planned a monthlong holiday in Europe, going from London to Paris, to the South of France, Italy, and then home. It spelled A for adventure B for badass and T for trouble!

My first stop was London, where I met an attractive Israeli over a very pink cosmo at some bar, and after some small talk and a connection of sorts, we ended up at my hotel having my rendition of wild, unbridled sex. I wish I had taken a picture of the look on his face when I summarily said good night and don't let the door hit you in the ass on the way out. It was priceless! It was also my first step into what turned out to be unworkable, at least for me, but one of my life's most important lessons.

The truth was, like it or not, I needed the emotional connection. I couldn't just have anonymous, emotionless sex. I did, however, complete my trip to France and Italy and had a few memorable liaisons in both countries, including one with a very hot American photographer who was living in Paris.

I met Robert at Les Deux Magots, a popular brasserie in the heart of the city. I was seated outside alone, people watching along the Boulevard Saint-Germain, and sipping a somewhat potent cocktail when I noticed a gorgeous man staring at me.

It didn't take long before he was seated next to me, and together we people watched and chatted as if we were old friends. It turned out he was an American in Paris. Imagine, traveling all that way only to meet an American at the most famous bistro in Paris.

But he was hotter than hot, so I overlooked that fact. He was tall, dark haired, with smoldering blue eyes and movie star good looks. Just my kind of guy. We made a date to meet later that night at his apartment. I was traveling alone, but my good senses kicked in before leaving the hotel to meet him, and I recorded all his details on a small tape recorder that I brought with me. Name, rank, and serial number, for sure, along with his address and a description.

Upon arriving at his apartment, I told him that I was traveling with several other friends and that they expected me to return to the hotel at a particular hour. I suppose this was my "go-to" safeguard just in case Robert happened to be more than just a pretty face or more than what I had bargained for.

We ended up, as one might have imagined, not going to dinner or a movie, but wrapped in each other's arms half naked, in a lip lock on the living room floor. That was followed by a long round of hot and steamy sex, conducted without the use of either a sex toy or any wild fantasies. He stroked my leg and slid his tongue around my ear and kissed my lips passionately. His dick was hard, fully engorged, and he slipped inside of my wet pussy with ease. We moved together breathing heavily until he shot his cum into my pussy and collapsed on the floor beside me. Dripping with hot cum, I made my way into the bathroom nearly legless from our encounter.

For the next several hours we lay naked on the floor wrapped in each other's arms until I released myself, got dressed, and left. I never saw Robert again, and while the sex was great, the evening wore me out.

PURGATORY 101

I met my first husband at the funeral of a fourteen-year-old classmate.

In hindsight, that should have been a major cause for alarm, but I was too young to heed traffic signs, red lights, or the warning of impending hazards, all of which were being sounded loud and clear.

For purposes of this "truth exercise," and to avoid giving him any notoriety, I will call him "Vincent." He was tall and awkward, and his hair stood straight up on the top of his head, like un-mowed grass. It was like a Chia Pet's hair, and I loved it. But then I was sixteen and had long since given up the Chia in favor of my pet cat.

Vincent was not yet fifteen years old. He had one brother and a domineering and possessive mother, which should have also been cause for alarm. I was neither alarmed nor deterred, as we oozed words of love and lust, betraying our backgrounds and our values, and hurtling headlong into a fumbling teenage affair. It was the first time for me having sex that dark and rainy night on the wet grassy mound in Griffith Park.

I was so naïve that I had no idea I had experienced an orgasm while making love in a park. It just felt like I was falling out of a building. I really hadn't known what that feeling was that night. Here I was having my first sexual experience ever, my first climax, without the aid of any fantasy, real or imagined, and didn't even know it.

There was no vibrator, no Edward Scissorhands, no third person, just two young, stupid teenagers having sex in the rain at 10:30 at night. It was so dark that you couldn't see your hand in front of your face, not that we were looking. Other than the sounds of our heavy breathing, the silence was deafening.

I can't remember ever having repeated that particular event, although as I recall, wild sex on burning hot sand with Ira, my second husband, did play a part one year.

But that night, I remember cold, wet grass blades sliding between my moist legs while Vincent's hot lips moved from my breasts to my thighs, stopping everywhere in between. My clothing was nowhere to be seen, at least at that moment. We were still half naked and breathing heavily when the police car drove up onto the lawn and took us into custody. It was the '50s and this was a curfew violation.

For this infraction, we were to be parted like Romeo and Juliet, and punished with eight hours of jailtime in the Hollywood precinct quarters. Our love letters were confiscated, and we were reduced to the status of teenage criminals, rather than lovestruck adults, ready to marry.

Our parents celebrated our incarceration, leaving us to rot in a hell called jail for the entire eight hours, only surfacing at the very last moment to pick us up. It goes without saying that the verbal abuse that followed was almost harsher than the eight hours we spent in our separate jail cells.

Little did I know then, but the very first sexual experience I had rendered me pregnant, at the age of seventeen. Once I had reached the age of realization, I knew that my parents' obsession with keeping us apart only served to drive us together. Rebellion was the operative word at that time for both of us. Lacking that interference, the "Chia" and I would have been over for good long before. The truth was that I never "really" loved him, and it was always just that thing called "puppy love."

The entire experience taught me a great lesson. In the years that followed, I never stopped my son from seeing anyone he chose. I would support his often insane notions of marriage at fifteen and ask with a hint of sarcasm, "When is the wedding? Just tell me what to wear and I will be there."

No weddings took place, at least not while he was still in his teens, and when one theoretically did, someplace in Florida, he was long past those years, and I didn't care one way or the other if he married or not.

The truth was, I hoped it might calm him down and take him from being a hopeless playboy to a captivating but settled young man. Not only didn't that happen, but on top of everything else, he remained angry and never forgave me for divorcing his father. I was a headstrong, obstinate teenager, determined to keep control of my body, something I had failed to do on that grassy mound. Right, wrong, or indifferent, Vincent and I had conceived that night and, once discovered, my parents immediately made the decision to terminate the ill-fated pregnancy and our illicit affair.

The 1950s was a time of innocence and rock 'n' roll, where if grass was something you smoked, you were a criminal or one of those outcasts your mother warned you to stay away from. Bill Haley belted out "Rock Around the Clock," the "Pachuko Hop" was cool, and we danced like fools to the beat of Frankie Lymon and the Teenagers, flipping our white hankies back and forth to the beat. Black music was making its mark, and songs like "Work With Me Annie" and "Annie Had a Baby" were banned, while more mainstream black music like "Earth Angel," "Only You," and "Smoke Gets in Your Eyes" topped the charts.

Marijuana was the sin of criminals; girls wore skirts with felt poodles emblazoned on them; and in grade school, I was left out of a secret club organized by several eight-year-old classmates called "Eight Box Butterfly," which spelled SEX when it was finally deciphered. I was constantly taunted with the boxy symbol and spent hours trying every possible code and letter combination to figure it out.

I attended Le Conte Junior High School, where the highlight of my day was walking endlessly around the main school buildings in the same direction with a group of girls, all wearing white bunny shoes. No one who was really "cool" ever wore black-and-white oxfords because they were too square.

Every morning after leaving the house and rounding the corner for school, I plastered on the lipstick, the darker the better, but still thought kissing was a sexual crime. That was until my classmate Norman pinned me against the hall lockers and planted a hot, wet kiss on my virgin lips. Early on in high school, we grew up quickly, after one of the girls ended up pregnant and the disclosure shocked us out of our proverbial knickers. I grew up even quicker once I found out that I was facing the same fate. After our night on the grassy mound, I kept Vincent a secret from everyone, even using the services of his friend to go with me to my high school prom.

A few months after the infamous grassy mound incident, I came down with the flu, or so I thought, but that notion evaporated after a week of vomiting. My mother, who clearly had baby-dar installed, knew almost at once that I was pregnant. Along with that newfound suspicion came a series of long and pain-filled walks, boiling hot mustard baths, and some four-letter words I had never heard her say before. Her last resort, a roller-coaster ride, twice, on the pier in Santa Monica.

Unfortunately, this kid was in for the count and so Mommy Dearest went on the road less traveled, scouring the neighborhood pharmacies for someone who would refer her to a certain type of doctor to resolve the situation.

"There is no way on earth we are going to allow this pregnancy to go on," she bellowed. "What will our neighbors think?" *Back then, that was a very important concept.*

"But, Mom, we love each other, and we want to get married," I wailed, really believing it at that moment in time. I was seventeen, wide-eyed, and filled with optimism. Even now I am amazed that I really believed that crock of crap.

Today, ensconced in the best quadrant of my life, I would rather be boiled in oil and stranded alone on a desert island in the hot summer sun than spend one hour with the Chia creature, who, at one time, I so desperately wanted to marry.

My intended, Vincent, whose claim to fame at that time of his life was that he looked great in an oversized red letterman jacket, had no job or any prospects for one, even if it was bagging groceries at the local market. But in true teenage style, he declared with wide-eyed innocence, "I will get a job and take care of her. I love her, and we are going to get married."

It made little difference that both sets of parents were dead set against any union that joined Vincent and me, or my parents and his mother in any "unholy" alliance.

In short order, after exhausting all the neighborhood pharmacies, a doctor who would handle the "situation" with a semblance of skill was unearthed. Mother got his name from a local pharmacy on Sunset Boulevard. My parents, who claimed to love me more than life, had now made the choice to put my life in the hands of a medically unsound doctor, who had lost his license for the "murder" of a girl during a botched abortion.

It was "fait accompli," so to speak. This was an act of vile deception so great as to remain in my conscious mind for the better part of four decades. I was a lamb being led to the slaughter, an innocent being fed to the lions, a child being taken into the proverbial den of iniquity to be punished for the crime of sex. I thought for a moment we were in the Dark Ages.

Clearly, the idea of a besmirched reputation, of neighbors wondering where that little, screeching baby came from, was more important than the life of their only child.

DESCENT INTO HELL

I never knew this Butcher's name, only the killing field location. His derelict house stood next to a vacant lot on Commonwealth Avenue near Sixth Street in Los Angeles. Later in my life, I understood the need for a location like this. Suddenly, this dilapidated house became my reality. My parents had summarily dropped me off into this house of horrors, perhaps never to see the light of day again. Or so I thought!

The wood-shingled two-story abode appeared quite run-down on the outside, and it turned out it was not much better on the inside. The shingles were peeling from too much sun and not enough attention, and it bore the scars of too many years of neglect, too many owners, and a basic lack of money. Perhaps it was just the Butcher's way of staying totally under the radar of an entire community in disrepair. Inside this aging eyesore were the same signs translated into the furniture and the draperies that hung by wisps in every room, as if to cover the ravages of time from any prying eyes. It barely did the job. Several ancient couches sat in solitary splendor in what passed as a living room. The arms were frayed and had seen better days, but that was decades before. The throw rugs covered a multitude of sins that had been committed on the wooden planks underneath, and one could only imagine their condition.

I tried to think what this place must have looked like in its heyday. The gleaming floors of teak or mahogany, the beautiful velvet draperies skimming the floor with their elegant tiebacks, the winding staircase leading to what must have at one time been beautiful bedroom suites.

The aroma of cinnamon and pine crept into my thoughts. I could almost smell it and kept it at the forefront of my mind. Walking through my new prison, my nostrils stung at the smell of alcohol and my lips tasted the dampness from the dank room with its stirrup-like device that held the secrets of an abortion doctor. I kept repeating the words *cinnamon and pine, cinnamon and pine*, until the scent almost became real.

I kept focusing on my own private little world of fine smells, allowing them to creep into the reality of my desperation.

I was now half naked and duly imprisoned on this metal apparatus, with no one around but the Butcher. I held tightly onto the heart-shaped amethyst that hung around my neck. It was a gift from Vincent and the one thing that was going to bring me back from the hell I had been banished to, or so I thought. No one was there to rescue me. I could call out all that I wanted and the only voice that would answer me back was my own. He stuck a towel into my mouth.

"Bite down on this and don't scream, the neighbors will hear you," the Butcher demanded.

I obeyed, bit down on the towel, held the small amethyst heart tightly, and screamed as if I were being murdered anyway. In truth, what was murdered that day was my innocence.

That night, alone in the darkened room, as I lay sobbing, a young girl came and sat beside me. She was the Butcher's niece. Her stomach extended beyond her toes. Her name was Anna, and she was going to have her baby at some Catholic home somewhere in Los Angeles named Saint Anne's.

She leaned in and whispered hesitantly, "I would never let him touch me."

I was silent in my shock. *How could this be happening? How could they do this to me? They gave me to a murderer! They must hate me!* I made my way into the bathroom and threw up.

Her lack of confidence in the Butcher, the man who was her uncle, made me wonder why my parents didn't love me. *How could they have thrown me into this den of disgust? How could they have risked my life?* I snuck down the long and darkened hallway, past the aroma of death and alcohol, to the telephone. A long string protruded from in between my legs.

A black rotary dial phone with a heavy lead-like receiver sat perched on a table in a tiny alcove. I lifted the receiver and dialed. The clicks of each number shattered the silence of the empty hallway. The dial clicked slowly as I called home, Hollywood 6-2-3-1. The rings shattered my eardrums, and each one seemed to last a lifetime as I crouched in the shadows.

A laugh echoed from down the hallway and broke my concentration. I felt like a cornered animal as I cowered on the dirty floor. The rug was old and tattered. It had a faraway feel to it, like something from the Far East or maybe even from Persia.

Yes, that was it, I thought, the rug must be from Persia. I had seen stores with rugs just like it in the downtown area of Los Angeles. I suddenly felt a bit more relaxed, peaceful for that moment in time, as the ringing of the phone continued. Once the rug had been beautiful, a blend of rich blues and pinks. A splash of red in the middle and the edges all done in cream. It had a picture in the center, but in the dark, I could barely make it out. It looked like a woman dancing. *I thought how wonderful it would be if I could be out dancing somewhere right now.*

Instead, I was in a dark hallway that reeked of alcohol and dampness, wearing a hospital-type open-back gown that told a tale of shame and near madness. *My parents must have been mad to do this. The incessant ringing! Oh my God, what if they aren't home, what will I do? I thought of death and Vincent as I began to hyperventilate. I thought of my baby and my life. Was I in a dream? Where was I anyway? OMG, I want to go home.*

At last, someone picked up the phone and I heard my mother: "Hello," she said in a questioning tone.

"Mother, mother," I whispered, fearful of the noise in the hallway and the laughter that broke the sound of my own heart pounding. "Mother, mother, it's me. Please come and get me. He is going to kill me, I know. I want to come home." I cried silently, but desperately.

"No, we are not coming to get you until this is over," she chimed back in an unwavering voice.

"Mother, please . . . mother . . ." She hung up the phone.

The silence was deafening as a dial tone buzzed in my ears. My plaintive wails turned me inside out. My mouth seemed to be open but no sound came from inside, as I struggled to keep my own death rattle quiet.

I was surely going to die this very night, and no one cared, not even my mother. I had been right about her all along. She was indeed a heartless person, punishing me still for the loss of my sister. I would never forgive her.

That was until I grew older and wiser, and realized that they both did me a great service. I can't imagine what my life would have been at twenty with two kids in diapers, and no husband to lean on or count on for anything. Vincent turned out to care more about playing pool with his friends than he ever did about me or being a father.

The Persian rug closed in around me as I wrapped myself in a corner of it for safety. It seemed like days went by, with me in my Persian cocoon. With each breath, I could smell its history. My nostrils were weeping from the pain of the carpet. Beaten within an inch of its life, it had seen so much sadness, so much pain and agony. People coming and going, its fibers reeked medicinally, and the stench of rubbing alcohol made my eyes water. It smelled old, like my grandmother's closet. It was as if this carpet had seen a hundred years of life and death. I could almost hear the cries of babies lost forever into the stillness of the night, where only the eyes of a few could tell the tales.

A stream of light woke me from my seemingly catatonic state. Startled and confused, I made my way back to the room where I was to sleep that night. I had lost all concept of time and space and only wanted to rid myself of the smells of mothballs, alcohol, and death that surrounded me. I was seventeen! *Why did I need to be witness to all of this? What crime had I committed that I was to be punished to near-death?* I fell into the soft mattress and wept for what seemed like months. A sharp pain woke me.

This time I staggered in a half sleep to the small hospital-like bathroom that joined the tiny room that housed me. It was stark and covered with old, broken porcelain tiles that belied years of visits from girls just like me. I looked for some signs of life and saw none. The pain brought me back. It was sharp, like a knife through my insides. It was so intense it frightened me. I sat down and stared at my stomach and the blonde hairs that covered my clit.

How could I have done something so wrong that required a punishment such as this? What have I done except to fall in love? Is that a crime punishable by death? I love Vincent. He is my man, the person that I want to spend the rest of my life with. What did I do that was so very wrong, I wondered.

Then I saw it, the long white string that was dripping between my legs. *What is that,* I wondered. *What should I do?* My seventeen-year-old mind was darting from one thought to another.

Night covered the window like a blanket of ink, and there were no stars lighting the sky. *I am dying right here, right now, and no one, not a soul except the Butcher's niece cared one single bit about me. I had gone to hell alone for love.* I tugged on the white string. Nothing happened, so I tugged on it again, harder. I pulled and pulled this white string to nowhere, ignorant of the consequences of my actions.

It lay there in the toilet beneath me, this thing, this apparatus that had just been pulled from deep inside of me. *What the hell is this, and what had I done? Oh my God, please don't tell me that I am going to have all that pain again. Please, God, don't let him do that to me again.*

I remembered the moment, a day earlier, when I had felt what seemed like a tongue and lips on my pussy, but no, how could that be? I was lying flat on the Butcher's instrument of torture with a towel in my mouth to keep me quiet.

The tongue was warm, and the lips were hot as they probed the outside of my clitoris and the moist, warm skin that surrounded it. I felt nothing but disgust and wished it would be over. Please make it stop. What was he doing to me? He was giving me head. The Butcher was giving me head. I lost myself in guilt and anxiety but held tightly onto the heart that gave me life. I was dying! The Baby Killer had his tongue in my pussy, as a prelude to an abortion that

I didn't want. Oh my God, help me, someone please help me. I am going to die on his table.

Death must have been too good for me, too easy, as there I was, staring into the toilet bowl at this large rubber bulb, tube, and string, all of which had been inside of me. *That must have been why I was having the pains. I can't let him do that to me again. Oh no, please no more.*

The cold tile floor became my bed for a time while I tried to understand what had just happened to me. I dragged myself back to bed and lay there comatose until the sun peeked into the bathroom window and startled me back to my surroundings.

It was only weeks later that I learned a girl had died on the Butcher's table the day after my third visit to him.

Home was never the same after that day and night. I harbored such resentment, such unbridled anger that I couldn't forgive and I couldn't forget. I was forced to return to the Butcher's lair on two more occasions. The first, because I nearly bled to death after the procedure that left me without our baby.

The second, the bleeding stopped totally, and I needed to go back to the Butcher for treatment. I remember that day as if it were yesterday. This time my parents enlisted the aid of Vincent, asking him to come to the house as backup.

Fear gripped me, and I locked myself in the bathroom and refused to open the door. Fear and terror were the only friends I had at that moment. My father tried climbing through the small bathroom window to "rescue" me. It was at that moment that I picked up a cobalt blue glass jar of bath salts that was sitting on the counter and heaved it through the windowpanes, narrowly missing him. That was when they reluctantly called in their version of the "troops"—Vincent. They were smart enough to know he was the only one who could talk me out of there with promises that never materialized.

"Your parents said we can get married if you just go back to the doctor."

He stood outside the locked bathroom door pleading with me. I finally opened the door and fell into his arms, only to be swept away by my parents to the Butcher and the house of horrors on Commonwealth Avenue. Death would have been better than the lies.

It was only later that I discovered the Butcher of Commonwealth Avenue killed a girl the very next day. That could have been me. The coroner's office could have been called to the house of horrors to take me away in a black body bag and dump me off on a cold metal slab for an autopsy. The coroner would have slit me open as I lay naked on that stainless-steel table, eyes wide open to the ceiling. A vacant stare into the world I had left because of my crimes.

I would have been unresponsive, motionless, dead. *"She was only seventeen years old. She had her whole life in front of her, and now look at her,"* they would have said. My parents would have cried hysterically.

My mother would have been inconsolable. *"She was my baby, my light, my life, my only daughter. Take me instead,"* she would have sobbed, as she fell to the cold tile floors at the morgue. *"What could have happened to this poor young girl,"* the coroner would wail. *"She was so young,"* he would say as he proceeded to determine the cause of my untimely death.

It serves them right. It's no less than what they deserve. They killed me. My mother and my father killed me. Listen to me, you guys up there cutting me open. No need to do that, I will tell you everything. Go now and arrest them. Arrest them for premeditated murder, two counts. They killed me, their only beloved daughter. Count two, the murder of their unborn grandchild. Go on now, don't waste any more time slitting me open, just arrest them and make them pay for what they did. Oh, and while you're at it, please tell Vincent that I love him, and say a prayer for my little baby.

Of course, it didn't happen that way at all. I woke out of my tormented sleep to the sounds of the street. Cars racing past, motorcycles on one wheel, dogs barking, chatter. All around me, incessant meaningless chatter. I couldn't shake it from my mind. *Where was I, and what was happening around me?*

I opened my eyes and saw the ceiling bearing down on me. My hands reached out but there was nothing but air around them. My breathing got heavier. The room was sparse and unfamiliar.

I kept hearing voices chattering from every side. Then a single voice, a low monotone saying, "You're fine now. There is nothing to worry about. You will be bleeding for the next day or two, no longer than that, and then you will be just fine and dandy."

Suddenly, I realized where I was, in Purgatory. I was in Hell! I was on the Butcher's Block lying face up on the cold metal table he used to torture and maim. I had been on that cold wet table twice before. Just like a dead person, placed into a cabinet at the morgue. Confused and startled, I sat up, suddenly throwing the towel on the floor beside me.

"What the hell are you doing to me?" I screamed.

"Nothing, nothing at all," he whispered.

Why did you have your tongue on my pussy two weeks ago? Was I all right then? What were you looking for? Why did you do that? Do my parents know what you did to me? You molested me, you perverted Butcher.

I was dazed from the pills I took to relax me before going to Commonwealth, but then no one could blame me for being upset and anxious. I had nearly killed my father with the blue glass bath salts bottle that I heaved through the bathroom window that morning.

I think I am going mad. I am losing my mind. Where am I, and what the hell is happening to me? Is this Kansas, or am I home yet? Where in the hell is Toto? I am going insane for sure. I am barely seventeen years old, and I am going insane. Someone, please rescue me, please. And while you're at it, tell Vincent I love him. In my young mind, I vowed that I would never love my parents again, for the sin they had committed. Later in life, I thanked them for their foresight, and for the fact that they had saved me from being a single mother twice . . . but again it was too late. By that time, they were gone.

My relationship with Vincent was born out of death but continued to flourish in the back alleys of Beverly Hills and secret corridors of Hollywood High School, until I reached the age of eighteen and found myself knocked up once again. I alternated between laughter and tears at the prospect.

A CONSPIRACY OF ANGELS

It's impossible to imagine what might have become of me had I been born to normal parents. Perhaps if my mother had proceeded with her New York stage career instead of marrying my dad, things would have been different, better. Maybe she should have wed Babul, the perfume magnate who plied her with kisses all over her arms or the bloke whose family owned a bank in Canada and sent a railroad car for her. At least he had his own railroad car. Even if she had remained divorced from my father instead of running back the first time he wagged his finger in her direction and decided he wanted to have kids after all.

The final scenario was unworkable, even in theory, as I would never have existed, at least not in their lives. Sometimes I wonder what it would have been like to be the child of wealthy parents. Or better yet, wealthy and normal, but that was not to be. How often I wished that the next time around I would be "to the manor born." But I'm still here and have yet to see whether I will return with a platinum spoon engraved with the name Gates hanging from my lips, as a plant in someone's rose garden, or worse, as the child of a cross-country truck driver with a wife named Mildred. I choose the talc-powdered bottom, engraved platinum utensils, and life as the child of really rich parents. They don't even have to be normal.

Not that I lived a life of deprivation, though at times, my world seemed to be like a prison with my mother as guard and warden. The walls of my domain only as far as she could see or hear me.

My mother wasn't a bad woman, just needy, and required a total life commitment from me in return for her decision to have given birth. Obviously, I had no say in that event, but her personal covenant to abandon all for the sake of having a child weighed heavily on my life.

Fortunately for me, I never knew of this "pledge" until later in life, and so I just grew up thinking my mother was narcissistic, possessive, obsessive, and just a plain bitch. My father, on the other hand, was a compelling victim. The abused husband who quietly endured endless high-pitched bantering from my mother and greeted my pleas that he leave her with words of love.

"Your mother loves you," he would say. "She's doing the very best that she can. She doesn't mean it. Go on, go tell her you love her."

It was hard to correlate those words with the welts on my legs caused by the yardstick she had just splintered on me, but off I would go to wrap my arms around her from behind and pretend everything was okay. It was never okay until my father had been dead for a decade.

My father, Norman, cut a dapper figure. At six foot one, 175 pounds, he was well-built and towered over me like a building. He reminded me of Howard Roark from *The Fountainhead*. His hair was bright red and his complexion pale and covered with freckles. He was so pale that he once got third-degree burns after falling asleep on the beach in the hot Miami sun.

As a result, he was forced to sleep on his knees and elbows for a week and never returned to the beach. My mother, the sun worshipper, loved the beach, where after only a few moments, she turned an extremely dark shade of brown. On the other hand, she hated what she termed the "whining and caterwauling" of my father's beloved operatic music. They were, in a way, like chalk and cheese.

As a child, I was doomed to have the same dots as my dad, enduring the calls of freckleface and redheaded gingerbread from my classmates. I wanted to scrape the freckles off or bleach them out. Neither worked, so I just tried to burn them away, several times, with the aid of a toxic suntan machine.

My father grew up in New York, one of two boys born to Victor and Rebecca Kenner. In what I suppose would be classified as a "normal" childhood, my father bloomed. He was intelligent, educated, witty, and a lover of the arts.

My father was an intellectual who fancied himself a playwright. His creative side washed over into my life, long before I even knew it existed. He also was an avid listener of opera, no doubt because of his intellectual side, and the fact that there were no televisions in people's homes in the 1930s. He could also count himself a dedicated, caring son and brother.

My father and his younger brother could not have been more different. Uncle George was a wild party animal who enjoyed all the hedonistic pleasures reserved for any single guy in the 1920s. He boozed, he smoked, he caroused. He drove a Ford convertible, and I'm told he was often seen driving with his hair billowing in the open air, a woman under one arm, one hand on the wheel, stopping only to take a swig of booze. Into the night they would drive, reckless, irresponsible, careless, and young. He was a wild, unrepressed soul with a wickedly good sense of humor. He died at the age of twenty-three in a tragic automobile accident.

I was named after my uncle George. My parents just added the "ne" onto his name once they found out I was a girl. Uncle George was the polar opposite of my father, who remained staid and conservative his entire life. My dad was brilliant and the thinker in the family. George was more outgoing and, for all intents and purposes, a bit of a madcap. He regularly squired my mother around to speakeasies and bars, events, and just plain crazy nights. That mother, the "speakeasy" one, the Broadway star, was a far cry from the one I spent a good part of my life with and never really knew.

Back then, before I was even a thought, life was ordinary and it was good, at least that is what I've been told. Every Friday night my grandmother on my father's side made Shabbat dinner, and my father sat at the table with his parents and brother George, but without my mother.

For thirteen years after they married, my father ate Shabbat dinner with his family and my mother stayed at home alone. The reason seems archaic today and downright ludicrous.

My grandmother Rebecca refused to accept the fact that my mother had been a performer wearing next to nothing on the stage in New York City, a veritable den of iniquity, and she wasn't Jewish by birth. It was irrelevant that she converted before marrying my father. "Tsk-tsk. A crime of all crimes, a performer, no less," my grandmother would hiss, as she rocked back and forth in her favorite chair. "And she's not even Jewish." That was a crime that held more significance than a divorce.

A fact was a fact, and this was irrefutable. That fact dissolved into nothingness decades later when my grandmother, alone and old by the standards of that time, moved to Los Angeles and formed an unbreakable relationship with my mother.

Now and then, I think about my grandmother Rebecca, who, in my eyes, was old at sixty-five. It seems funny now but back then, I thought my grade-school teacher Miss Downey was ancient at twenty-seven and personally vowed at the tender age of seven never to get "that old."

After Grandmother Rebecca moved to Los Angeles, it was like a miracle had transpired. Mom's "Jewishness" suddenly stood out like a proverbial sore thumb, as she cooked matzo brei and gefilte fish, all while celebrating her born-again religion. My mother became far more Jewish than anyone I knew, other than my grandmother Rebecca, celebrating holidays with the finesse of a "balabusta."

Mom's key to success was her way around the kitchen, and what she could do with the likes of kreplach, borscht, stuffed cabbage, and other delicacies, much to the delight of my grandmother. The two things I remember most about my grandmother are that her house always smelled like mothballs and when she kissed me, the sharp hairs on her upper lip stuck me like tiny needles. Now I wonder why she didn't just pluck them out.

Even though I know that my grandmother was a great cook, I only remember the smells of the kitchen from my mother's hand

and not my grandmother's. The fresh tomato soup with rice and potatoes that I would nag my mother to make. The tiny kreplach that I would fry in butter the next day until they were crispy.

She made beet borscht with boiled potatoes. I used to love it with gobs of sour cream, the colors of red and white standing apart, brightly separated. I hated it mixed together like my father always wanted, blended so that the beets were blobs of liquid, and the dark red color of the cold Russian beet soup turned pink from the sour cream.

Mom would never ask me before pouring the pot, sour cream and all, into a mixer and instantly turning it monochromatic. There it would sit, pink in a glass in front of me, (my dad loved his borscht in a glass). It looked remarkably like a strawberry milkshake.

In the meantime, I would moan and complain, begging for normal beet borscht with boiled potatoes, sour cream, and beets all very much standing alone, not blandly blended.

"Next time," she would say. "It's too late now, dear. I've already put all the beets into the mixer."

How about asking me next time, I would think.

My father attended Penn State, went out for *some* sports, and excelled at running, though he never ran very far from my mother. He went to Wharton Business School and then stepped onto the floor of the New York Stock Exchange as what was referred to as a Customer's Man.

To his credit, he braved the crash of 1929, extracting all but one of his clients out of the market before it happened, protecting them from total ruin. Then he stood on the sidelines watching helplessly as millionaires dove out of buildings or sold apples on street corners. Unfortunately, while he saved the capital of many of his clients, he never fully recovered.

He spent his later life recounting this phenomenon over and over to me as the reason not to take any risks, or to buy anything that you couldn't pay for in cash. In retrospect, I ended up being an avid risk-taker and adventurer, something my father would not live to see.

I don't know exactly when my father first laid eyes on my mother, but perhaps it was in one of the many shows on Broadway that she starred in or maybe one of her many news articles.

Her demeanor was impressive enough to force my father to stand, flowers in hand at the stage door, waiting amid a flood of fans to meet her.

The term was "stage door Johnny." Whatever it was that my dad had going for him—personally, I thought he was incredibly good-looking, tall and lanky—my mom chose him over all the other wealthy men who pursued her. Looking back, I realize my dad was one of the smartest people I have ever met.

My mother was stunningly beautiful. Forgetting that she was my mother, as I am a bit biased, she was gorgeous. Her platinum blonde hair framed a perfectly formed face, with rouged, pouty lips and sultry dark eyes. She was a stunner who literally and figuratively pulled men into the web of her life. Those were the days of the speakeasies, the absinthe, of Helen Morgan warbling "Bill" or "My Man," as she perched, half-dead on the top of her piano; the booze; the flappers; the theater. Yes, the theater and my mother, and then there were the cigarettes.

It was all the rage. Lucky Strikes, the cigarette that means "fine tobacco"; Camels, the one you would "walk a mile for" even without the filters; and Winstons, the one that "tasted good like a cigarette should."

My father was into all of it. Every movie star talking or not, had a cigarette dangling from their fingers or lips. They even lit cigarettes two at a time.

My mother and father made a stunningly beautiful couple, and they cherished me as a child. They were both successful in their own right with my mother starring on Broadway and my father a Customers Man on the floor of the New York Stock Exchange. His brother George squired my mother around in New York while my father was writing a special play.

My mother and I and Uncle George. Sadly he passed away at a very early age and I never had a chance to meet him.

The air of every cinema was clouded with the "remains of the day," smoke hanging like a noose over every seat. My father smoked Camels, three packs a day.

Hard to imagine how something so bad for you could create a generation of followers so hellbent on showing how mature they were by puffing on what I would call a "death stick." Even today followers linger, not even slightly dissuaded by the addition of the serious health warnings on each pack. My dad probably would have thought twice had he seen that artistry, but he continued puffing away until he was close to death.

THE BIG LIE

It was midnight, January 17, 1920, when America went dry. There wasn't a place in the country (including your own home) where you could have a glass of wine with your dinner and not be in violation of the law.

The Volstead Act prohibited the manufacture, sale, and possession of alcohol in America. This period of dryness went on for thirteen years. Unfortunately, no other law in America was violated by so many "decent law-abiding" people.

Overnight, almost everyone in the country became a criminal. Ordinary people hid illegal liquor in hip flasks, false books, and hollowed-out canes. In speakeasies, where you knocked on unmarked doors and whispered a password, they drank bootleg liquor out of teacups just in case there was a police raid.

The year was 1925 and mob-controlled liquor created a booming black-market economy. Gangster-owned speakeasies replaced neighborhood saloons, and by then, there were over one hundred thousand speakeasies in New York City alone. Mob bosses owned plush nightclubs with exotic floor shows and the hottest bands. In Harlem, at Small's Paradise Club, waiters danced the Charleston and illegally carrying trays loaded down with cocktails. Popular stars like Fred and Adele Astaire entertained at the Trocadero. And at the Cotton Club, Duke Ellington led the house band, as tap dancer Bojangles Robinson and jazz singer Ethel Waters packed the house.

There were no headlines on this story until 1934: Gerrie Worthing, aka my mother, ran away from her home in Michigan and went to New York City. Using the $100 she had "borrowed" from her mother's purse, Gerrie fled to New York to follow her dream. My mother was fourteen years old! Today, it is shocking to realize that my mother's narration of her life, to me at least, had all been a lie. It was one carefully crafted to deter me from living my dreams of being a singer of some importance. The big lie remained in place long after my mother passed away.

Today, it is hard to imagine that my mother, the one portraying that puritanical New England affectation to me, was, at fourteen years old, dancing her way to stardom. Women had only gotten the right to vote in 1920, and we were just entering the Jazz Age.

Flappers frequented the nightspots dancing the Tango, the Black Bottom, and the Charleston, with bare arms and legs flying through fringe. It took nearly a year before the private detective sent by my grandfather located my mother. She returned home for a mere moment before heading back to Gotham, her mother Lydia in tow.

One of the stars of the speakeasy days was a brassy, bold, peroxide blonde who called herself "Texas" Guinan, known as the "Queen of the Night." Who could have known that decades later, I would be involved in the heart of it all, the New York nightclub scene, dealing with a rather "dangerous" cast of characters and well-known celebrities, and would also be known as the "Queen of the Night!"

New York has always had its demimonde, where the rich and famous flirt with fast living and rub shoulders with the decadent and the criminal elements. The 1920s setting was a constellation of smoky speakeasies and celebrity-crowded nightclubs, awash in bootleg liquor and underworld figures.

"Texas" Guinan, a wisecracking, besequinned, and outrageous woman, ruled as Gotham's nightclub queen. As a symbol of the exuberant twenties, Texas was right up there with Lucky Lindy, Babe Ruth, and Silent Cal. She was born Mary Louise Cecilia in Waco, Texas, in 1884, twenty-seven years before my mother saw the light of day. Educated in Catholic schools, Texas grew up a great storyteller.

In later years, she wove a mythical account of her youth and convinced reporters that she had ridden broncos, rounded up cattle on a fifty-thousand-acre ranch, attended the elite Hollins Finishing School in Virginia, and run off to join a circus, all of which were pure fantasy created by her inventive mind.

As the country went to war, she was acting in silent movies, a career that lasted until 1922. Texas starred in thirty-six movies, mostly two-reelers, though of course, she inflated the number to three hundred, which was better for business. Weaving fanciful stories wasn't her only talent. She could sing a bit, act a bit more, and she possessed self-assurance and ambition to spare. All of it she parlayed into a modest show business career before becoming the top nightclub hostess of her time.

Upon settling in New York, Texas dyed her brunette hair flashy blonde, gussied up her blowsy figure in glittery clothes, cultivated the right underworld connections, and went to work as a nightclub hostess.

In just a few years, prohibition had made gangsters into millionaires, venal politicians into corrupt fat cats, and Waco's own Texas Guinan into the mistress of Gotham's nightlife. Guinan began holding court at the King Cole room, which would become a favorite of silent screen's lover Rudolph Valentino, the legendary actor John Barrymore, Mrs. W. K. Vanderbilt, and the serial bride of a long string of millionaires, Peggy Hopkins Joyce (aka, at one time or another, Mrs. Everett Archer, Mrs. Sherburne P. Hopkins, and Mrs. Count Gosta Morner). My mother and Peggy became quite close over the years, and she gifted my mother an engraved bracelet that I still have today.

Clearly, the King Cole was a place to see and be seen, no small thanks to the club's new flamboyant hostess. Texas reeled in customers like no other speakeasy hostess during the Prohibition years.

Pleasure-seeking patrons, respectable and not, elbowed one another for the privilege of having Texas empty their wallets. Then came a business venture between Texas and Larry Fey, a man of questionable past and present. The venture was a club called the El Fey.

The club was frequented by well-heeled Wall Streeters and Ivy League collegians who loved the big-city high life, famous athletes, prominent politicians, and mobsters galore.

As the twenties began to roar, the El Fey Club attracted anyone with money to burn and a penchant for illicit fun. It rivaled Jack and Charlie's 21 Club as New York City's best-known speakeasy and was favored by writers Dorothy Parker and Robert Benchley. George Raft, then the top Charleston dancer in town, made the El Fey a regular stop. It was the hot spot for the time.

It was not unusual to see screen cowboy Tom Mix, the indefatigable Peggy Hopkins Joyce, who had befriended my mother somewhere along the way, and the legendary Harry Thaw, who had killed architect Stanford White in a jealous fit over his young wife Evelyn Nesbit at the El Fey. They and other notables thronged to the club for a taste of the high life and decadence.

It was into this world of illegal liquor, mobsters, high-rollers, and unimaginable decadence that my then fifteen-year-old mother threw herself. As I consider her options now, what else could she do but lie to me my entire life?

Nights at the El Fey, and later at Texas's other clubs, blended alcohol-fueled mirth and sportive bedlam. Armed with a clapper, a police whistle, her ever-derisive wit, and sporting an array of gigantic hats, Texas impaled big spenders with insults and made them love it.

"Hello, sucker" was her blunt welcome to fat cats on a spending spree and became as common a parlance, as "Give the lil' girl a great big hand," which was her introduction as a performer walked onstage. Then came the inevitable breakdown in the relationship between Fey and Guinan, and she wanted out.

Fey made the mistake of threatening Guinan, whereupon she brought in her own personal group of "in-house" enforcers to the party, and Fey quickly backed down. Texas, known for being bold and brassy, then launched her first independent venture, The 300 Club.

My mother was one of her entertainers and a most important one at that. A photo in the New York City papers, date unknown, announced brightly: GREETINGS OF THE SEASON FROM "TEXAS" GUINAN. (The photo is of my mother.) It read: "Gotham's most famous nightclub hostess presents 'Gerry' Pratt. Pratt, a former local girl who once starred in Earl Carroll's *Vanities*, is one of the reasons why most visitors to the "big city" put Texas's place on their list. Gerry is one of her entertainers."

The new club at 151 West 54th Street was a hit. To be part of Broadway's status elite, you had to be part of the scene at The 300 Club. The club became the target of undercover police operations who were relentlessly trying to destroy the illegal liquor trade. The club was raided night after night, and Texas was hauled off countless times. Some nights well-heeled customers accompanied her, but true to form she would reappear the next night.

Then one night while Texas was clad in a garish costume, police came down on the club once again and this time Texas sounded off, singing "The Prisoner's Song" as police escorted her to a waiting car: A rather gruff detective wittily retorted, "Give the little girl a big handcuff."

At the 47th Street police station, true to form, Texas entertained a horde of arrested guests, reporters, photographers, police, and federal agents with her renditions of the song. It became a veritable party at the police station. The "Texas" show lasted, off and on, for nine hours. Smack dab in the middle of all the drama was my mother, still at the club, dancing her way to stardom. She was barely sixteen years old. Three days after her nine-hour jail stint, Texas faced another challenge, bible-thumping Aimee Semple McPherson. McPherson was a relentless self-promoter, but she was Guinan's exact opposite in every other way. McPherson's principal mission was the reform of wayward souls, and according to her, "Texas" consorted with the devil and was headed to certain doom.

McPherson arrived in New York with her hair glamorously permed, sporting a white gown, her arms laden with flowers, and headed to The 300 Club for a closer look. She swept into the club at three in the morning, after a surprising quick stop for a Black Bottom lesson, of all things, in the Village.

Texas welcomed her guest, calling for "a hand for the brave little woman." A historic meeting followed as the glamorous evangelist stood beside Texas in the so-called den of iniquity. There was no way to calculate the public relations value of this historic meeting.

With the club's patrons cheering, McPherson spoke to the room: "This is an experience such as I never had in all my life," she exclaimed.

After using some religious terms to address the throng of people, Aimee called it a night after inviting them to her revival meeting later the next day.

Texas and her girls, including my mother, didn't disappoint, and on the way to another night of festivity, they showed up chastely cloaked in furs, at McPherson's Glad Tidings Tabernacle on West 33rd Street.

Both Texas and McPherson were no strangers to the camera action and, as they clicked, Texas and her group sang and listened intently to the religious fervor spouted by McPherson. Shortly after, Texas declared McPherson "a marvelous woman," and the two shook hands as the paparazzi buzzed.

Then, her priorities firmly in view, Texas gathered her flock. "Come on, my chicks, let's get on to the club." My mother was swept into a waiting car.

In 1927 police locked The 300 Club for six months. My mother was only sixteen years old but had already been part of a fast and furious life for more than two years. I would be nearly four times older than that when the lie was finally exposed in a series of old newspaper clippings. By then it was too late to confront her, as she had already gone to her maker.

The New York Yankees won the pennant by nineteen games; Babe Ruth hit his epic sixty home runs; Lindbergh flew the Atlantic nonstop; the stock market ascended before suffering a tremor in August, then continued its climb to the brink.

In Washington, President Calvin Coolidge, a man of few words but of profound intuitions, chose not to run for reelection in 1928. My mother was just seventeen and about to burst onto the New York scene in earnest.

The stock market crash of 1929 would signal the end of the "party," but my mother was dancing her heart out and going strong. In 1931, Al Capone landed in jail for income-tax evasion and in 1933, prohibition was officially rescinded.

Who could have guessed that my mother's world would collide with a world she didn't know at all and that everything would change? As the youngest daughter of WASP parents, Mr. and Mrs. R. L. Pratt, my mother was brought up in a very strict Episcopalian home by an overbearing father who used a ruler on her hands if she failed to wash them properly.

Her father would stand at the door with a wooden ruler in one hand and demand that my mother and her sister, Dorothy, hold out their little hands, palm side up, then palm side down. If a trace of dirt remained, Grandfather Pratt would smack the palms of their hands, whack! whack! whack!, until they were red as beets from the pain.

"Now go and wash your hands properly," he would bellow, "then come back to the table and sit down, and don't speak until you're spoken to."

This, of course, was my mother's perception of Grandfather Pratt, née Worthing, mother's stage name. Other than the wooden ruler saga and a few other choice reminders, I don't remember either of my mother's parents, my grandparents, perhaps because I saw them little or perhaps because I have blocked out the memory. All I know about Grandmother Pratt is what my mother told me. That she was a vain, selfish, and self-centered woman, consumed by her looks and always staring into the mirror. That never sounded so bad, at least to my ears.

I have come to find out that this entire time was fabricated by my mother and fueled by my father to keep me in line and, in their own way, to protect me from the sins of a life she had already lived.

The story about Grandmother Pratt being so vain and obsessed with herself, always looking into the mirror, was consistently vomited into my ears by my mother, who of course never, ever told a lie. *Supposedly*, Grandma was a typical "stage mother" who, after failing to live her own dreams, forced those dreams on my mother. At one point in my life, that almost made sense. Years later, I discovered clippings and news articles all about my mother and they completely dispelled the version told to me about her life.

The stories about my grandmother, her vanity and random abuse, were highly doubtful, since the clippings I finally found revealed that my mother ran away from home at the tender age of fourteen and my grandparents had to hire a private investigator to find her and bring her back home. This must have been painful and devastating to them, especially at that time. She was finally located in New York City, working with the famous Jonathan Logan.

My mother's childhood was all but denied, and at eleven she was dancing and flaunting positions that today I couldn't even draw. I believe that this was my mother's own doing and that it was her desire to become a star, and not the manipulations of a vain, obsessed woman, my grandmother, forcing her dreams onto my mother. Newspaper articles from the time support this notion rather than my mother's reinterpretation of the facts.

Dressed in crinoline, her hair crimped into "flapper" styles or finger waved, my mother twisted her body into pretzel-like positions and danced, and danced, and then danced some more. She finally danced her way to Broadway.

She was only seventeen when she appeared in Earl Carroll's *Vanities*, and *Ziegfeld Follies*, and slightly older when she starred in shows like *She Loves Me Not*, *Naughty Naught*, and *The Wind and the Rain*, her reviews already flagging her as a future big star.

The *Billboard*, April 21, 1934, announced in their "legitimate" column: NEW YORK, APRIL 14 – GERRIE WORTHING [MY MOTHER] UNDERSTUDY FOR POLLY WALTERS IN "SHE LOVES ME NOT," PLAYED THE LEAD IN THAT SHOW, WHILE MISS WALTERS WAS TAKEN ILL. AS A RESULT, SHE HAS FOUR FILM BIDS.

The Detroit News, August 29, 1934: ROYAL OAKS GIRL BECOMES A SHUBERT BROADWAY STAR; Daily News, Saturday, September 15, 1934: LOCAL GIRL EARNS PLACE AS LEAD IN BROADWAY SHOW.

Photos of a scantily clad Gerrie Worthing echoed from the pages of national newspapers and magazines.

Gerrie Worthing, my mother, was a very talented woman with great skills in both acting and dancing as evidenced by these photos. Her love for my father and desire to have children sadly shortened her career.

ANGELS IN SIN

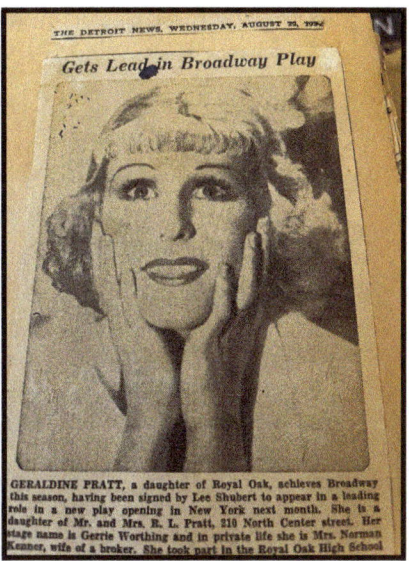

These are a few of the photos and news clippings
from her successful career on Broadway.

A smoking, sensual Gerrie, dressed as a dance-hall hostess, peers seductively from the newsprint. My mother! My mother? She was scandalous and risqué, sides of her I never saw and never knew about until after she died.

The year was 1934 and my mother, the conservative, puritanical, steel magnolia, the old-line New Englander who never slept with anyone before my father, headlined in the *Cincinnati Post* on October 8, 1934: DECENCY CRUSADE FAILS TO ENGULF BLASÉ BROADWAY; LATEST STAGE PLAYS RISQUÉ DESPITE HULLABALOO. Center stage in a beautifully profiled photo, was my mother, Gerrie Worthing.

My puritanical mother in an article that begins, "New York, October 8 – What with the Legion of Decency scaring the sin out of the movies and some of the elder sages predicting a cleaner theater, you would think that by this time the Puritans would have landed on Broadway and had the situation well in hand. Well, they have not..."

The article goes on to describe a risqué play, with some degree of nudity, playful cuddling, and: "All this time David is romping with the cuddly Joan [my mother] and finally, there is a bedroom scene in which she disrobes with an abandon that has the most shock-proof customers popeyed. Charming Gerrie Worthing is all that she should be, in the role of the blonde who is not all that she should be – if you know what I mean." Who would have guessed? Mother had suitors by the score. Day after day, they arrived bearing gifts. Railroad cars were sent by the son of a family that owned a bank in Canada. Flowers adorned the backstage. One suitor stood out from the others, perhaps because he was young and handsome.

My father, bringing a small bouquet to the stage door, emerged the victor. And to the victor go the spoils. Interesting that my father's middle name was Victor, and his father's first name was the same.

Soon, the newspapers announced their surprise wedding in a few startling paragraphs.

It read: From "Your Broadway and Mine" by Louis Solbol, Monday, April 20, 1931. "Later at the Hollywood restaurant... a dimpled blonde dashes madly up the stairs.... She halts, breathlessly...

'I've been married for three weeks to Norman Kenner,' she explodes. 'Do you think I ought to tell the newspapers and get my picture in?'"

An April 25, 1931, column in the *New York Herald Tribune*: "Announcement today of the secret marriage of Geraldine Pratt Worthing, New York dancer and daughter of Mr. and Mrs. R. L. Pratt, and Norman Kenner, Wall Street broker, on March 27, comes with interest to Royal Oak, as well as to the theatergoers of Broadway.... Geraldine has been on Broadway for three seasons, appearing in *Ziegfeld, Earl Carroll, George White*, and "Texas" Guinan productions.... She expects to advance, rather than retire, from stage work, after the marriage.

"Mr. Kenner, who has been on Wall Street five years, is writing a play with a friend and expects to produce it himself, which may give his bride a prospect on the legitimate stage."

Another article proclaimed their wedding and went on to say: "To the surprise of all concerned, Gerrie Worthing married young stockbroker Norman Kenner, in a civil ceremony yesterday. We all wish her the very best."

And so heralded my mother and father's respective goals, neither of which came to fruition. My mother was twenty and my father was twenty-three.

My mother's needs soon became clear. She wanted to have children, a lot of them. She was a nurturing woman. In spite of what the newspapers heralded, my father soon demanded that my mother quit the stage.

I never knew my namesake, my uncle George, because he had died in a horrendous car crash years before I was even a thought. My mother was left devastated and changed forever. The rumor had circulated that my mother was with him that fateful night. The story went on to say that she was in the car and had been badly injured, but I was never able to confirm that.

Another story emerged that had both of my parents in the car and hurt badly enough both emotionally and physically to be unable to attend Shiva for my uncle. At this late date, there is no one of sound mind who can verify either story, but somehow I suspect that one of them is true.

To most onlookers, my mother and Uncle George seemed like a couple as they partied around Manhattan together. My uncle George, his dark hair always slicked back, those smoldering, sensual eyes and swarthy good looks, made him a natural with the ladies. He had women clinging like vines and booze neatly tucked away in a silver canteen, his initials boldly displayed on the front. It said G. K., oddly the same as my mother's and mine. He was a depression-era party animal who adored women in general, and my mother in particular.

WHERE ANGELS FEAR TO TREAD

It is hard to believe that my father and Uncle George were brothers given the opposite ends of the social scale they inhabited. Uncle George was the party animal of the family, preferring the bright lights, jazz, blues, and smoke-filled bars. My father, on the other hand, preferred to spend his evenings in the Holland Hotel, curled up on a couch writing the great American play. They lived at the hotel in the early days of their marriage.

Uncle George and my mother, who was usually dressed in some scandalous, nearly naked outfit, would crawl around the New York nightlife scene together. For years into my parents' marriage, my mother and Uncle George appeared to be the "couple."

While they cavorted around the New York nightlife scene, my father stayed home, listening to his beloved opera and writing. In my mind it was like Nero fiddling while Rome burned, although not exactly the same.

Unfortunately, the great American play idea slipped through my father's fingers and failed to see the light of day or contribute to him realizing his dreams.

He passed away leaving only the notes of his theatrical ambitions on a cluster of stained and yellowing lined legal pads. My tears were to stain them even further, as they fell over the sheets like rainwater.

An irony that failed to materialize until after my father's death was that my mother had desperately longed for me, while my father couldn't understand the need for children. My mother ended up divorcing him because of it, only to remarry him after he mellowed his position. She actually fled New York for California to apparently show him she meant business. As luck or life would have it, my father and I grew incredibly close, like two peas in a proverbial pod.

Strange, but that same emotional reversal happened with my father, after my mother came home one day with a dog she rescued from the shelter. Initially, my father thought her quite mad, referring to her as Clyde Beatty, the well-known lion trainer from the circus.

"Is Clyde Beatty there?" he queried, thinking she had already arrived with her "treasure."

"Who?" I was in the dark about what was about to transpire, or what already had transpired.

"Wait and see. Your mom got a dog, a rescue dog."

A short time later, there was the knock on the door, and I opened it to see my mother holding a slightly disheveled miniature dachshund in her arms.

"Say hello to Brandy."

Once the initial drama had faded, my father loved that little dog almost more than he loved me. His name was Brandy, but I never found out whether or not mother named him or just took the name he'd already been given. He was a knocked-down, dragged-out brown and black miniature dachshund who had seen better days.

In truth, he defied all odds, living a very long life, despite the fact that he regularly consumed Hershey's kisses, a no-no in dog world.

A connoisseur of cleverness, he would steal them out of the green glass dish on the coffee table and proceed to unwrap the silver foil with his teeth, consuming the milk chocolate inside with vigor. It should have killed him but never seemed to cause him any harm or sleeplessness.

When my father was hospitalized toward the end of his life, my mother and I would stand in the hospital parking lot under the area of his window so he could see Brandy and blow kisses to him.

It haunted me for the rest of my life that I wasn't present, either in the room or the parking lot, when my father suddenly took a turn for the worse and passed away. He was three weeks from his sixty-sixth birthday. I still miss him every day and regularly celebrate his life.

I could never do anything quite right where my mother was concerned, or so it seemed in my child's-eye view of the world.

Growing up, my perception was that my father should leave my mother and allow me to take care of him. That scenario, at least in my mind, would have been preferable to what seemed to me as their constant arguing. I used to call my father "Poppy Seed." Why, I don't know, but for me, it was an endearing term that showed how much I loved him. Until her death, I saw my mother as the bad guy in our relationship and in theirs. Sadly, I never really saw the person obscured beneath my perceptions of who my mother was.

The one thing that I remember about her, good, bad, or indifferent, is that she had no censor, no filter or boundaries. One might say that she was truthful and honest; another might declare that she was rude and tactless. Maybe she was a complimentary combination of both.

Now, looking back, I realize how very childlike she was until the day that she died. I realize that she had essentially given up her childhood to pursue her dreams. Imagine never knowing what it was like to be a teenager, to play outside with friends, to be young. She never really grew up emotionally. Later in life I think she turned the clock back to become childlike, a bit giddy and emotionally young. I only wish I could have recognized that amazing trait in her, but back then it was only an annoyance and embarrassment.

It was difficult, if not impossible, to take my mother anywhere, because you never knew what would erupt out of her mouth.

One extraordinarily embarrassing incident occurred when I was about fifteen. My parents had taken me to my father's all-time favorite restaurant in Hollywood, Don the Beachcomber.

This hot spot was once called the "Original Tiki Bar." The owner Donn Beach aka Ernest Raymond Beaumont Gantt, a Texas-born former WWII veteran and sometimes fantastic storyteller, filled the place with Polynesian fare, including a bamboo bar with matching barstools, fishing nets on the walls, and colored fishing weights in every shade of blue and green. He also was a first to "cross market" with a gift shop and Chinese grocery right inside the door.

He became famous for making powerful rum drinks that sported small, brightly colored paper umbrellas and had intriguing names like the zombie, cobra's fang, navy grog, mai tai (a favorite of my mother), and the missionary's downfall.

Donn was quite the shrewd businessman, even going so far as to install a sprinkler system on the tin roof of the restaurant so that customers would think it was raining and stay for another drink.

I had been going there since I was about two and was always welcomed with open arms and smiling waiters. I had my very own chopsticks that were housed in a beautiful carved bamboo container with my name on it.

The containers were reserved for celebrities and very special guests. I always felt like a celebrity, and I loved the food and the brightly colored drinks with the little paper umbrellas. My drink of choice was the Shirley Temple, but it always looked like the ones my parents drank.

Truly *the* place to see and be seen, as a young girl I saw and said hello to the inimitable Joan Crawford, as she sat shrouded in a darkened booth sipping an umbrella-adorned drink. She must have been both shocked and appalled when I called out to her as we were leaving the restaurant. There she was sitting alone, wrapped in a black, coal-like cloth that embraced the paleness of her skin.

She was stunning, at least the child that I was thought so. I can still see her now, poised, posed, and regal in that darkened corner booth. She was magical to me then and even now, as an adult.

Drinking was something that was not in my mother's skill set. At the tender age of only twelve or thirteen, I knew how little it took for her to get legless. The mere act of waving a mai tai under her nose usually did the trick, but sadly that never quite satisfied her desire to obliterate the drink.

Once she had a sip or two, my mother was off to the races, so to speak, and anything or anyone was fair game for what she deemed as harmless fun.

On that one particular night of embarrassment, we were seated next to a table of eight people, an unusual assortment, as I recall. I clearly remember the woman directly behind my mother had a necklace on with a drop at the back. Right across from her at the large round table was a man wearing an obvious toupee, a clear and present disaster just waiting to happen.

Barely one mai tai later, my mother turned, pulled on the drop hanging from the woman's necklace, and chimed out, "Ding-ding." The startled woman turned and laughed, which only served to encourage my mother.

Then without warning she rose, smiling, and walked around their table to the other side, where the man with the ill-fitting toupee was seated. At first glance, she looked harmless enough, and with one hand outstretched, she greeted him.

"Hello, I'm Gerrie Kenner." She smiled, and as he reached out in a gesture of surprise and good will, she took her other hand, grabbed onto his ill-fitting toupee, lifted it off his head, then dropped it down again carelessly, nearly covering his eyes.

At that precise moment, my father and I, mouths open in shock, headed for the door, so I have no idea what transpired after that. For us, it was the ultimate night of horror. Here we were at my father's all-time favorite restaurant, his Friday night dinner-out spot, where he usually dined with his closest male friend Sam Levitt. He was well-known here. This was his refuge, and we had just suffered the ultimate humiliation, at least in our eyes. .

For my mother, my childlike mother, it was great amusement. She and her mai tai were having what she might celebrate as a smashingly good time.

Now, one might think that she was appalling, rude, and vindictive, but that was not who she was. I realize now that she was just very young and immature in her actions. I only wish I had recognized her behavior for what it was back then. We might have had a much different relationship.

The day before I lost my mother to her own willful desire to leave this earth, I was dressing for a Halloween party at Paramount Studios. She was living in an assisted-living condo in a high-rise building in Westwood, on the sixteenth floor, above the actions of the city.

That night we were on the phone, and I was describing my rather scanty outfit to her. I was headed to Paramount Studios along with a guest list of about five thousand other assorted people. I was going as seduction, half naked, with brightly colored feathers glued onto my bare torso, a pair of tiny shorts that barely covered my ass, and stilettos adorned at the back with more feathers.

"What are you going to do about covering your 'coochie'?" she asked. Her question stunned me to a point of absolute silence, but those words echo in my ears today.

Back then, I was embarrassed by her comments, but only wish she were here today to "embarrass" me again.

The morning after the party, I sat at Ben Frank's Restaurant on Sunset Boulevard, covered in feathers from the night before and surrounded by friends of all shapes, sizes, and genders.

I wondered out loud how I was going to be able to get over to see my mother that afternoon. In that instant, another haunting decision was made. I opted to leave it until later so I could get the feathers off my body.

Sadly, later never happened. The next time I saw my mother she was lying on a bed in the emergency room at UCLA, unresponsive even to my pleas and tears.

As it turned out, my mother had been in distress earlier in the day, however, the housekeeping staff at her condo failed to alert the front desk. No one was notified when my mother didn't answer the door for the housekeeper, or when she failed to go down for either breakfast or lunch. I phoned around dinnertime, only to find out that she had not even come down for dinner. I immediately panicked!

"Someone needs to go up there right now and check on her." The fact that I had to tell them what should have been standard procedure infuriated me even further. I raced to the facility, my heart pounding like a jackhammer. By the time I arrived at her apartment in Westwood she had been transported by the fire department to UCLA Emergency hospital.

What had happened to her? The clock stood still! An hour seemed like a lifetime, and the pain was unbearable. More guilt piled onto my now adult shoulders! It had only been that morning, the day after a night of partying, that I stressed out about going to see her at the retirement home.

Rest seemed to be more important than visiting my mother that morning, at least at the time. After all, there was always tomorrow, or the next day, or the following Saturday. Sadly, that was not to be, as there were no more days to be had, no more moments to put off, no more time to find the words of love that I couldn't seem to express.

Quite simply, she was gone forever, never to know how much I loved her, how much I appreciated her, for who she was, and who she wasn't.

If I had one wish, it would have been that she regained consciousness so that I could have told her with passion how much I loved her.

The only positive thing that came out of that day was that my son finally responded to a request of mine and showed up at the hospital. I don't know what I would have done if I had to deal with her eventual death alone that night alone, awash in my tears of regret.

At least he came through without a boatload of drama or a contentious, disrespectful attitude on a night that I needed him the most. For that I am eternally grateful.

Over the years, there were many other incidents where my mother's mouth got the best of her, and it got to a point where my father refused to take her to visit their closest friends for fear she might say something that would "insult" them.

Funny, looking back, some of the things that she did and said were quite humorous. Once she apparently broke into raucous laughter when visiting some friends because the wife had all the white furniture covered in clear plastic.

My unfiltered mother could never understand why anyone would cover their furniture with plastic and couldn't help but ask. They were never invited back after that.

One Thanksgiving, Raymond, my then husband, my mother, and I were invited by a girlfriend of mine to her home for dinner.

She had a number of grown children and a few grandkids who were clearly a bit overweight.

First, my mother sailed gleefully into the kitchen to deliver a running commentary on the cooking of the turkey that had fallen apart on the cutting board.

"This turkey isn't done right, it's falling off the bone." Her words trailed behind her as she made her way back to where we were sitting.

"No wonder those kids are so fat, the way she feeds them," she chortled in a voice loud enough to be heard in the next county.

Oops! I died a thousand deaths, hoping my friend hadn't heard my mother, but we were never invited back, and maybe that was for the best. That woman became part of my inner spring cleaning later that year and was dropped from the rosters of my life. Interestingly enough, the person who told me about doing a spring cleaning of your acquaintances was a hot and hunky "porn" star with a twelve-pack who I went out with while living in New York City in the '90s. I met him at a hotel one night while out with the girls, and as it turned out, he was starring in what turned out to be an X-rated show in the Village.

The very next day I told my closest gay friend, Mitch, of my encounter with a smoldering hot hunk named Ryan Idol.

"What? Did you say Ryan Idol? OMG, come with me right now," he ordered.

The next thing I knew I was standing in a porn shop in front of a row of videos staring at my new "hot date" who was in full color on the covers with an assortment of men.

"You can't sleep with him. You know that. I don't care how hot he is. That is not happening."

"Okay, okay, but we're going to see his porn show in the Village," I replied. I immediately bought the tickets and counted down the hours until the show.

We arrived early and sat in the very front row mesmerized as Ryan performed totally naked for my benefit, bumping and grinding inches from my face. It was, admittedly, one of those unforgettable moments in one's life. After the show he found us having drinks at a nearby bar, sat down next to me, and finished the evening with us, much to my delight.

We went out a few times and shared some incredibly hot and passionate moments on my couch. But, thankfully, I was wise enough to balance the hot from the not, and other than those steamy moments, I erred on the side of caution and stayed clear of having sex with him. It was one of the most difficult things I have ever forced myself to do, and I argued back and forth with my decision, the pragmatic me versus the sexually charged me. Sex or no sex, but good, bad, or indifferent, the sensible me overruled. His last known address was a prison in California where he ended up serving time for the attempted murder in 2009 of his then girlfriend. In retrospect I dodged a hail of bullets. For a time we stayed in touch, and years after our first meeting he relayed how he eliminated people from his life with an annual spring cleaning.

Fortunately, I was not one of them until long after we met and he moved to the West Coast.

It's funny how life works and how the spring cleaning of my proverbial closet brought back the memory of Ryan. As time moved on after my mother's death, I began to see her in a totally different light. I came to the realization that since my mother was loved by so many people, she must have been a very special person.

That aha moment happened to me one day when I was in the midst of a seminar called Actualizations. I don't really remember what was going on or why I was standing up sharing, but there I was, and I recall saying to the group of several hundred attendees that I didn't want to end up being like my mother.

I sat down and suddenly it hit me. Why not? Why wouldn't I want to be like my mother? People loved her.

One of the families that she babysat for gave her a trip to Europe, another a Caribbean cruise, and another $3,000! No one had ever done anything like that for me, not even close. So, my mother must have been a pretty amazing woman to have people want to do such special things for her.

Too bad I didn't see that while she was alive. Then I could have done something to honor her. Instead, I just pushed her away, pushed against, denied, defied, and on some levels disliked her and her behavior. That child inside her that I should have embraced and loved I pushed away. And now it was too late!

Unlike me, my mother loved children and would have had a dozen if she could have, but sadly, she only had two and one of them died at only three weeks of age, my sister, Vicky. The guilt of her death lived inside of me from the time I was five until I was decades into maturity and was able to finally let it go.

Vicky, who never got to experience real love, or devastating pain, and who I never got to meet. However, in my child's perception, the burden of my sister's death fell on my small shoulders.

I had contracted the German measles, which in turn caused my mother's stand-in doctor to give her a Rubella shot. This course of action ended with my sister Vicky being born with a hole in her tiny heart.

It was a real-life domino effect. In those days nothing could be done, and three weeks later with tears, remorse, and what I viewed as the condemnation of me, my parents buried her at Hollywood Cemetery, one block from where we lived.

At first, we visited her tiny grave frequently, but as time marched on, no one went to clear the weeds, no one went to shed tears on that tiny grave, no one honored her short life, or tragic death. She was just a distant memory in everyone's mind but mine.

Me, the evil girl who got the German measles and caused my sister to be born with a hole in her heart. I would like to say that eventually I let that go, but in reality that persisted as a lie to myself, and I held onto the guilt until both of my parents were gone.

My relationship with my mother was to be strained until the very end of her life, even during times when I tried really hard to make her happy.

It's only now that I realize how brave my mother really was. After my father died, she moved alone to Desert Hot Springs, over one hundred miles south of Los Angeles, actually buying a double-wide mobile home without even one word of discussion with me, her only daughter.

This was the woman who I thought couldn't even write a check. She struggled with what she wanted for her life and what she ended up with. I am certain that the old-fashioned morays of the time influenced all her decisions.

She was, it turns out, a warrior woman long before I even thought of that term. Sad that we never found common ground until it was too late. The truth is, we were alike in so many ways, and neither of us had any idea.

Her ashes currently reside in a beautiful white Cottura urn covered with butterflies and hummingbirds. It is perched on top of an antique wooden chest in our bedroom overlooking our king-size bed. She now has a bird's-eye view of our life in the raw, awake and asleep, something I doubt she has much interest in.

Looking back, the interactions between my mother and I were memorable, to say the least. Comedic at times, heartbreakingly painful at others. One time, I scaled the banister of her ground-floor apartment in West Hollywood in fear that something had happened to her.

I had recently relocated her from her double-wide home in the desert because she not only crashed her golf cart into a wall, but she fell in her home and couldn't get up for several hours. I was worried and felt she was too far away, and with my international traveling I wanted her closer. That day I called and called well into the evening and she hadn't answered the phone. It was ten o'clock at night, and I was worried and couldn't sleep. I had gone to bed a bit earlier but phoned one more time, and there was still no answer.

I got up, got dressed, and jumped into my car for the short drive to her apartment. I lived about fifteen minutes away in Beverly Hills at the time. I arrived at her apartment, which was on the first floor, and tried to enter using my key, only to find the chain was on the door.

"Mother, Mother, are you there." I banged on the door again. "Mother, it's me, answer the door, please." The sound of silence echoed in my ears.

Now I was really concerned. What the hell could have happened to her? Had she fallen or had a stroke or a heart attack? Was she passed out? Did she slip in the shower and break something?

My mind raced in fear that something horrible had happened. Why else would the chain be on the door and my mother not be answering when I called out to her? It could only be that she was injured or maybe even dead.

My heart was pounding out of my chest. I was hyperventilating, fearful at what might have happened to her. I hadn't even told her that I loved her that day. I needed to get into that apartment and fast.

I made my way around to the front of the building and noticed immediately that the sliding door leading into her apartment was open, and it was 10:30 at night. Frantic, I climbed over the railing that surrounded her small porch, pushed the living room drapes aside, walked into the darkened room, and promptly fell over the coffee table.

"Who's there?" she called out. The sound of her voice enraged me. I screamed back, "It's me!" Suddenly, the lights went on.

There she was sitting up in bed, seemingly incensed.

I was angry and shouted, "I've been calling you all day." My heart was nearly pounding out of my chest as I mentally struggled to make sense of what was happening.

"I didn't want to talk to you," she calmly replied.

What? I got out of bed at 10:00 at night and drove over to see how you were, and you refused to answer the door because you didn't want to talk to me? Was she kidding? What the hell was wrong with her anyway?

I tried to breathe deeply so that I could bring myself down from the anxiety I was experiencing. I could hardly believe my ears when she said in an offhanded, matter-of-fact way, as if ordering lunch, that she just didn't want to talk to me!

There it was! Simple, straightforward, truthful, honest, uncensored, my mother! What can one say to a statement like that? She didn't want to talk to me, so she didn't answer the phone or the door.

Just keep breathing. Breathe, relax, this is not really happening. This is your imagination not reality. How could this be real? Your mother loves you and she would never do anything to hurt you, would she? Breathe!

It was during the scream fest that followed that she shrieked five words that stabbed me in the heart and would change my emotional life forever.

"Your father never wanted you," she bellowed, spit flying from her rageful mouth, her face red with anger.

The truth was like an arrow piercing my heart. For a moment in time, I felt like I was dying, as the words penetrated my soul and cut a piece out of me. *I am dying. This can't be happening. This can't be true. OMG, please, God, let this be a bad dream.*

I **was** dying for sure, bleeding from the open wound she had inflicted on me with her words. I couldn't move and I couldn't speak. I just stood there, paralyzed with pain.

My father and I were so close, he loved me, what the hell was she talking about? How could she speak of the dead like that? My father was dead, and she was disrespecting him to me. Of course he loved me, of course he wanted me . . . didn't he?

Somewhere buried deep in my psyche, I already knew that truth, but while he may not have wanted children way back then, we were bound by the deep love of a father and his daughter. That bond wasn't even broken at his death.

I knew that on so many levels I loved my mother beyond mere words, but it was difficult, no, nearly impossible to express that to her. She needed so much from me that I often felt I had to be both daughters, the one I was and the one that she lost. Sometimes I even felt like I needed to be all the other children she wished she had. But I was only me, just me, laden with the guilt of my sister's death. I couldn't seem to express my love or my pain to my mother. I never knew why, but looking back, perhaps it was because we were so alike. So much the same yet so different in how we expressed ourselves. Why couldn't I get those words out even now? I struggled with them, those words of love, and I lost my battle, and then, just like that, she was gone in what seemed like an instant.

Now, having her staring down at our bed from her whiter than white Cottura urn seemed to be both perfection and punishment for all of the days I failed to show her my love. Even in death I had failed her. She had wanted to be spread in the Pacific Ocean, but doing that would take her away from me again. My heart cried out for the loss I had experienced on two occasions.

Once, during my troubled life with her, and now, when all that remained were ashes of what was once a brilliant performer, a mother, a wife, a warrior, and above all, someone who I loved and lost.

I couldn't bring myself to honor her wishes, so instead, I spread her around the world in locations that I loved: my garden in the Hamptons, an offering to the Pacific Ocean, and at last, there she was, perched on an antique chest in a gorgeous white Cottura urn covered with beautiful birds and butterflies.

She was close enough for me to reach out and touch what was left and to talk to her in death, as I had never done in life. I've even asked for her sage advice now and again, which she has given and for which I am forever grateful.

Perhaps she can hear me when I say:

"Mom, I wish we had taken the time and put the energy forth to really know each other. I miss you more than words can say, and I celebrate the amazing woman that you were."

THE POISON APPLE

There is no way to measure the emotional and physical crime that was committed against me during that illegal, immoral abortion. It was raw and devastating, and before my thoughts totally cleared, my criminally negligent parents, seeking to whitewash their guilt, negotiated a deal with me: A 1956 Chevrolet Impala in exchange for never seeing Vincent again. A notion born out of death but destined to die in reality. Even though it seemed like a fair enough deal for me regardless, I had absolutely no intention of giving up my man. Imagine, if I traded the love of my life for a blue-and-white two-door Chevrolet, which I named "Little Evil." Not happening! Later in life, I would have traded Vincent for a bag of Cheetos.

A friend of Vincent's escorted me to the senior prom, and Vincent waited outside so that we could steal some time together. The friend's name was Jimmy, and he had been adopted by parents who really loved him. I used to wish over and over on every star that I could see in the sky that they had adopted me, that they were my parents. But they belonged to someone else.

They belonged to Jimmy, lucky child that he was. In an act that today I can only classify as borderline insane, a mere two days before prom, in an effort to be tanned and fabulous, I stood directly in front of an ultraviolet ray tanning machine at the gym. There I was, pale as a slice of white bread, flicking the "on" switch over and over to get a quick "fix," using the machine to replicate an instant tan. When I finally emerged from the room, my eyes were swollen shut, and I had a large, purplish-red streak emblazoned across my chest. I looked like the victim of a gang assault.

Prom night, I slid into my beautiful pale pink, spaghetti-strapped dress, wondering how I could mask the huge purple blob that traversed from one shoulder to the other, and wishing I had bought a dress that covered up my breasts rather than bring attention to them. Lucky for me, ice packs had taken down the swelling in my eyes and they were no longer shut. Eyes wide open certainly was the far better look.

Shortly after my graduation I decided to take a break from Vincent and dip my toe into the dating pool. I was just eighteen, still very naïve, and although I had given up believing in Santa Claus and the Easter Bunny, I was soon to get a jolt of reality. I had begun attending services at a Buddhist temple and was starting to use meditation as a tool to learn more about the "me" trapped inside. One day I met a young man named Steven at the services, and he seemed nice and interesting. When he invited me to see the infamous comedian Professor Irwin Corey, I accepted. We met that night at the Playboy Club where Professor Corey was performing and laughed until our sides were nearly split. Afterward Steven asked if I wanted to go to a party in Trousdale Estates at the home of the daughter of the namesake of a well-known brokerage house. I was having a great time, and so I said of course. But first we stopped at the home of a very well-known and extremely famous singer. He was an international superstar, and his songs were regularly number one. I will call him "Billy John." I was nervous when we got to the door because he was one of my all-time favorite singers. Steven rang the bell several times and just as we were about to leave the door swung open, but no one was there.

We entered the palatial home, which featured an indoor swimming pool where one might have a living room, and as I looked over my shoulder toward the front door, there stood this famous singer naked as the day he was born.

I was shocked and embarrassed and couldn't walk fast enough in any direction. I finally reached the living room after passing a naked young man on the diving board, then breathlessly fell into a waiting chair. A few other people were already seated waiting for our host to return. When he did, still naked, I didn't know where to look and finally, in desperation I walked out to the patio to play with his enormous sheepdog. After about an hour or so of more surprises we left and headed to the party. I was young, and still in shock, so once there I couldn't wait to tell my story to anyone willing to listen. I sat on the couch and one of the guests sat down next to me.

"You won't believe what just happened," I said breathlessly.

"Really? Tell me," She said.

"I was just at Billy John's home, and he answered the door totally naked."

"OMG, really?" she seemed genuinely surprised.

Just then, my mouth fell open as a naked girl ran across the living room floor followed by a naked man in hot pursuit. I looked up at the wall of glass that separated the living room from the swimming pool and saw naked people swimming around laughing.

"Where is the bathroom?" I queried. I made my way there just to compose myself before heading into the kitchen, where several other girls were gathered. Since they were all clothed, I thought that was a safe place.

"You won't believe what I just saw," I said breathlessly.

"Must have been Joseph and Angela. Naked again. I saw them," one of the girls said. "You came with Steven, didn't you?"

"Yes, why?"

The girls looked at each other knowingly and then started laughing.

"Do you remember when he put that hand towel over his dick at the last party at the Playboy Mansion? He always was the first one to get things started."

They laughed in unison. Shocked, I headed out to find Steven and get the hell out of there, still totally confused about what was happening. He was talking to a group of guests when I approached,

"I want to go home now, please."

"Of course, let's get out of here."

We thanked the hostess and left the party. I was confused, shocked, and angry, and I couldn't really understand what was happening. I was still very naïve and this entire scene was brand new to me.

"I'm so sorry," he said. "I had no idea this was a swingers' party. I would never have come here if I did."

"I didn't know what to say or do and I was totally uncomfortable," I told him. I was still in shock.

"I'm really sorry. I promise it will never happen again."

My mind was racing a mile a minute, and I found it hard to believe that he had no idea where we were going or what the agenda was. His apologies continued all the way to where my car was parked, and while I listened, I learned an important life lesson. I naively made the mistake of going out with this man and it turned out badly. With all his apologies, I wasn't going to make the same mistake again. I would never see him again, and that turned out to be the right decision. Months later, I happened upon a magazine article about the Playboy Mansion and Steve specifically, that talked about how he was the go-to "party person" for events and that he knew exactly how to get things started. He would drape a tiny hand towel over his erect penis and walk into the group of partygoers naked and ready.

I made the right call and remembered that to this day. If a person shows you who they are, believe them. You can make an honest mistake once, but if you do the same thing again, expecting different results, then the burden of what happens is on you. Einstein said that repeating the same thing over again expecting different results is the definition of insanity. This one incident influenced my life to this day. It was the first and the last experience of its kind, although I did continue dating a few different men. I struggled between sanity and rebellion before returning to Vincent to upset and nearly destroy my parents, and, as luck would have it, myself.

Some months later, we eloped to Las Vegas. I was already throwing up again and knew what my fate was to be. I also knew Vegas was the town of good luck, but little did I know it would play such an important part in my life. The Little White Wedding Chapel in Las Vegas, Nevada, would soon be introducing us as Mr. and Mrs.

PRISONER OF DARKNESS

The preacher was a tall and lanky dude with long, slicked-back hair, who looked like he doubled at one of the lounge shows in Vegas for Elvis Presley. I was nineteen years old and my husband was eighteen, but we were ready to take on the world. In truth, we were so ill-equipped that we were barely ready to take on each other. We drove back to Los Angeles in our beat-up car, holding hands like a couple of infatuated newlyweds, exactly what we were. We moved immediately into an apartment in a complex owned by Vincent's mother. It was a good thing that we had her, as truthfully no one else wanted us.

The apartment was small, very dark, and smelled like mothballs. There were two windows at the front that were covered with dingy beige curtains that had been recycled more than once and showed wear and tear no matter what part of the room you were looking at them from. The carpeting was olive green shag and it resembled dying grass. It wasn't an expensive shag carpet like the ones you see in the *House & Garden* magazine. It was just ordinary in its appearance, significantly worn down, but suitable for this tacky rental unit that we now called home.

Our new home was furnished in traditional 1950s fare with a threadbare couch, covered in large cabbage roses of white, pink, and green. In its heyday, it must have looked presentable, but then, years later, without the aid of a simple cleaning, it was worn, tattered on the skirt, and faded. It looked like something that might have been retrieved from a dump yard, or from the home of a recently deceased relative who had owned it for fifty years. A lone, soot-covered, tattered brown chair stood beside it.

A laminated end table was on either side of the tatters, and there was a rectangular glass and laminate coffee table in front of this Mexican modern ensemble. Cream-covered shades stood smartly on top of the discolored brass-based lamps, and a metal floor lamp sprang up from the other side of the room.

Clearly, this was not *House & Garden*, but more like Cartoon Express. The entire apartment reeked of old age and mothballs, and I had to wonder who the hell had been living there before us. The darkness of the two rooms nearly buried my youth, and in the morning, I could hardly breathe, suffocated by the despair of the place. There was no escape, and only my dreaded regular doctor's appointments allowed me to be free of this prison for a time, to breathe the fresh air and see the sunlight that escaped me each day. I was a prisoner of my own doing, a convict sentenced to life in this shabby prisonlike apartment for the crime of being pregnant. What was I to do?

Over the next months I wallowed in shapeless maternity garb, the kind with little butterflies or bees all over the front, or horizontal stripes that made me look even fatter than I was. They were in pale, nonexistent colors that melted away my identity. I was, for all intents and purposes, nonexistent. Pregnancy obliterated me, emotionally and physically. My outfits were indistinguishable from a pup tent, and my body ceased to exist. Unlike the svelte bare maternity outfits that adorn celebrities, I was destined to look like an engorged papaya at the age of nineteen.

I was a shadow of the person I longed to be and thought I had been in a previous life.

I lived for the drama I could create while Vincent fixed our car in the driveway. It was like the do-it-yourself projects I had read about, but far from the trendy life I dreamed about.

He would come upstairs into our dark and musty apartment, covered in grease and smelling of dirt, the road, and exhaust fumes, his hair still standing straight up on end. It made me wonder what the hell I ever saw in him. I never figured that out even years later.

His hands and fingernails were caked in black gunk, and the hair I once found so cute, so fascinating, now looked amusing and ridiculous. The playful way he would tell me to get off his lap now became just another annoyance, as my belly grew fatter and fatter. Then there was the incessant morning sickness. Not the flu, of course, but this retching and vomiting that tore into my guts every morning and had me hanging over the bed or the toilet bowl every night. My appetite waned and all I could think about was sleeping this pregnancy away. It went on for nine agonizing months.

I feel a bit dizzy and tired. I'm sick, sick of hanging over the edge of the bed retching my guts out. No sex, what the hell has happened to the sex? I want this over and I want this over now. Maybe if I take just one more pill, I can sleep tonight, just one more. Okay, I think I feel a little better now. Just a little more sleep for me and I will be fine.

The sound of broken glass brought me back to where I was, the kitchen, but I was still a bit groggy. Vincent had gone out with his friends, again. That seemed to be a typical day for him lately. He didn't really enjoy seeing me drag my oversized girth around the small, dark apartment so he would go off with his friends to play pool, or hunt chicks.

I had just dropped a glass down the garbage disposal. Then, in my cloudy state, I made the mistake of trying to retrieve it with my bare hands.

Blood was everywhere, on my hand, on the counter, on the floor. and in the sink. *What the hell did I do? I thought I was just going to pull some garbage from the disposal and the broken glass was there. I didn't even realize I had done that.*

I wrapped a double bed sheet around my hand, lay down on the couch, and waited for Vincent to return and take me to the hospital. *It serves him right. Where in the hell was he anyway? I just sliced my hand open and am bleeding all over the house, and where was he? Probably out playing pool with his buddies while I bleed to death on the couch.*

I drifted in and out of consciousness. At times I felt as if I were floating above the whole ridiculous scene, watching some Peter Sellers movie about the clumsy Inspector Clouseau.

What in the world had I just done? I suppose I could have phoned someone, anyone, but I was nothing if not dramatic then and I rather liked the idea that Vincent would come home, drunk, after a night out with the boys, and find my lifeless, pregnant body on the couch.

What would he do? How would he cope? The knowledge of his failure to be there would be overwhelming, and he would die a thousand deaths. The punishment fit the crime, and for that I was grateful.

I would call no one. I would wait and let the drama unfold, as a good soap opera does every moment of every day. General Hospital *or* As the World Turns, *this was my life, laid bare for all to see. No, not all. It was my life, laid bare for Vincent to see. It would serve him right to find me dead or dying on the couch. I was nineteen, pregnant, and bleeding to death, and where the hell was he? With his stupid friends, that's where!*

As luck would have it, I did not die, nor did I lose enough blood for a transfusion. I merely wallowed in self-pity for several hours, my hand wrapped in a bed sheet that had turned bright red, until Vincent returned home to our barrio apartment.

A late-night trip to the emergency hospital, twelve stitches, and a stern warning from the doctor not to drop any more glasses into the garbage disposal, and I was good as new. My hand healed perfectly, with a small but meaningful scar at the base of my right pinkie, and Vincent went on disappearing with his friends. Clearly my near-death experience had not impacted him nearly as much as I had hoped it would.

For me, I realized my naivete had put me in a dangerous position where I could have ended up bleeding to death or losing the baby right there in our apartment. Maybe then Vincent would have paid more attention.

At last, the olive-green shag carpeting proved far too much for me, and on a fateful day in October, with my belly still swollen beyond my toes, we moved to Vincent's mother's bungalow in Burbank.

It was a tiny place, with two small bedrooms that reeked of mildew and Mexican food. Mother was anything but the stereotypical Hispanic mom that is sometimes made into a cartoon.

She was sleek and elegant, with a heavy Hispanic accent that belied the fact that she was born in San Diego. She was also very skilled and clever and used the accent regularly for her benefit.

It allowed her to consistently pretend that she didn't understand English and gave her time to think things through before replying, only to reply in broken English. It was an art, and she was the craftsman.

There were four of us in our new Burbank abode. The husband de jour was a man named Howard who was her seventh and eighth. She obviously didn't learn anything the first time she married and divorced him, because she decided to marry him again, years after their first divorce was final. It was a compounded mistake indeed, but one that she finally rectified after our son, Greg Alan, was born. Howard was balding, introverted, and slight of frame.

His background was German, and it was clear right at the onset of our arrival that he didn't like either of us and considered us a huge burden. He just sat on the couch in perpetual silence, staring out into the backyard, no doubt secretly wishing we would just vanish.

The house in Burbank was a step or two up from the olive shag-carpeted mausoleum that we had lived in rent-free for months, but only just a step or two. However, the inclusion of Howard into the equation basically put it on the same playing field as the mausoleum.

I was heavy from being pregnant and dragging my overstuffed body around depressed me beyond words. I couldn't sleep very well and spent hours working on poses in bed that would give me a few restful moments.

Most nights, I slept on my stomach like a beached whale, searching in the sand for a delicious treat. It was quite the feat and one that I cannot replicate today, no matter how hard I try.

Sleeping on my stomach seemed to work for me at the time, but later on, I worried if that was why Greg Alan was born with a slightly squashed head.

Howard was a bitter and angry man, who became even more so once we moved in. Some days he seemed permanently affixed to the overstuffed sofa, barely glancing up for hours at a time.

The '56 Chevy sat in the driveway, not running most of the time, and Vincent spent hours covered in grease trying to look like a mechanic in repair mode. It was really quite amusing! My father, on the other hand, probably didn't know the difference between a wrench and a hammer. He was more of an intellectual, and truth was that is the kind of man I should have married in the first place.

The nine months seemed to be never ending as I dragged my inflated body around. I was feeling much like an African elephant. *Was I cursed? I wondered if I would have to carry this load for another nine months or even longer? How did elephants do it? I no longer walked, I waddled.*

Sleeping on my stomach wasn't an option any longer either. So, I hardly slept anymore, but rather rested, one gigantic side of me propped up with two fluffy pillows.

I didn't binge on food or indulge myself, as I had no desire to eat and never had food cravings. It seemed to me that I just lounged around getting fatter and fatter, wishing I had never had sex at all. When Greg Alan was born, I weighed the astonishingly low figure of 116 pounds. With all the blubber I thought I had put on I had only gained sixteen pounds.

There I was, relaxing on my side, daydreaming that, in some diabolical way, maybe this was just that, a bad dream. But it wasn't, and I continued being both pregnant and bored with my routine of waddling around night and day.

Nine months and one week behind me and I was still fat and flabby. Now I was late, and that was the very last thing that my body or me needed or wanted. I cried, I wailed, I screamed, I went slightly crazy, and then I went to the doctor again. I just wanted this torture over! My very short female doctor finally decided to induce labor, a process that I caution against even after all these years.

Two weeks before my twentieth birthday, I entered the hospital young and naïve, and my first input of information came from a nurse who confided in me that I should not have a spinal block for delivery.

Instead, she suggested general anesthesia, since a seventeen-year-old girl had recently died after having a spinal block. This certainly wasn't a great way for me to start the process of childbirth. I was already quite terrified since I was alone and had no idea what to expect. That rather unsettling news was accompanied by the screams of other patients coming from the delivery rooms.

After the nightmare of childbirth, I often lamented that I was nineteen and alone in an ordeal that I would never forget. Those few days crafted my lifelong attitude about giving birth, and I never considered doing it again.

There I was, lying in this stark, vacant room all alone, because in the '60s hospitals did not appreciate the value of having a loved one in the room with the expectant mother.

The screams were penetrating my ears as I lay alone in the hospital bed, wondering why I was getting this IV in my arm and what the hell they were trying to do to me. Every so often Dr. Anne would come into the room, climb up on a box, and stick a few fingers into my private parts. Her visits became more and more frequent until finally, the moment had arrived.

After what seemed like a lifetime and an abundance of drama later, our son Greg Alan came into the world, with a small bit of fanfare and an enormous amount of straight black hair.

No one was allowed in the delivery room except Dr. Anne on her box and the nurses. For me it was a day of monumental decisions. The blackboard in the room from hell, where I was confined prebirth, looked like the scribbled notes of a grade-school kid. They were actually anesthesia decisions being made by my practical, nearly twenty-year-old mind in relation to the type of knock-out drops I was to receive. The choices were anything but vast. General or spinal, my final answer was based on the fact that a girl a few years younger than me had died days after getting a spinal. Contrary to what the doctor had suggested, I opted for a general. In my mind a sleepy newborn was better than a dead or permanently paralyzed mother.

During that stressful time, I decided other issues that weighed on my shoulders. As an adult, of sound mind, I recognized incredible pain and knew enough to understand that our body helps us forget quickly.

Therefore, in order to never forget the experience of childbirth, I made a mental note about its unbearable nature and agreed never to experience it again. Therefore, Greg was destined to be an only child from the get-go. In a move I could only classify as spiteful, he went on to have at least four kids that I know about. That was the final tally at the end of his terminal illness, a failed bout with cancer. Sadly, that illness had in fact turned him into an irrational person and even more malevolent toward me than normal.

Unfortunately, he departed the world long before he could experience some of the "joys" of real fatherhood.

Of all those struggles, the anger, the resentment, the awkward tween years, the defiant teens, and all the rest that I had lived through, suffered with, and died a thousand deaths from, I think I regret that almost more than anything. No, I **know** I do. That after decades of his emotional abuse nearly destroying me, I admit that I reveled in the thought that one day, down that road, he would experience the devastation that comes and never leaves when your child treats you like an evil stranger.

I wanted him to have that experience, times four, to know how it felt. He managed to duck out on that one for sure. His children were far too young to have wounded him as he had wounded me. When he passed, the oldest was eight, too young to have done much beyond watching in stunned silence as his father became consumed by the ravages of cancer.

His illness was to deprive him of any of the joys that his children might have brought into his life as well. But then, Greg knew everything, yet failed himself by not adhering to his doctors' instructions following a fifteen-hour surgery to save him from the disease. After being diagnosed with cancer of his tongue and mouth, he underwent an operation at the eminent UCLA hospital in Westwood in November 2009. He emerged, days later, unable to talk and in need of rehabilitation therapy, but still his combative and angry self. Several years later, he unilaterally decided that he never had cancer, and that the eminent hospital had operated on him without just cause. Another error in judgment by a young man who was too "smart" for his own good and ended up outsmarting himself.

PROMISES AND PIECRUSTS

Other than his American Indian look at birth, Greg Alan was nothing unusual. At first my mother thought he had been hit in the face with a board, since it was squashed like a marshmallow that had been sat on, but red, the coloring of a Native American Indian. His road to the light of day had been rough, not forty miles long, but more than an inch and the exit door was nearly closed, so he struggled to free himself from imprisonment. His face clearly took the brunt of that struggle.

As luck would have it, the years were very kind to him. By the time he was six months old he had the face of an angel, and as he aged, he became movie star gorgeous and a veritable magnet for women of all ages.

His father and I had long since divorced, with Greg taking sides, and so he fought ferociously against me, but clung to every word his absentee father uttered. I often wondered if his struggle with our divorce influenced the anger and mayhem that he inundated me with each day. Fortunately, or not, it was that very anger that closed him off where I was concerned, and in the end, kept me from ever knowing the answer.

Before Greg even started school, Vincent and I were drifting apart for a million reasons, the most important of which I forgot the moment we moved in together. I didn't really love him but foolishly was punishing my parents, and in the end, myself. But then, who knew? Vincent was more comfortable in bed than at work, and only showered every four or five days, whether he needed it or not.

He carried a rage inside of him that exposed itself with physical abuse to the inside of our apartment, and to me. One day he hit me so hard that he shattered my eardrum, and another he took his anger out on Greg, whose only crime was to pee in his diaper while Vincent was holding him.

He was barely three months old. We were living in a small apartment in Burbank, alone and on our own with our son.

Vincent had picked him up before his diaper was totally on and he peed on him, hitting him in the face. I thought it was quite amusing but stifled my laughter for fear of reprisal.

Vincent turned red with rage, flinging Greg from one side of the room onto the flowered couch. He didn't even understand or care that he could have injured or killed our son. What if he had missed the couch or if he had rolled onto the floor? It was just the first of many such rageful incidents that I had to deal with in the few years that I was with him. His narcissistic personality allowed him to believe that he was always right and never made mistakes, when in actuality, he made them regularly.

One morning he put his fist through the bathroom door in our apartment because I woke him up. As I recall I had taken the advice of my mother when it came to techniques of waking up a slothful person. She suggested a glass of cold water worked quite well, so that was my crime that particular morning. I tossed the water onto a sleeping Vincent, and he rose like a phoenix out of the ashes of our bed, fists flying in every direction. I never asked my mother for wake-up suggestions again.

A few weeks later, I was feeling emotional and sat on Vincent's lap. He immediately pushed me off and onto the floor and said, "Get off, you're wrinkling my pants."

It goes without saying that I never sat on his lap again. The one-time fairy tale had turned into a horror story right before my eyes. My parents had been right all along. Vincent was not the right person for me or for our son.

My relationship with Vincent slammed into a wall before the third year of our marriage. We had been drifting apart for some time, with Vincent running amok with his ne'er-do-well friends from high school, and then there was a period where he pretended to go to college. Toward the end of all the drama, I had a short but tumultuous affair with a guy named George who worked in my office, and who made love to me as if there was no tomorrow. It was my first affair as a married woman, and I never regretted it. He was dark-skinned, very good-looking, and had a strange foreign last name that began with an A. I would sneak over to his tiny apartment near Western Avenue in Los Angeles, and we would play the song "Strangers in the Night" as we had hot sex on his couch hour after hour. After our lovemaking we embraced, and then I would drive home to the "Little Shop of Horrors," a small apartment in Burbank that Vincent and I rented. It became part of my routine and a couple of nights a week I would "work late."

It was a fantasy! George and I would get naked, his hard dick pressed against my slender belly. Then he would slip his hardness easily inside of me and pound away, until he shot a load of hot cum into my waiting vessel.

I was so young, and it was scary at times, partially because I feared getting caught, and the other part because I feared getting pregnant. Neither event occurred, however, and the end of the affair came as abruptly as the beginning. One day it was just over. Months later, Vincent moved out and I filed for divorce. It was the end of a short chapter in my life and the completion of the somewhat bumpy road of my youth.

I had given up my teenaged years in favor of what I thought was true love but was really nothing more than my ego trying to prevent my parents from being right. In retrospect, they were right, and now it is far too late to tell them. Vincent had been my first lover and my first "love," but not my last, not by a long shot. I was twenty-one when parallel events changed my life forever. The events happened in rapid succession, literally within weeks of each other. First, Vincent moved out, then I shattered my leg in a skiing accident, and both events were devastating in their own special way. I remember Vincent and I parting ways after his mother offered him a particularly fast muscle car. So much had proceeded this event that it is all quite convoluted now, but suffice it to say,

Vincent was lying about almost everything. I was totally over him and his lies and wanted out.

One massive lie involved him going to college. His mother was paying a small fortune for him to attend the University of Southern California when all the while he was playing pool with his high school buddies.

This monumental falsehood continued for more than a year while we were married. He would leave for "school" each morning, books in hand, returning after his definition of "school" was over for the day. It took a lot of costly tuitions before "mommy dearest" realized that his entire time at college was a fraud and any "report cards" were forged, as he hadn't been attending school at all. What shocked me was there were no consequences for his unconscionable actions.

Of course, she was angry and yelled, screamed, and threatened, empty threats of course, just before she asked her ninth husband to give him a job in the stock market.

That was her definition of a consequence! On the other hand, I was done with him and his lack of motivation and personal hygiene, and his flagrant, continuous lies. My consequences where he was concerned were to get a divorce.

Shortly after we divorced, he started working in the stock market for his stepfather, the ninth and final husband, only to violate his most basic rule, don't hold any stock overnight. This ended up with the company losing large sums of money, and Vincent finally losing his job.

I suppose it didn't really surprise me that his mother's attitude toward his lying and cheating was insipid, and forgiveness arrived almost immediately along with a gratuitous amount of money.

His list of lies had gone on for so long and were so outrageous that my patience had finally disappeared, and only anger and disappointment were left.

After he was out of the apartment and I had a chance to breathe again, I made plans to go skiing with a girlfriend. Always the adventurer, this was brand new for me as—newsflash—I had never been skiing in my life before. *What could possibly go wrong?*

We drove in my VW Beetle hundreds of miles to June Mountain in California on the way to our amazing adventure.

My sense of wild abandon and recklessness began on day one when I rented skis, boots, and bindings. The optimum word here is rented! Had I done a bit of research into this adventure, I would have made the commitment to purchase equipment and not rented from a shop on the slopes.

I have always been a bit of a risk-taker, and this day was to be no different. I looked the part attired in trendy ski garb, spent the appropriate amount of hours on a bar stool, and then we set off to hit the slopes.

I picked a slope with a catchy name, Boardwalk, but had no idea that it was for advanced skiers. I just thought it looked interesting on the map of trails. So, there I was at the top of Boardwalk, on my rented skis, about to take my very first pass down this run. I suppose that on some level, I knew this was meant for more advanced skiers and not a starting point for newbies, but there I was skis pointed downhill, and it seemed a bit late to change my mind.

I began snowplowing to keep from going too fast, first run and all. The icy wind was hitting my naked cheeks, stinging them with the freezing cold as I advanced down the slope. My snowplow position was now a thing of the past, and my skis were parallel, and I was picking up speed. Suddenly, my ski hit a sitzmark, a hole in the snow, and there was a cracking sound that echoed in my ears. My next clear memory, I was looking up from a snowbank into the patchwork blue sky above. The rented bindings on my ski boots had failed to release and my leg snapped over my left boot like a dried twig.

It was the ultimate **oops** moment! I lay prone in the freezing snow, smartly dressed in my trendy ski garb, but confused, disoriented, and not knowing what to expect next. Skiers passed by at high rates of speed, some stopping to offer assistance, others not.

What had I done? What was I going to do? Was I just going to die here in the freezing cold? OMG, the pain, the excruciating pain. It seemed like there was an endless line of skiers offering hand waves or assistance before the snow patrol finally arrived to cart me off on a gurney.

Being young, a bit headstrong, and stupid, I was embarrassed at my plight, rather than at my stupidity when they arrived to haul me down the mountain. I could only hope that no one of any consequence had seen me.

Imagine that! Two spiral fractures in my leg and I was worried about someone of "consequence" seeing me being carted off on a gurney.

A ski trip that had started in June Mountain ended up in Mammoth Lakes, when I was transported by ambulance nearly thirty miles with an air cast on my shattered leg.

My next memory is of the ambulance arriving at the doctor's office and a hot and hunky doctor walking out into the snow to carry me into the hospital. The injuries were serious, and I ended up in surgery for hours and in the Mammoth Hospital in excruciating pain for a week, with metal pins in my knee and ankle. The only good news the accident brought about was that I enjoyed five days with the hot, hunky doctor visiting me two or three times a day before I was pronounced ready to go home.

That stupidity ended up leaving me with metal pins in my knee and ankle and a cast the length of my leg that was to remain for five long months before a walking cast replaced it. I think the pain of that break lasted longer than the pain of my breakup. The failed trip down the side of the mountain may have seemed like the ultimate embarrassment in my young life, but that was nothing compared to what lay ahead.

Since my girlfriend had long since taken the car and gone home, I had no choice but to reach out to my abusive, soon-to-be ex-husband Vincent to come and pick me up.

Vincent and I became a historical blurb very quickly and I had no one to cry or complain to, as both of my parents remained distant and unmoved. The ride back with him was nothing if not an exercise in silence, with two people who had absolutely nothing to say to each other, good, bad, or indifferent. Vincent and I were soon divorced, and he went to the proverbial other woman.

Her name was something that began with an E, although I cannot for the life of me recall what it was. She went on to have one child with the Chia Pet, before learning his true character, or lack thereof, and divorcing him. There were moments when I felt sorry for her and wished we could have at least had an open line of communication. I might have been able to prevent some of her pain.

Our break-up had ended with a bribe, much like when I had been bribed with a '56 Chevy to stay away from Vincent. Vincent's mother had bribed him to stay away from me with a super-fast muscle car, a Pontiac with a 350 Hemi engine inside. Considering the bribes, I was worth far more than he was, clearly, at least where his mother was concerned. It wasn't long before he married the girl whose name began with an E.

Greg was three at the time and not quite a handful, but on his way. By the time he reached the tender age of eight, he had packed his bags and run away a few times, lit the rubbish container at the back of our apartment on fire once, and stolen a modest number of Hot Wheels cars from local establishments. I drew the line at everything, even making him return the stolen Hot Wheels cars to their rightful owners. Sadly for Greg, nothing made up for Vincent's intentional absence.

I spent six long months in a leg cast as a result of my skiing accident. Six months of my life in pain, with my leg propped up on a wastepaper basket at my office. At the time, I was working for a real estate company on Robertson Boulevard. It was about an exciting as my broken leg.

Three of us in a small office with nothing to look at during the day but each other.

After nearly six months of being wrapped in what seemed like white concrete, I was aching to break out of my prison. True to form, a month after getting the cast removed, I flew to Mexico by myself and ended up scuba diving in Acapulco with full-on tanks strapped to my body. Fearless always was, and still is, the best definition of who I am. Truth is, there was nothing I really feared back then, not even being alone. It may have *seemed* crazy scuba diving nose to nose with a moray eel and other assorted sea creatures a mere month after recovering from a devastating skiing accident, but for me it was "business as usual."

By then, I knew that being single was far better for me and my adventurous life than being trapped in a loveless relationship with anyone. My mantra over the years became, "If it's broken and you can't fix it, next!" I adhere to that today!

Nothing could stop me then and nothing really stops me now. Looking back, there is nothing I would change other than not marrying the Chia Pet when I was nineteen. That would have solved a plethora of problems, and I could have dodged the courtroom drama that Greg created.

Greg Alan, or just Greg as we called him, struggled with life almost from the moment he was born. He always longed for what he didn't have, rather than be satisfied with everything that was right there at his fingertips.

Even as an adult of fifty, he longed for the one thing he really didn't have and never managed to get, which was his father's love. He wore his anger and contempt like gang colors for all to see.

His childhood had been marred by waves of stealing and setting an occasional fire in the trash bin, most of which were masterminded to receive the long overdue attention from his father. At arm's length it is clear to see that some people don't have the capacity to love anyone other than themselves. Sadly, Greg could never step back far enough to recognize the futility of his desires The stunts he pulled rarely worked and only served to upset everyone involved, eventually destroying my relationship with his stepfather, Ira.

Greg was without a doubt a handful who really spiraled out of control the day he turned thirteen. Truthfully, it wasn't just about wanting the attention of his dad that made his wheels turn. He was motivated by a cauldron of anger against me, of course, for leaving his father in the first place, but also aimed at everything and everyone who was postured along the sidelines watching and waiting. Those "posers" included Ira, and a stepbrother who seemed to live the charmed life, as well as an assortment of other siblings, all of whom were treated differently than Greg, at least in his mind.

The year was 1974 and I was already married to Ira, a criminal and personal injury lawyer. Greg turned thirteen that year, and I watched helplessly as his head seemed to spin around, and his wheels flew off in every direction. He seemed to be possessed by the devil himself, in need of an exorcism, and truthfully, he never recovered. In an instant, he went from "difficult" teen to impossible one, and I had no idea which way to turn for help.

We were living in Tarzana, a town in the San Fernando Valley, where South of the Boulevard held some significance. A happy collection of two adults, both in need of some R&R, a teen in need of an exorcism, and three dogs all ensconced happily ever after in our South of the Boulevard home. At least that was the dream but not the reality.

The sign of the devil within him was only just rearing its ugly head when, one day, shortly after he turned fifteen, I overheard him negotiating to buy a bunch of pot to sell. *What the hell was going on?*

The red flags were dropping all over the place, and it was time for Ira and me to have a very serious discussion about Greg and his future.

Ira was working at the Van Nuys District Attorney's office, and we knew this needed to be dealt with quickly and effectively and not put on hold even for a minute. Then before we had a chance to talk about how to proceed, I discovered several one-hundred-dollar bills stuffed under the cushions of our living room chairs. That was the breaking point and the one that caused Ira to call in some favors.

What followed was a flurry of phone calls, a court hearing, and after the dust settled, Greg was sent away to a special rehabilitation camp for troubled juveniles with assorted problems, located in the San Bernardino mountains, called CEDU. It turned out he would have been far better off at home than in a center that became rife with charges surrounding the abuse of youngsters in their care. Unfortunately for all concerned, the real camp would not be exposed for what it was until years later. The mere location of the camp totally isolated the residents with escape from the prisonlike surroundings the only option. CEDU was billed in some ads as a boarding school for troubled youths and a youth-oriented drug rehabilitation center, neither of which provided a very accurate picture. In later years, they actually called the facility the nation's first emotional growth boarding school, but that too was totally inaccurate.

The questionable therapy procedures utilized to allegedly help "fix" troubled youths included sleep deprivation, marathon therapy workshops lasting days on end, and humiliation at the hands of other residents. Many of these controversial therapies had their roots in Synanon, a substance abuse program that was founded in 1958 by recovering alcoholic Charles Dederich. His methods were supposed to "help" addicts by humiliating and isolating them, forcing them into hard labor and depriving them of sleep.

Numerous programs sprang out of Synanon and flourished for a time with the help of daytime television. Many a troubled juvenile that had been sent to CEDU adopted the fight-or-flight attitude, with flight being the eventual winner.

Greg ran away a total of three times before Vincent decided to take him home to stay with him and his new wife. The placement exercise essentially lasted longer than his stay at CEDU. By then Vincent was married again and had a new baby, so this exercise became not only one of futility, but a serious mistake in judgment.

Within days, father and son were sleeping in the car, thrown out by his new wife, and within a week Vincent was calling me to announce the immediate return of Greg Alan to the school.

The problem was the courts were no longer involved in the matter, nor would they be paying for the rehabilitation since Vincent had officially removed him. Of course, Vincent called expecting that I would share the joy of paying over $1,350 a month to the rehab center.

"You must be kidding me. Are you completely insane? You took him out of there, you pay for it. I am not paying one penny more than the one hundred fifty dollars the courts ordered."

Of course, after a few more colorful expletives, I launched into a verbal attack that left him speechless, perhaps for the only time in his miserable life.

"We struggled to get him into this program, and the court was paying all the costs but one hundred fifty dollars. Then you decide to go and take him out, and now the cost is thirteen hundred and fifty dollars! You can damn well pay for it yourself! I am not paying one single dime. You did this, you live with it," I exclaimed.

Of course, after the smoke cleared, I did not pay any money toward the madness Vincent had singlehandedly created. Greg was returned to CEDU by his father and approximately a month later, he ran away again, but this time he ended up at Ira's office, of all places. Of course, we took him home and tried to make the best of what seemed to be an unhealthy and dangerous situation. Little did I know the day we attempted the assimilation of Greg into our life would be the beginning of drama on steroids.

We had recently moved into a large home on Doheny Road in Los Angeles, and so we turned one of the bedrooms into a room for Greg. His presence was unexpected, and while we were filled with a good deal of apprehension, we welcomed him with open arms and a stern warning that he best never be buying drugs to use or to sell. Sadly, those words landed on deaf ears.

I am not sure what we could have done to have eased his assimilation into our lives, because what we did failed to work. Our new home was set amid lovely trees and a heap of celebrity neighbors. It boasted two living rooms, formal and casual, a dining room that could seat twenty easily, a library, a forty-foot master bedroom, and a one-thousand-square-foot guesthouse. There were four bedrooms upstairs and a maid's room and bathroom downstairs. Greg's new room was home to a custom-made four-poster bed with a set of stairs to help you climb into it.

When we sold the house a year later to Stevie Nicks of Fleetwood Mac, that bed was the only thing she requested be part of the sale.

BROKEN PROMISES

Growing up, Greg was never known for his tidiness, but his flagrant disregard for even the basics of cleaning his new room went beyond words. One needed a ladder to be able to climb over the piles of dirty clothing that he "hung" on the floor. Perhaps a better course of action would have been classes on the art of cleaning and directions to the room that housed what is commonly known as the washer and dryer.

At least with those two issues resolved, he could gather his dirty clothes off the floor, carry them to the laundry room, and fling them into the wash. Sadly, those classes were never held. In some ways, he was sixteen going on six, headstrong, willful, angry, sullen, and full of his own importance, and in other ways he was sixteen going on twenty-six, headstrong, willful, angry, sullen, filled with his own importance, and a magnet for strippers. He appeared to be on a collision course with himself.

What went on inside of his head was a rage against his father that he never expressed but rather directed at me. In my heart I knew that Vincent didn't have the capacity to love anyone, but like most kids, Greg needed his father to love him. Sadly, to this day Vincent is totally incapable of loving anyone but himself.

Greg's rage continued to gain tread and grow exponentially over the wrongs committed against him, real and imagined, by his father, though most were real.

The love-hate turmoil pounding inside of Greg's head must have, at times, made him think he was going mad. Not a day went by where I didn't suffer at the hands of his misplaced anger. I tried but could never figure out what to do about it, and I suffered because of my failings.

He loved his father, no doubt about that, but the anger and disappointment he also felt for him propelled the rage even further. As Greg got older, Vincent, pretending to care, used him to reel in women.

His movie-star good looks made him a magnet for women of all ages, shapes, and sizes, so Vincent took him to strip clubs and party houses. There it was, a veritable buffet of sex, drugs, and women in every direction, and right in the middle of it all was Greg, with his raging good looks and hot, sexy body. Of course, Vincent was right there too, along for the ride of his life.

Truthfully, there were times when I couldn't help but wonder how this incredible specimen could be my son. He was smoking hot, with a body that screamed sex. No wonder some of my girlfriends were lusting after him. Over the years, I spent a great deal of time cleaning up his messes, believing the tall tales he would weave for my benefit, or the benefit of anyone within earshot. Everything was always someone else's fault, as Greg never took responsibility for anything.

He was, in my humble opinion, a master manipulator, using his good looks to ply whatever he wanted from whomever he wanted it from. He always looked older than his years and, in fact, we looked closer in age than any mother and son should. Some people might have even thought we were dating.

Years later, I wondered how significant a part the age issue played in our lack of a close relationship.

After all, some kids want their mother to look like a "mother" and apparently, Greg was one of those kids. I often played mind games, picturing myself with my hair graying, respectably pulled back in a bun, wearing minimum makeup, if any. (Men in general, and Greg specifically, claimed to dislike makeup.)

There I would be, dressed conservatively, a schoolmarm outfit of checkered or paisley print, wearing sensible, low-heeled shoes, an acceptable outfit for a PTA meeting. The visual was positively terrifying.

No question, this was how he would have preferred me to look, and that became more obvious as he grew older. What he wanted me to do was to grow old with grace and not Botox.

I was, in his mind, destined to look the part of a PTA mom skirting on grandmother, parent, cleaning lady, driver, chauffeur, seamstress, cook, and bottle-washer, but above all, appropriately aging mother. That was never going to happen no matter what sort of aggressive behavior he employed. I was determined to be true to who I was, who I am, and who I wanted to be. Me!

As an independent thinker, I had other ideas in mind. Good, bad, or indifferent, I never embraced the PTA mom with graying hair smartly pulled into a bun "look." My outfits resembled Gaga on a stage belting out a tune for all to enjoy. I was thin, blonde, and shapely, and had zero intention of changing that look or attitude for Greg or anyone else. Four husbands and three divorces later, and I am still an independent, strong-willed individual with no thought of changing.

In his mind, no mom should look like a slightly older girl-friend, decked out in a leopard Dolce & Gabbana corset dress, tits slightly bulging from the low-cut top enticingly.

Then there was me, Greg's mom. There I was, looking every bit the celebrity, made up like a movie star, teetering on a pair of four-inch Gucci stiletto pumps, a Fendi Spy Bag at my side, and a perfect, totally jeweled Sidekick in my pocket.

It was obscene, a horror, and a nightmare for him. There were the stares from strangers and his barely out of the teen years friends. "Shit, Mom, everywhere we go people stare at you. Why are they asking you who you are? Do they think you are some damn movie star or something? They want your autograph and all of that. It's embarrassing. They just stand around and stare and they think you and I are together. I mean, what's up with that anyway? Let's not go out for dinner, let's just stay in tonight."

I would have barely enough time to roll my eyes and sigh before he began bellowing once again.

"Oh God, I don't want anyone else asking if we are an item. I don't want any more of my friends blurting out, 'This is your mom? She looks so young.' I am sick to death of it. If one more guy stares at you or gives you a look, I am going to punch him out."

Those words literally became Greg's mantra, and, sadly, I had to endure those words day after miserable day.

At a time when I would have thought he would be proud of how I looked, how I dressed, how I carried myself, those words echoed against the wall that separated us and made me sometimes question whether I was right or wrong.

I questioned whether I should fall victim to the whims and wishes of my only son and start to look and act like the "mother/grandmother" he wanted me to be. The good news or the bad news, depending on your perspective, was that I never changed who I was, not for him, not for anyone. I am who I am and dammit, I'm proud of that.

He continued to carry on about me even though his father could wear anything he wanted, fuck anyone he wanted, anytime he wanted, and do or say basically whatever the hell he wanted. It made no difference because Greg still idolized him and put him on a pedestal, off-limits to criticism and basically untouchable.

Right, wrong, or indifferent, I refused to buckle under to his almost obscene requirements of me, and now I will never know for sure whether that change would have brought us closer or continued to keep us at arm's length for his life and mine.

His willful, unbridled anger tore at my heart and almost emptied out my soul. His words could cut to the quick, and he used them like daggers rather than entry-level, exploratory conversations. It soon became clear that some of Greg's friends didn't share the same conservative value system he held when it came to me, and that they liked what they saw.

It was hard to forget the night that Nick, Greg's best friend, a hunky and hot fireman, pressed his lips against mine and passionately kissed me for what seemed like an eternity. His kisses made it clear that more was desired, wanted, and needed. I may have wanted it and I did, but there were still signs of intelligent life inside of me, so I reasoned, how could I? I was, after all, Greg's mother, chauffeur, cook, cleaning lady, seamstress, parent, but above all, above everything else, I was his mom.

As tempting as Nick was, as much as I would have loved to have his rock-like six-pack and his hard cock pressing against my naked body, I had to refuse, reject, walk away, and give up on his advances. He hadn't been the only one, but he was, after all, a very memorable one.

Greg wore tight well. That day the skin-like white T-shirt showed off a mass of rippling muscles, more than God or I had ever imagined possible. His arms bulged with strength and the veins were like tributaries flowing under his skin and standing out as he leaned into the car. I couldn't help but think how ridiculously hot he was, although hot was not a word I felt comfortable using when it involved my son. I felt incredibly guilty just having those thoughts. I tried to eradicate them from my mind.

According to many of my girlfriends, he was undeniably a hunk, and some of them knew him very well, far better than I would have liked or approved of. I found out quite by chance that at least one of my so-called friends had slept with my son, and that was a shock that essentially ended our friendship.

The hot, muscular guy in the Coke ad had nothing on Greg. He was six foot two and dark, with skin like pounded coconut shells. His jaw was square, and his cheekbones sat smartly under his eyes.

My only son Greg was blessed with movie star good looks and never had any problem finding women to party with. One woman's obsession cost him dearly and ended badly for everyone.

ANGELS IN SIN

A *GQ* cover, January issue, sprung to mind, although he never saw himself in that light.

He was a sexually charged person, a Scorpio, the symbol of raw, rampant sex. I am a Scorpio and believe that one hasn't lived until they have been bitten by the sting of the almighty Scorpio. Somewhere in his Scorpio background lurked a Gemini moving in or out of him, as he had the ability to sting severely, but also to charm you into the ether. I hardly ever saw the latter when we were together, however, but then, I am getting ahead of myself.

Dedicated and loyal, an intrepid private eye, always trying to figure things out, the Scorpio loves sex just for the sake of sex. Greg was the typical male Scorpio, light on the outside with a very dark underbelly. Personally, I have always loved the female version of myself and have always refused to date the male version of me, finding the sting too painful to bear. However, if my memory serves me correctly, I did have a short but meaningful liaison with a successful Scorpio screenwriter who I met in Hollywood. I took a screenwriting course from him that ended up in a sexually charged romantic liaison that lasted for months. How many, I cannot recall, but significantly more than one or two. Obviously, I overlooked his dark underbelly in favor of his amazing wit and great looks.

I think over the years, I have gotten as bad as a lot of men who don't recall the names of those they have slept with. Maybe not quite that bad since I usually recall the names eventually. This particular Scorpio was memorable, and I do recall his name and face, though for purposes of this memoir, he shall remain nameless. He did, however, write a fantastic screenplay that was made into a wildly successful movie that starred Eddie Murphy.

Greg was a womanizer, and a good one at that. He had taken after his grandfather on his father's side and was hopelessly in love, or should I say lust, with every coffee-colored chick with big tits that he laid eyes on.

The breast man was a predator who usually ended up convincing the lamb that she needed more mutton on her, and so big tits were generally the order of business for all of his many girlfriends.

He kept an encyclopedia-sized black book with notes alongside each entry, giving inside information as to the likes and dislikes of the lady of the evening, and spelling out personal information for the predator to dine on, just in case he lost track of who he was with. But then, there was one big-breasted chick in particular who nearly finished our entire family off and made them but a memory in some forgotten diary. Her name was June aka Raven, and she was almost Greg's downfall, and in many ways, she changed the trajectory of his life and mine.

Moonlight and Madness

I was just twenty-three as I stood at the edge of the softly beating waves, the moon was dancing across the water, and the sky was black as India ink. The pungent smell of flowers permeated the air, and a warm breeze filled my nostrils until they flared open in acceptance. I was in Oahu for the second time in a month and a single woman. I could hear music, even though there was none playing, but I was in Hawaii where the air was fresh, the pungent floral smells hit all of your senses and I was in love, or at least in lust. The moon was the only light silhouetting the frame of a slender man with closely cropped hair who was standing waist deep in the dark, dancing waters. He motioned to me and obediently I ran to the water and into his arms. Clearly, I was ignorant of the fact that our two-bedroom love shack was actually a military retreat for soldiers and their families, and the surrounding waters were often filled with great white sharks, eager for leftovers that were tossed into the ocean. But then, I was just twenty-three.

My lover, Ron, and I had met a month earlier in a bar in Oahu, and this was both my return and, as it turned out, our swan song. Our relationship had begun and ended over a series of gardenia-clad Blue Hawaiis, a bar, and some recklessly spoken words.

The warm summer night, the scent of fresh flowers, and a few leis scattered in the water had convinced me the month before to follow this hot guy to a nearby apartment, where we had wild and crazy sex for hours, and played silly games on my stomach with whipped cream and strawberries.

I was nearly a virgin and more importantly I was free. My leg had recently healed from the nasty double spiral fracture and now I had one thing on my mind, hot sex, then falling in love, and my lover in Oahu fit the bill. At least I thought so.

Unfortunately, only the hot sex was real. In spite of the fact that my heart, my mind, and my body told me that I had found love again, it was not to be, for my lover, the dark and handsome Ron, was married with two small children. Who knew? All I came away with were two fabulous trips to Hawaii, some amazing memories, a few pressed gardenias, and a broken heart very much in need of healing. Welcome to my life!

My youth gave me more than just an overactive sex drive. It gave me the ability to heal quickly. My healing happened at warp speed after I met and bedded another guy with a three-letter first name and a dick the size of a baguette of French bread.

I met Lyn at the Luau restaurant in Beverly Hills, over a very blue drink, with an umbrella resting inside the lip of the glass. Now it seems like there was always a pink or blue drink involved in my escapades, with or without a gardenia or colored paper umbrella. We exchanged furtive glances, moved closer to each other and further away from the bar, all the while holding onto these enormous blue drinks.

Finally, we were cozying up hip to hip, then belly to belly, leaning on a couple of bar stools. He was tall and good-looking, and who knew then what special surprises he had to offer.

In retrospect, he did absolutely nothing of interest professionally, but physically, he caught my eye. I was in the mood to forgive and forget the other handsome but married guy with the three-letter name, Ron, who had held me, and my heart, by the dancing waters in Oahu. So, forgive I did, and forget as well, as Lyn and I made our way to his apartment that night.

After some more small talk, he started kissing my neck and slowly began to remove my top and then my tiny skirt.

He kissed my naked breasts and lightly ran his tongue over my nipples until they were hard as rocks. Once we were both naked, we had sex until we were totally worn out and he had no more cum to shoot into my hot pussy.

After all was said and done, he could lay claim to having given me some of the best, if not the most, climaxes, I had experienced in my twenty-four years. I was quenched and thought he had the closest thing to a porn star dick I had ever seen in my life. It was a full four fingers in breadth, and he nearly impaled me on the length. He was the first uncircumcised man I had ever been with and ended up being the only uncircumcised man I was with for the rest of my life. His penis resembled an elephant's trunk, and it was all I could do to keep from laughing out loud, until it was fully engorged and was no longer a laughing matter.

Sexual rapture is meant to last for only a moment in time, and that moment lasted one night. Either by my choice or his, we never saw each other again. In retrospect, I doubt that I could have functioned during the day if I were being impaled on a baguette-sized, fully engorged dick on a regular basis.

We parted ways, practically anonymously, only exchanging our first names and a lot of kisses and caresses. Over the next few months, I partied now and again, had some more nearly anonymous sex, and then seemed to settle down for a year or so while I watched Greg act up.

Then one night on the way home from the Cocoanut Grove and a Supremes concert with a girlfriend, I met someone special. It started innocuously enough at a stoplight, where this good-looking young man pulled alongside of me and asked for directions to the Marina del Rey. Only later did I find out that he knew the way extremely well, but his pickup line worked the charm.

We bantered back and forth, through a stoplight or two, and then I gave him my phone number. The following day he called, and we made a date to go to dinner.

He was a law student whose name was Ira Seltzer. He was a very bright, engaging guy who made our first date special, even though we went with another couple. Easy on the eyes with a very outgoing and fun personality, he seemed to find humor in almost everything. It was memorable for other reasons.

His friend brought a woman, a beautiful blonde, who was unique both inside and out. That date was the first and only one for them, but she and I became inseparable friends, sisters from another mother, and our connection has spanned decades and continues to this day. Friendships like that don't come into our lives that often, and this one has been special since day one. She has gone on to change the lives of so many women with her incredible work around incest and abuse, and she has even written books on the topic. I am blessed to call her my sister and my friend.

For Ira and me, it was to be a far longer date and commitment that ended with us marrying in Las Vegas, a year and a half later. By that time, we were spending nearly every available moment of time together, and Greg was already looking at him as a stepfather, whatever that meant to him. With law school finally in the rearview mirror, Ira went to work at the district attorney's office, and we settled into a somewhat normal life, at least for me.

Today, I wonder what normal really looks like, not only to me, but to others around me. I think my view may be somewhat bizarre and politically incorrect.

ANGELS IN SIN

There is nothing like the brilliance of a ride in a hot air balloon over the Masai Mara just as dawn breaks. From high above you can see herds of buffalo, zebra and wildebeest as they make their way over the terrain. On each of my three ventures into the air we landed in the midst of a herd of zebra and wildebeest to enjoy a waiting breakfast as the sun rose over the Mara.

The breathtaking majesty of Victoria Falls in Zimbabwe just as the sun hits the water creating a beautiful rainbow. No matter how many times I have stood at the base of the Falls, climbed to the top or flown over in a helicopter, I am always without words at the sheer magnitude and magic of it.

I was transfixed in Bombay, India as a giant cobra assumed the position and expressed his feelings about me taking pictures of him. I stayed a measured distance away.

ANGELS IN SIN

The cobra's benefactor plays a tune to get the snake to rise and show its' hood which generally happens when the animal feels threatened. I just stood and watched in amazement.

Hard to believe but this snake charmer seems totally unaffected by the fact that a python is now wrapped around his neck and the cobra is standing at attention right in front of him. I could not take my eyes off of this sight.

Outside of Delhi I am transfixed once again by the sight of a dancing bear who performs for me without hesitation. Moments later I would find myself part of the act.

Part of the act as the dancing bear's owner places the front half of a python around my neck. Notice that the snake is around two of us as its tail curls over the shoulder and down one side of the laughing Indian man beside me.

ANGELS IN SIN

Once again I am tempting fate and the elements while in a market outside of Bangkok Thailand. I could not resist the adorable little monkey at one of the stands and he came to me and laid in my arms with his little paw on my chest for what seemed like forever. It was so magical.

This particular occasion I found myself in Banff Canada and booked by a friend for a massage treatment. Clearly that was not on my wish list, so I cancelled the spa treatment and booked a sled drive instead. Again, I cannot resist wildlife and this pup in training stole my heart.

There I am, driving this team of eight dogs, which surprised even me. I started out with the driver and me in the cozy seat below him. Once we got to our destination he asked if anyone wanted to drive the sled back. There were two other couples from Georgia in sleds. Of course, never saying no to anything I raised my hand and said "ME." Not to be outdone by a lone woman, one of the men chimed in "me too." As luck or destiny would have it, I took my sled team back to the start without one issue, and it is not easy as you slide dramatically when changing direction. Unfortunately, the other couple, with their husband driving hit a tree shortly after takeoff. Luckily no one was hurt.

ANGELS IN SIN

This is a great look and I enjoyed every minute it took to get this way. Here I am covered in Dead Sea Mud from the Dead Sea in Israel. It may look a bit strange but it feels amazing and it is said to have a detoxifying effect and that the natural oils help balance the skin. I just loved how it felt on my body.

The pyramids made an incredible backdrop for my ride on a horse in Egypt. Seeing one of the Seven Great Wonders of the World was truly jaw dropping. I visited the Valley of the Kings and just the magnitude of what I saw made me ask many questions that have never been answered. Just looking at the way the Pyramids and the Great Sphinx were constructed gets your mind burning with questions. It is truly an experience to behold!

A delightful pyramid of Egyptian children decided to gather to greet me near the pyramids. It was such a joy to witness them forming a beautiful group of smiles and it gave me such pleasure.

The Khan Al Khalili Bazaar in Cairo, dates back to the 14th Century and this is me right in the center of it. I strolled through the stalls overwhelmed with the treasures being sold and of course returned with some amazing artifacts. This is a must see just for the experience as there is nothing quite like it. Today there are over four thousand shops spread across the winding alleys.

ANGELS IN SIN

Talk about up close and personal this was totally amazing. It was in Kenya at a famous animal orphanage that I was able to touch a baby elephant. The Sheldrick Wildlife Trust elephant orphanage and rescue which I visited in Nairobi National Park is where the magic took place. I have been there several times over the years and one time I was blessed when the caretakers were teaching an orphaned baby rhino how to eat grass. The baby was only a few weeks old and I got to stand within a foot of this beautiful baby for an hour watching it learn how to eat. Sadly, I did not have my camera then as I was heading to the airport, and it was packed away.

The Eastern Cape of South Africa at an animal rescue provided several incredible up close and personal encounters with wildlife. Meet Blade a stunning Serval, three-months old. I actually met Blade when he was only six weeks old, and he played on top of me as I lay in the grass at the rescue. I watched him grow into a beautiful representation of the species and it was fantastic knowing that he had been saved and protected as a newly born baby.

Standing in an opening in the rock with the wonder and magic of the Great Wall Of China behind me. There are no words to describe the feeling of walking on this great wonder of the World. Once in a lifetime does one get this opportunity. We had a Chinese English interpreter with us so no tours ever.

One can see Mongolia if you look over one side of the Great Wall Here I am being fanned by a lovely Mongolian woman who followed me up the steps to the top, and as I rested, she cooled me down from the climb.

ANGELS IN SIN

My view of the Great Wall from one perspective. It goes on for what seems like forever. We climbed to the Wall from the Simatai side and not the tourist side. It was heavenly.

The Forbidden City, Beijing in the background was just another part of the phenomenon that was China. The people, the food, the incredible cities and how far into the future they create their visions.

There is no sight that can compare with the trove of life-sized terracotta warriors that were discovered buried in front of the mausoleum of Emperor Qui Shi Hwang in 1974. There are over seven thousand of them in a variety of positions along with chariots and horses. Emperor Qui ascended the throne at the age of thirteen and apparently was obsessed with immortality. He spent a good deal of time in search of an elixir that would provide it, but his search was unsuccessful. His answer was to continue his supremacy by having this army created and buried by him. To date over two thousand of these warriors have been discovered and their presence continues to mystify and delight science and tourists from all over the world.

ANGELS IN SIN

The dramatic art of Face Changing I captured while enjoying this incredible display of near magic. The performers change their faces with the wave of a fan or a movement of the head. It was mesmerizing and as close as I was to the stage in the small theater, I could not see how it was done.

More of the dramatic art of Face Changing captured by me while enjoying this stunning, near magical performance. One must see it to believe it and then, even up close and personal, it remains a mystery.

ANGELS IN SIN

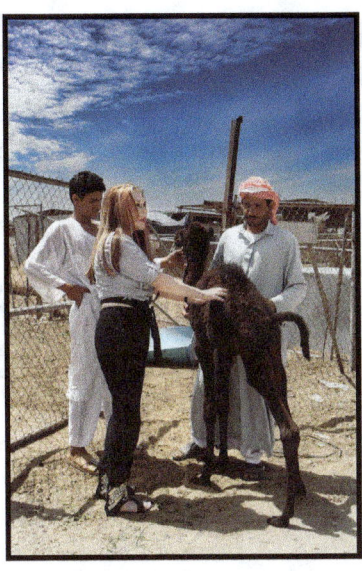

A first for me to be up close and personal with none other than a baby camel. It was magical as the two of us greeted each other in Doha. That was an amazing experience to say the least.

Another first in Doha at a hospital that rehabilitates wounded animals. This beautiful falcon seemed right at home with his handler and medic. It was truly a sight to behold and to be so close to this amazing bird,

The skyline in Doha is not what I expected. As I always say, never expect anything and always expect the unexpected. Majestic, futuristic buildings line the sky and it is another sight to behold.

Never say no to any challenge is what I always say. So when I was traveling alone in Thailand I spotted a beautiful temple. I enjoy going into temples, mosques, and churches around the world, so I respectfully walked inside. There seated on the temple floor were beautifully dressed people, so I sat down and joined them. It was not long before I realized that I had just crashed a wedding. Another first for me and what a first it was.

ANGELS IN SIN

Another unique moment with "Bob," a bull Elephant that I rode on while in Zambia one year. I went specifically to do an elephant safari, and Bob was my companion and trusted guide, along with a live guide of course. This was just a special moment I shared with Bob.

This is zip-lining at its finest hour. Over a thousand feet above the jungle floor I zip-lined to eleven platforms going at very high rates of speed. There is a brake so that you can slow down before colliding with the next platform. We reached speeds of 55 mph for sure, and it was exhilarating and scary at the same time. Nothing like zip-lining USA style for sure. This is a MUST do for all risk takers.

Gathered together with my dear friend Ann and her family outside of Paris. This was one of those beautiful moments that you cherish for a lifetime. My friend Ann had a chateau in Chamonix and she invited me there on several occasions. It was a sight to behold indeed, and many magical moments were shared by us. I am forever grateful for her friendship.

My soulmate Paul and I at the "Face Changing" theater in Beijing. This was one of the magical moments that we have shared in our journey together.

Normal to me is *not* having friends you've known since grade school, especially when you're sixty. Normal to me is *not* living six blocks from where you were born, or where you grew up, or where your mother, father, sister, brother, or aunt live. Normal to me is *not* living in the same town or the same state you were raised in. Normal to me is *not* working for the same company for thirty years until you get a gold watch.

Normal to me is *not* ending up as a senior citizen playing bridge, or mah-jongg, or living in a fifty-five-plus community, where everyone knows everyone else. Normal to me is living life to the fullest, taking risks, and experiencing everything that it has to offer, the good, the bad, the ugly, and the who knows, no matter what.

What that means to me is *not* playing it safe, but rather jumping off that cliff without a net, crashing a wedding in Thailand, going to see a risqué sex show in the Pat Pong, clutching a baby monkey in my arms at a marketplace in Bangkok, or balancing a six-week-old wild Serval cat on my chest in East Africa. It means traveling around the world alone, no tours and no travel buddies. Alone means just that, by yourself. Looking back, I have no regrets and there is very little that I would change.

In my defense, I have had an amazing life, experienced incredible adventures, crashed weddings, flew twice in a hot air balloon over the Serengeti, climbed the Great Wall and was fanned at the top by two Mongolian women, canoed twenty-six miles down the Zambezi River with a hot actor from Hollywood, looked into the mouth of a hungry lion more than once, zip-lined from one thousand feet above the jungle onto eleven platforms in the Eastern Cape of South Africa, traveled on seven safaris in four countries by myself with only my Maasai guide as company, and so much more.

I have taken risks without regard to my safety much of the time, but I have lived, I have loved, I have lost as well, and I have no regrets.

Ira and I had some good times, some great times and some "I just can't believe we did that" times. We partied with some amazing people, we dined at great restaurants, we made love naked on a mound of hot sand on a beautiful white beach, the waves crashing around us. We laughed, we cried, we shared many great days and nights, weeks, months, and years together. I watched as he tried cases and won, tried cases and lost, and finally, left the DA's office, stepping jauntily into private practice, with a little help from me. But together, we did it!

Of course, he had to have "the look" of success. We had the expensive cars, the homes, the housekeeper, the "flash," the fun, and the trials and tribulations that go along with a relationship that was free-falling and wound up tightly with complications.

At the end of the day, we were different in so many ways. He loved an open-door policy at home, but I wanted people to call and ask if they could come over.

I hated not having my privacy at all times, even though I have always been a very social person. Looking back, I suppose my being social had to be on my terms, which meant don't just appear at the door. While Ira loved being surrounded by his friends, watching sports for an entire weekend, I had little interest in sports and hated the loud, unruly noise of the almost nightly gatherings.

Then there was Greg, who managed to create dissension, almost daily, with his challenges to authority, his overwhelming need for Vincent to really "be" his dad, and the angry, sullen, disrespectful attitude that he assaulted us with.

One day, sometime between Ira and I separating and me announcing my departure for the wildly irreverent city of New York, I made a decision that changed my life in a monumental way. I always had a fear of fire, a healthy one brought about by the fact that I had seen a man burned to a crisp in an explosion near my workplace on Santa Monica Boulevard when I was in my early twenties. The sight of him being taken away on a gurney, blackened beyond recognition, never left my memory.

So, when I discovered that Tony Robbins was going to be in town doing Unleash the Power Within and the famous Firewalk, I decided to sign up. I had heard so many tales and rumors about the Firewalk being fake from people who had never even done it that I was determined to do it myself before making any judgments. It was in a sense, another life lesson because I discovered that people often provided advice and information about things they have never experienced and didn't really know about, so I learned not to listen to the noise. I made the decision to find out for myself firsthand by going and doing, and not asking those who didn't know but loved to advise.

In those early days of Tony Robbins's career, the audience numbers were in the hundreds rather than the later thousands of eager men and women anxious to make any sort of contact with Tony Robbins. I was hellbent on doing one thing and that was the Firewalk.

It was being held at a Sheraton Hotel in the San Fernando Valley, and I arrived right on time that Friday night. Like most self-help seminars, there is a certain amount of seemingly tedious work at the very start that can have some unexpected consequences going forward.

The beginning of the evening was spent doing, as I describe it, some inner healing work, exercises that were allegedly meant to heal your body from within. I was skeptical but open and did the work even though I didn't really see the value at the time. My mind would be changed by the following morning. At that moment, I was totally focused on walking over red-hot embers in my bare feet, as crazy as it sounds.

During the evening we were led out to the parking lot where we could view the pathways of flames dancing into the blackened sky and embracing the once black coals.

At around midnight we returned to the parking lot essentially to do the Firewalk. I watched as barefooted person after person walked over the now red-hot embers and emerged on the other side, triumphant. But I continued to stay on the sidelines, waiting for something earth-shaking, I suppose, to happen. The Universe was to oblige in a matter of minutes.

I watched and debated with myself arguing both sides of the issue.
I came here to do the Firewalk.
Yes, but I don't think I want to do it now.
But, my sensible side replied, *this is why you came in the first place.*

Yes, I know, but no one will know if I don't do it. My mind raced between the diverse thoughts and my seemingly intelligent argument.

But you will know, and you are the most important person of all.

At that precise moment the Universe stepped in and made my decision easier. I was watching the spectacle of fire, and suddenly two dwarfs were assisted over the hot embers and my sensible side won the debate.

If they can do it, then so can I, I declared to myself.

With that, I walked over to the line and got in as the coals were turning dark. I mused how they would be much colder by the time I got to the front of the line. But, once again in its wisdom, the Universe provided me with the real challenge and proved me wrong. A life lesson to be sure. The Universe never gives you anything that you cannot handle.

Moments later, I was at the very front of the line staring blankly at the darkened coals when I heard someone say, "More hot coals."

From the side I could see a man pushing a wheelbarrow filled with red-hot embers toward my pathway. He dumped them and raked them, and there I was staring into a sea of fire. I should have thanked the Universe but there was no time.

I mumbled, "cool moss, cool moss," and stepped off, careful not to run. Somewhere in the middle of my journey I felt a hot ember burn the inside of both feet, but I kept walking until I reached the other side and a box of wet grass. I stepped out of the pathway, feeling triumphant but wounded, and vowed not to return the following day due to my "injuries."

I limped back to the room where the event was progressing, took my seat, and completed the final hours of the seminar before making my way to the car for the trip home.

I arrived at about four in the morning, feeling very sorry for myself, and literally took off my clothes ready to fall into bed. Just before that I examined my feet and saw clusters of fully formed blisters on each of my insteps. They were swollen with liquid and extremely painful. Too tired to provide medical treatment, I simply donned a pair of socks and fell into bed. I was certain that I wouldn't return that day, but I did have an early morning hair appointment that I intended to keep.

I awoke two hours later at six thirty and readied myself to shower and go to the hairdresser. Imagine my shock when I took off my socks and saw that the blisters had fully healed and were crusted over. It was like weeks and not hours had passed. The Universe was calling out loud and clear telling me that the healing work I had done earlier was valuable after all and in fact more than that, my eyes had been opened to some other truths. I was shown definitively that the Firewalk was real, there was no denying the heat of those burning embers on my bare feet. Exhilarated by my findings, I had an immediate change of heart and couldn't wait to get to the seminar and share my experience. It was moving and life-changing, another life lesson. It was at that moment I became empowered to leap off any cliff, of any height, without a parachute, land safely on my feet, and face any challenges the world intended to throw at me.

As strong and resilient as I was before, I was now impervious to so many fears that cripple most people. Even at my young age, I had faced a lot of challenges that might stop another person in their tracks. I was a single mom without funds and no real job after I divorced Vincent. It became clear to me very quickly that I was not going to get much monetary support. At the end of the day, he gifted me with the paltry sum of $15 a week, hardly enough to put food on the table for Greg and me. Clearly, I had to make money and fast.

I started working wherever I could, as a proofreader for an advertising agency, as an editorial assistant for a very popular car magazine, and finally a short stint at a fashion company, which ended up being the start of a new life for me.

Using my favorite tool, the newspaper, I got a job working as a showroom girl for the edgy fashion designer Betsey Johnson and ended up taking on several small fashion accessory lines to supplement my income. That too ended up as a life-changing decision, as so many decisions in my life seemed to do. I was still single but dating Ira and trying very hard to build some kind of business.

The two accessory lines I took on were a plus in my mind that only added to the edgy fashion line I was selling.

Unfortunately for me, the new sales manager on the scene had an entirely different read about what I was doing and, without hesitation, fired me.

But as I always say, when one door closes, another opens, you just need to be smart enough to walk through. A very important life lesson learned and never forgotten. That incident turned out to be the start of my twenty-five-year-long fashion career.

Subsequently, I assembled a few more accessory lines, went on the road, and ultimately opened my own fashion accessories showroom at the California Mart in Los Angeles, showcasing more than two dozen amazing lines.

Over the years, my success grew, and I ended up not only selling but developing lines, traveling around the world alone designing and manufacturing handbags, belts, and jewelry. I loved every part of this business, except collecting the commissions that were due.

Ira and I were married by this time, and I was able to be instrumental in helping him leave the district attorney's office and go into private practice. Our family dynamics were tenuous most of the time, with Greg playing one of us against the other and constantly making me choose between Ira and him.

I started meditating, trying to find some peace and tranquility in my life, and that worked for a while. I started jogging as part of my meditation. I was getting up at four in the morning when it was black as ink outside. just to jog away from the stress that was rampant in our home. Then as more cracks appeared in the foundation of our marriage, my meditation gave me a clearer perspective on what was real, what was imaginary, and everything in between.

We had been married for about seven years when my life took another radical turn. I had taken a business trip to Texas where I was attending an industry show and it was day two or three of the four-day event. I was staying at a lovely hotel in Dallas and decided to go to the bar for a drink and some downtime that evening.

It just so happened that a young, gorgeous musician was playing in the lounge that night. I sat mesmerized by his voice, the song he was singing, "House on Pooh Corner," and his engaging smile, and ended up still there when the last set was over. It didn't take long before he had joined me at my table, ordered drinks, and was engaged in communication with me that was warm and comfortable.

His name was Keith, and little did I know that he would change my life and who I thought I was. Up until then I identified myself with my "look"—my nails, my hair, my lipstick, my clothing. I was so much more than that inside, but the life I was leading with Ira never really revealed the who that I was, beneath the facade.

Keith saw through my exterior walls and immediately knew who I was inside. It was so refreshing, so real, so exciting. Our conversation flowed like liquid gold, and we were mesmerized with each other, hardly taking our eyes off one another for the rest of the evening.

The moments turned into hours, and then we moved out of the lounge and upstairs to my room. For the first time in a long time, maybe in my lifetime, I made love to another person. It was magical for both of us. My heart was in motion, and somehow I knew this was not the end, but rather the beginning of something that was life-changing.

Over the next year, our relationship grew and I grew, and I was able to love the me who was shrouded by a faux exterior. I fell in love with Keith and he with me, in spite of my situation and the fact that I was thirteen years his senior.

One month we met secretly in San Francisco at a dear friend's home and then in Texas, whenever we could. Our phone calls were punctuated with words of love and feelings that I hadn't shared with anyone in years. Sadly, our relationship was ill-fated, and his desires to have a normal life with children and a white picket fence overshadowed his feelings for me, and we parted ways, with love. The year that I had with Keith changed me for the better, and I wish that I could have given him the life that he wanted, but recognized that I couldn't, and loved him enough to let him go. He taught me to love myself as I had never done before.

Shortly after that emotional upheaval, Ira and I had what I would classify as a massive blowout, during which I divulged my love affair, and he divulged his one-night stand. Just goes to show how little we know about those we live with.

He had been screwing the secretary at his friend's medical office. Tempers flared, a phone flew from one side of the room to the other, and we didn't come out on the other side until divorce court.

Oddly enough we remain extremely close friends to this day, and we value the relationship that we have and love each other for who we are as people.

I never saw Keith again, but I thought of him often, especially when I looked at who I had become since knowing him. He changed me and made me appreciate the person I was inside, rather than just accept the fake shell I displayed on the outside. People like that come into our lives for a reason. We just have to recognize it when it happens and be open to the magic they bring.

DIAMONDS AND DRUGS

Greg was barely twenty years old when he crossed paths with "Raven," the chocolate-covered one-woman demolition team, with tits the size of watermelons. She was the embodiment of everything deranged in our society. Unfortunately, Greg, the naïve "tit" man, got caught up in her web of sex, drugs, and deception and our world changed forever, and not in a good way.

As luck or misfortune would have it, he found her number and picture while scrolling through the neighborhood trash paper, known for back-door sex ads. There she was, a 56D cup, with cheeks that protruded like golf balls, and an ass big enough to land a 747 on.

He was young and impetuous, and thought little of the consequences of his actions. In fact, in his naïve mind, there was no such thing as a consequence, thanks to his indulgent grandmother. Consequences were reserved for the less sophisticated type of person, he reasoned. But there were grave consequences for his actions, ones that would leave two families reeling, and Greg behind bars facing murder charges with the death penalty at the end of the road. His reckless acts would ricochet on and off the front pages of newspapers from coast to coast for over a year, and then return to the headlines a few years later. During all of this time, he remained, as always, a defiant know-it-all and oblivious to the path of destruction he left behind.

She was a master of deception, this woman called Raven. A shade of black equal to slate, who hid behind a photograph that depicted her as she once was, an attractive black woman, endowed with breasts the size of ripe melons.

Once upon a time she had starred in porn movies, but that was long ago, and long before Greg happened to find her. Behind the deception lurked a 280-pound woman who had fallen victim to far too much plastic surgery and drugs.

She had surgically enhanced her cheeks and breasts until she looked like a cartoon character with apples for cheeks and watermelons for breasts.

She had become a caricature of who she once was, surviving on a myth and her history as a low-level porn star in a Russ Meyers movie.

June aka Raven had come a long way. She had worked the major cities from Toronto to Miami, the Vatican and back, plying her trade of drugs and women. Her unusual looks and a commitment to pretend to be transgender, male to female, made her quite popular around Hollywood, where she plied her wares.

To add credence to this deception, she kept a large penis in some sort of liquid on the nightstand by the side of her bed. She also surrounded herself with pre- and post-transgender people, some of whom would end up testifying at the trial of her accused killer, my only son, Greg Alan.

The "relationship" between them was a rocky one almost from the start. He would call her dozens of times each day, mesmerized by her sultry voice and heavy breathing. She sounded like an eighteen-year-old virgin as she purred seductively into the phone; however, she was anything but that, this predator Raven. She was a black widow, a purveyor of death, a drug dealer, seductress, manipulator, arsonist, prostitute, madame. She was all of these things and more, with a network that stretched nearly around the globe.

The naïve Greg thought he knew what he was dealing with, but he really knew nothing. There was danger at every turn in this relationship, and he had no idea he was walking over landmines every single day. For months they never met in person but carried on their marathon phone calls daily. Regardless, they were strangely joined together as a result of the gifts and money she showered upon him. She knew exactly how to capture her prey and was a skillful hunter.

He was in awe, as the gifts poured in nearly every day. Hundred-dollar bills stuffed inside a teddy bear with a Rolex watch entwined around it. Gifts magically arrived by limo at his home, and that was just the beginning of an avalanche of money and presents. The mystery that surrounded their lack of personal contact only served to enchant and interest him even more.

The gifts were lavish and at times shocking, as wads of hundreds, and a mountain of expensive watches continued to arrive by car and driver. In his mind, this beauty he had ensnared looked exactly like the picture in the five-and-dime rag sheet he regularly perused.

In his naïve mind, she was his dream woman! Her skin like a Hershey's chocolate bar and her giant tits like luscious melons. There was plenty of her to enjoy, and he thought he was about to be the one to explore her, siphoning every bit of juice from her chocolate body. He could hardly wait.

"Hi, honey" her words oozed into the phone like liquid silver. "Hi, baby" would be his reply.

"What's my big boy up to today?" she asked.

"Just hanging out. Let's get together, baby." He would endeavor to make a date.

"Not today, I am not going out today, honey. How about tomorrow, we could get it on tomorrow. I'm going to send you a little present, honey," she purred.

The emptiness of their routine chatter was accentuated by the fact that during the first three months of this daily, rather rote relationship, they still hadn't met each other. This game of hide-and-seek played itself out day after day, week after week, until one afternoon, he finally reached his boiling point. He was not used to being put off by any woman, and this infuriated and confused him. They had been speaking for hours on end either from his father's office, the palatial Beverly Hills home of his grandmother, or the simple mobile home of my mother, but had never laid eyes on each other. It would later emerge that was because Raven had a lot to hide. She knew she was far from the fetching weight and youthful looks she displayed in the decade-old picture from that rag paper.

The truth was, she looked like a different person altogether, but she had fallen hard for this gorgeous, impetuous, and rather reckless young man, and she wasn't about to lose him. So she just kept delaying the inevitable. She was far older and wiser than he would ever be and had immersed herself for years in a very dark world, one filled to capacity with prostitutes of all shapes, sizes, colors, and genders, including those barely recognized by modern society.

She was well-connected in the international drug world that stretched from Miami to Boston to New York and Canada, and on to Italy, and was aware that her connections could, and would, provide her a safe haven from the prying eyes of law enforcement or curiosity seekers. She had friends in high places who would protect her, and so she could deal drugs and women from her "castle in the sky" without concern. She was invincible, or so she thought. That was until she saw "his" picture. Greg's rugged, smoldering good looks appealed to her and enchanted her sense of sexuality to a point where she all but lost her sense of self-preservation. Day after day, she purred sexual innuendos and outright seductions into the phone. In that sense, she was a master of disguise. Day after day, Greg would breathe heavily, gushing seductive words back while making plans to ravage her body. He wasn't used to women saying no.

All to no avail. She continued with this perversion for weeks, that turned into months, and the games continued. Greg was overwrought with anger and confusion. He had fallen in love with her angelic voice, the vision he held of her, and the plans that she made to turn his world upside down. In fact, she did just that, but not the way he envisioned.

Truth was, his entire world was about to come crashing down after she broke yet another date with him. It was at that moment he decided that the only answer to this cat-and-mouse game she was playing was to confront her, whether she liked it or not. An ill-advised decision at best, and one he would live to regret. That day, he drove like a madman to the apartment where she was living and demanded that she open the door.

Cringing behind the flimsy wooden frame was a 280-pound aberration, pleading with him to go away. Then the door came crashing down, splinters from its framework falling like a meteor shower. It was then that he laid eyes on the person who had been on the other end of that angelic, sultry voice. That siren he had fallen head over heels in love with turned out to be a monster. The sultry, sexy, raspy voice on the phone belonged to a massively obese woman with cheeks that protruded like tennis balls, and a chin that jutted forward like the wicked witch from *The Wizard of Oz*.

His toes curled, and it felt like the house had literally fallen on him, but he wasn't in Kansas anymore. Horrified and speechless, he turned quickly and ran for his car, gunned it, and drove as fast as he could to get away from the horror of what he had just seen.

Confused and angry about the deception, he went home and locked himself in his apartment, ashamed and embarrassed that he had been so gullible. He tried to drown out his emotions with a shot, a few smokes, and an afternoon shower, but nothing could wash away the visual imprinted in his head. At the time, our world was marked by long periods of no communication, and were it not for that, I would have been caught up earlier in this monstrous nightmare. Thankfully, he was not speaking to me, and so I was partially spared, but only partially, and only temporarily.

Back at her apartment, Raven was enraged and seeking revenge, so she called her driver and made an impromptu visit to Greg's Marina apartment that afternoon. He had just stepped out of the shower when the doorbell rang. Her unexpected arrival took him by surprise, and he dropped the towel that was draped around his still wet body and ran to the bathroom, leaving the front door ajar. She seized the opportunity and strolled in, shutting the door behind her. Alone in the living room she methodically scanned the wall of photos Greg proudly hung of family members. Thankfully, I was not among them, as we were on the outs. There they were, Grandma, Vincent's mother, resplendent in furs and jewels, father and stepfather donning suits and sport coats, looking every bit the successful Beverly Hills matron and family, displayed for all to see. She must have been seething as she opened her handbag, took out a ruby-red lipstick, and methodically scribbled death threats on each photo before walking out, leaving the door open. A horrified

Greg hid in the bedroom, door locked, until he was sure that the coast was clear. Only then did he emerge, shut and double locked the front door, and called his father. His macho attitude prevented him from seeing the danger in this entire relationship, and he continued blindly for a while before totally getting out of town.

I wish I could say that this story had either ended happily or just plain ended at that moment, but as in all Hollywood soap operas, this was not one to end well. Raven was livid, unable to get Greg out of her mind, and she refused to accept his rejection.

Her constant phone calls went unanswered, and even her angry attacks in chalk on the outside wall of the gym where he pumped iron daily were ignored. She went from enchanted and engaged with him to disenchanted and enraged in a matter of days. After all, men usually paid well for her services, and she was prepared to give her all to Greg.

How dare he? No one is going to treat me that way. I will finish him, destroy him, make sure no one has him. Just watch me! I will ruin his family and him, starting now.

It was at that moment she made the fatal decision that if she couldn't have him, no one would. She was consumed with rage and vengeful thoughts, and for the first time in her life completely irrational. She had always dealt with life and death situations, with drug dealers and deals that fell apart, with hookers and angry johns, but the moment that door came crashing down, she forgot all she learned, and her only thoughts were of revenge.

She had been rejected! Who the hell did he think he was anyway? Men paid a lot of money for her services. Most of them thought she had once been a man, and she was able to charge those pathetic losers more because of that. Imagine, they actually thought she had once been a man with a dick.

To bolster that notion, she put someone's penis in formaldehyde in a jar on the nightstand by her bed. It was never determined who among her litany of acquaintances might have been missing a penis, but it served to dispel disbelievers.

Men, johns, were delighted to part with hundreds, if not thousands, of dollars to have sex acts performed upon them by her. Now this person, this loser, this Greg Alan, was rejecting her. Not a chance!

Raven intended to make everyone on her radar pay for what she perceived as this grave injustice. Her vengeance was immature and irrational in nature, but proved highly effective in nearly destroying Greg, his father, and his grandmother.

The first step on this pathway to destruction happened a day or two later when she set his car on fire, right in front of his condo. That same day she ordered hundreds of pizzas to be delivered to his apartment. That same week she called his house and his father's office thousands of times each day, rendering the family business nearly inoperable.

To accomplish this, she employed the services of a number of low-life druggies, who had enough fingers and phones to flood the family office with calls, every minute, for days at a time.

That strategy turned out to be highly effective. She wrote hateful epithets on building walls, which served to get some of the attention she desired. She left angry messages on gym walls and street corners near his home. At one point, she even called my aging mother at her home in the desert in a last-ditch effort to find Greg. My fearless mother just set the phone down and went about her business, leaving Raven to scream into the receiver to no one. In the end, when none of those actions worked, she resorted to something that she knew would. Unpredictable violence unleashed without regard for the consequences!

So, in the dead of night, she and several cohorts set fire to Vincent's business, which was located in the Santa Monica mall. The fire quickly got out of control and engulfed two adjoining stores, destroying all three in rapid succession.

Of course, that got their attention, and Greg was spirited out of town into hiding indefinitely, and all contact was subsequently severed. About this time, by some quirk of fate, I was ensnared into the drama that had become his life and into the deadly events that followed. Initially, Greg was moved from one hotel or motel to another, and from one family friend to another. A few months later, a small contingent of "thugs" arrived at her apartment in West Hollywood and beat the hell out of her, nearly killing her.

It was a not-so-veiled message that left her and her ego bruised and badly injured. But this was far from over, because even then, for whatever reason, she failed to get the message.

While in some ways Raven may have thought she won the battle, in the end she lost the war. For months she searched everywhere trying to locate Greg to no avail. He had, for all intents and purposes, simply vanished, dropped off the face of the earth. I ended up being instrumental in getting him out of town, in fact out of the state and to Arizona with his then girlfriend. But Raven's rage didn't let up and only increased with his absence.

Then came the final act in this drama. One steamy summer night in May, Raven was accosted as she left a building in the San Fernando Valley with a young male client. Shots rang out and when the smoke cleared, she lay dead on the sidewalk, shot five times in the head. Her companion, the great grandson of a famous author, was also shot, only he survived his wounds, but she lay dead in a pool of blood. The $5,000 she stored in her wig was gone, along with the lone gunman.

Suspicion fell on Greg almost immediately, and he was brought in for questioning. Law enforcement refused to believe that he was living out of the state when she was killed and did everything in their power to prove that. It was a dead-end street for authorities at that time as they simply had no evidence and Greg was not charged. Sadly, that moment of triumph was short-lived. In November of that year, he was arrested in the parking lot of the family office on Robertson Boulevard by a throng of gun-wielding cops and a low-flying helicopter and charged with first-degree murder.

It was surreal, and on some level, I refused to believe the charges. Up until then I managed to stay at arm's length from all the drama, but now I was dead center. Once the reality hit, I took a step back, put my investigative reporter hat on, and went on a mission to unweave this tangled web and help exonerate my only son.

He was arrested just before Thanksgiving and incarcerated in Los Angeles County Jail in the high-profile section, along with a cache of hardened criminals. His "neighbors" were murderers, serial killers like Richard Ramirez, the Night Stalker, the worst of a bad lot.

Suddenly, it was up to me, my aging mother, and my third husband, Raymond, to visit him so that he wouldn't lose hope. It was a given that neither his father nor his grandmother would be going to Los Angeles County Jail to see him. To set their bar that low would be unthinkable. This would be the first and the last time I ever visited a jail, except when I was a teenager arrested with Vincent for a curfew violation. This was substantially more significant, and surely no one could say that Greg didn't do things with flair.

This was something I never thought I would experience, and never had, until that day. There the three of us sat, looking through glass at my son and talking to him via telephone through the same glass barrier. He had done nothing, except to exercise poor judgment and align himself with a woman so corrupt, so lacking in moral fiber and values, that it boggled the mind.

She was a hardened criminal whose life was built on the backs of drug dealers and prostitutes, her income derived from promoting herself, her girls, and her immediate access to hard-core drugs and pay-by-the-hour sex.

It all seemed irrelevant now, because Greg was standing before a judge in a courtroom in the San Fernando Valley, flanked by a team of expensive lawyers hired by his grandmother as the charges against him were read. I was holding back the tears and anger trying to comprehend what had happened.

What followed was a circus of motions and emotions; motions on top of emotions, and an arraignment that took the breath right out of our bodies. Prosecutors were asking for the death penalty. One might think the killing of June aka Raven would be considered a public service, but that was hardly the case. It was like a living nightmare, a horror movie in real time that I was starring in, the lead character of a Stephen King novel. This was my son, my only child, and I **knew** he had nothing to do with her murder. I knew where he was, because, amid all of the drama, I had sent him to Arizona to stay and had spoken to him the night after she was murdered. He was still in Arizona, five hundred miles away, and had been working that day. But then, I was his mother, and my word was about as important as a roll of pennies in a bank robbery.

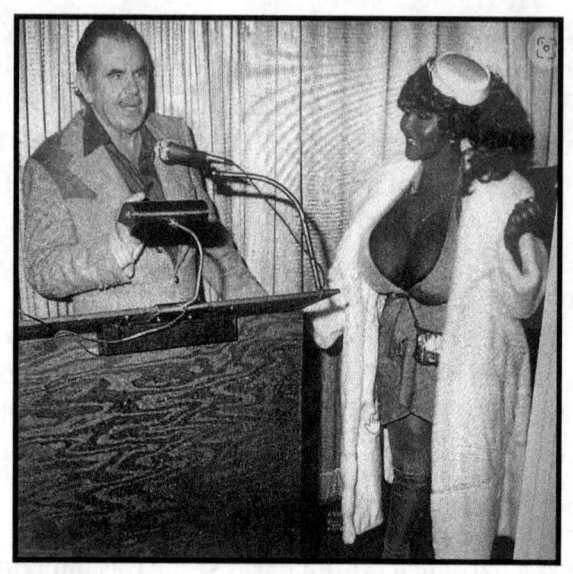

What started out as a flirtation ended up as a dangerous obsession that cost a life and threatened to destroy a family. This was not only costly financially but emotionally, as Greg was charged with the murder of the obsessed Raven. The ensuing trial stretched over nine months and took an unbearable toll that ended with his almost immediate acquittal.

A person has not experienced real stress and anguish until they have been involved in a capital case against a loved one. This case took years from my life but ended with Greg celebrating his freedom. Thankfully I recovered and was even stronger.

He remained in jail awaiting his trial until Ira, my lawyer ex-husband, was able to get him released into our custody. An ample bond had been posted by his wealthy Beverly Hills grandmother, Vincent's mom. It was under these pressurized circumstances that Greg temporarily moved in with Raymond and me, a move that lasted all of three weeks.

Even an arrest for first-degree homicide did little to change his attitude of entitlement. He maintained unrealistic demands to come and go as he pleased and ended up creating more turmoil in our relationship than we could handle.

It surprised me how out of touch with reality he really was, even as the defendant in a murder trial who was facing the death penalty. But then, his grandmother, Vincent's mom, had made an art out of making all of her grandchildren totally dependent upon her, a feat she was quite skilled at.

Whether it was hiring the most expensive lawyers that money could buy to defend her grandson or getting another granddaughter out of a bank robbery charge, there was no one better than her. So, it was not a surprise that he felt impervious even to the charge of first-degree murder. He knew without question that Grandma would get him off somehow.

It took only a few weeks of near mortal combat between Greg, Raymond, and I before we gave in but not up and he moved in with his grandmother, where there were no rules, even then. At our home, he thought this was spring break and that he could come and go as he pleased and bring the flavor of the moment home with him at whatever hour. So, for three agonizing weeks he rolled in at two or three in the morning, sometimes alone, sometimes with some young thing he had picked up at a bar. I stayed up worrying about his welfare and safety, and I suppose just worrying like the mother of someone charged with first-degree murder might do.

At the mansion in Beverly Hills, with Grandma overseeing nothing, he continued to go about his life in party mode, as if nothing out of the ordinary had happened. In the meantime, on both sides of the family, people were struggling to stay glued together. In truth, they were coming apart at the seams, as they tried to make sense out of the senseless and comprehend how any of us were living this nightmare.

When the trial finally began, it was nothing less than a three-ring circus and it seemed as if Barnum & Bailey had taken over the courthouse for a performance. Prosecuting attorneys were forced to call a variety of Raven's circus-type friends as witnesses. And so, the parade began.

This parade seemed to go on and on, with an end that became more unpredictable each day. The summer heat was stunning in its severity, but even more stunning was the parade of circus freaks the prosecutor called as witnesses.

It was a veritable fashion show of oddities, a collection of curiosities, an assortment of the absurd. One afternoon, as the midday sun beat down on the courthouse, prosecution witnesses began to arrive. Some were decked out in black fishnet stockings, fur, and the occasional hankie for effect. There they were, drug-addicted prostitutes, bizarre faux fashionistas, and transgender hookers, adorned with plastic diamonds, all taking an oath to tell the whole truth and nothing but the truth. It would have been a show worthy of a New York night spot were it not a courtroom in a courthouse in Van Nuys, California, now the scene of a murder trial where the death penalty was on the docket.

"Would you please state your name? What is your occupation? Please remember, you are under oath," the prosecutor repeated dryly. It was riveting to watch, and in some ways it was comical and what we might refer to today as a very bad reality show. But good, bad, or indifferent, my aging mother and I had front-row seats day after agonizing day, for the show of shows, and the performances of a lifetime.

Hooker after hooker took the stand, swearing under oath to testify truthfully. Each one was more outrageous than the next, in appearance and affectation, until finally the prosecution rested. In between hookers, the prosecution called their "star" witness, a bookish-looking client of Raven's who accentuated his look in court with coke-bottle-thick eyeglasses. Remarkably, he had been on his way to meet Raven at her den of iniquity and testified under oath that he could identify the man sitting behind the wheel of the so-called getaway car.

As it turned out he was not the star after all, but rather the weak link in this dramatic saga. It became clear to me immediately that he was not telling the truth and that the jurors needed to be convinced of that fact. The reality that Greg could be convicted of murder had already set in, so I did what I had to do behind the scenes to help his lawyers investigate the evidence.

With Raymond in tow, we walked the murder scene over and over, checking out each angle of this witness's story to see if he really could identify the driver of the getaway car. After a few dozen walks of the scene, it was clear to me that given his line of sight from where he was on the sidewalk looking down on the car, coupled with the fact that he wasn't wearing his glasses, it would have been impossible for him to have seen the face of the driver.

In an alternate Universe, had he been blessed with x-ray vision like Superman, and had his eyeglasses on, he might have been able to see through the top of the car and identify the driver. Since none of that was true and both x-ray vision and his glasses were absent that evening, his testimony was obliterated on cross-examination.

When at last the jury filed out to deliberate, I died a thousand deaths as I agonized over the verdict. I watched their eyes as they left the courtroom for any signs of what was to be. This truly was life or death, and I was at the end of their razor-sharp decision, holding on for what seemed like an eternity. I was weak at the knees, hyperventilating, and stunned, when the jury came back a mere twenty-six minutes later I held my breath, clutched my mother's hand, and perhaps for the first time in my life, I prayed to anyone out there to save my son.

"The jury has reached a verdict. As to, Count One, murder in the first degree, how do you find the defendant?" I could no longer breathe. I stared helplessly into the faces of the jury.

"Not guilty."

I collapsed back into the seat shaking uncontrollably. While Greg was visibly shaken, he quickly recovered as his lawyers started hugging him and glad-handing one another. It was as if he didn't really comprehend the severity of the entire trial and what it meant for him going forward. The weight was lifted, but I couldn't stop the shaking. It continued well into the next day, accompanied by a waterworks of tears of joy. The day before was embedded in my mind, and I continued to hear the words "not guilty" ringing in my ears for months after that.

Greg seemed almost impervious to emotional upheaval and simply carried on, business as usual, oblivious to the wreckage he had left in his wake. He did so seemingly without remorse, regret, or acknowledgment to the family left in shambles due to his reckless actions.

In all the years of life that I shared with him, I never quite got used to his sense of entitlement and his inability to show appreciation to anyone but Vincent, for anything, no matter how significant it was.

One notable fact that bears exposure was that Vincent was not in the courtroom that day when the jury returned their verdict. He was busy sailing off the coast of San Diego! Like everything else that involved his father, that didn't seem to matter to Greg, but had it been me, off sailing that day, his anger would have known no boundaries.

If I could have had one wish that day, it would have been that Greg learned something from this near-death experience. My wish never came true. In the end, he walked free, as if nothing had ever happened, and years later, two men were convicted of the crime. The killer and his accomplice had been tied to the murder of well-known Cotton Club producer and director Roy Radin.

Not surprising, both men worked for the private security company hired by Greg's wealthy grandmother to guard the family after Raven set fire to the stores in the Santa Monica mall. Was there a connection? We will never know, as most of the leading characters are long since deceased.

If there was, it would have shown without question the lengths that both grandmother and son were willing to go to be free of any responsibility. The sacrifice of a grandchild, a son, to me was unthinkable. I suppose that is one of the huge differences between us. My mother aged a dozen years overnight. I was fortunate enough to have been absent, thanks to Greg, during most of this nightmare and was spared some of the drama. No matter, effectively, I had done my nine months of motherhood, twice, and hoped I wouldn't have to serve another nine months. I was wrong!

THE PAIN OF SILENCE

The pain that followed the initial rush of good fortune with his acquittal became unbearable as he distanced himself from me once again.

He never once acknowledged my mother or me for being there in court every day, or for the emotional sacrifices and support we gave him through this unspeakable nightmare. He never acknowledged the work I had done to discredit the prosecution's star witness either. A thank you, I appreciate you, I love you, would have been nice but was out of the question for him. Even though I hadn't expected it, I suppose that on some level, I hoped he would grow up enough to recognize what he had done and how it had impacted us emotionally and physically. He left this world without so much as thanks, Mom, but instead continued in his relentless pursuit of Vincent's elusive love.

Over the years Greg broke many hearts, bedded many women, grew older, but not wiser, and kept that side of himself that I would have loved to have seen a secret, at least from me. It was only years after his death that I met a close friend of his who shared with me a Greg that I never saw and sadly never knew. Thanks to this amazing friend, a window was opened, and he was revealed to be a loving, loyal person who cared about others and was compassionate, kind, and brilliant.

He had managed to keep all of that from me during his life, only allowing me to see snippets of it after his death, and then only through the eyes of his friend.

His passing, like his life, was filled with drama. In 2009, after several years of silence, he sent me an email with the subject line:

"Dying Of Cancer." I was living in South Africa at the time and responded immediately with concern. More drama was the agenda.

Among his other talents, he was a "drama queen" and held first prize as a skilled manipulator. The "Dying Of Cancer" subject line in his email was unnecessary, and after more than three silent years a simple "Hi Mom" would have moved me to immediate action. I reached out that day asking for some additional details about his illness only to be rebuffed with an overdose of vitriol. He was harsh and rude, calling me a monster, which was anything but the case. I was concerned and trying to understand what was happening from halfway around the world.

True to form, Vincent had already worked his magic by canceling the medical insurance, which was being paid for by his late mother's trust, for all five of her grandchildren, including Greg. For a few sentences in his email, Greg railed against Vincent for that despicable act and then promptly put his upset aside, never to be addressed again.

The fact that Vincent knew his son was critically ill did nothing to change his decision, so at the end of the day it was up to me to ignore Greg's ugly commentary and pay the insurance company directly for the next year to keep his policy in force. My seemingly unforgivable sin had been to ask him for some details and the name of his doctor so that I could call and get more information about his life-threatening illness. Less than one week after his policy was set to cancel, Greg underwent fifteen hours of major surgery at UCLA for a cancerous growth in his mouth and throat without so much as a word to me. The date was November 5, his birthday. He must have thought the insurance fairy paid the family's medical insurance for the next year.

It wasn't so unusual for Greg and me to experience long bouts of silence. He spent most of that time trying to bond with his father, and that took him down a pathway of strip clubs, drugs, and hookers. Even though he never realized it, attention from Vincent was only provided when Greg gave him something in return, like being a magnet for chicks or sending him drugs from California to Colorado through a courier service.

It had been almost five years since I had seen Greg. Most of that time was spent in silence, at least from his side. The year was 2003 and I was living in South Africa but had not met Paul, my soulmate, my person, my fourth and final husband, yet. It was in August of 2003 that Greg became a dad for the very first time, and I made sure to be there for the birth of his son. Fences were mended temporarily as I put on my best grandmother hat and talked baby talk nonstop for weeks to his tiny creation. I returned to South Africa and a few months later suggested to Greg that we take a short vacation together to Panama, even entertaining the idea that I could buy a property there. His only child was now nearly six months old and I had been in South Africa for almost two years, so distance stood in the way of most plans. I rented a beautiful villa on the beach in Coronado, and we set out for what I had hoped was a new beginning. Our intersecting lives seemed to be tinged with a bit of magic, at least for the first few days. It was during our trip that he begged me to send him there to live. We were standing on the balcony looking out over the water when he paused for a moment and looked directly into my eyes.

"This is what I want for my life. I would love to live here. It is my dream."

It was a first, him being so honest, so real with his words, at least with me. The emotion flowed from his face and eyes, and I could not ignore the feelings buried deep inside of my only child. I was so moved by his words and wanted to please him so much that a few months later I rented the same furnished home for them in Panama, and they started the process of moving. He still had the condo in the Marina that his grandmother had purchased, so I suggested they leave everything in place and not move their personal belongings until they were comfortable with their decision. The lease that I signed was only for a year, so that made sense, at least to me. In typical Greg fashion he ignored me and proceeded to pack all his furniture into a shipping container, including his car, then advised me once the ship was on the high seas that he needed more than $6,000 to retrieve it on the other end. I was worn out with his demands and his sense of entitlement, but once again I had no choice but to comply. It was only later that I discovered he had told the same sad story separately to his father and grandmother, and they had also forked over the money for the container. This deception became a normal course of action for Greg over the years.

Initially, he had been excited to live there, but then once they had actually moved and the reality of living away from family and friends set in, he wanted to go home. It made little difference to him that I had spent many thousands of dollars to make his "dream" come true. They packed up and moved back home without a word of apology.

But that was just the beginning of a seemingly love-hate relationship with both Panama and me. They moved back and forth no less than five times over the next few years, and his life actually came to an end in Panama, the location of his dreams and, apparently, his nightmare. His back-and-forth moves to Panama were spurred on by a sudden love of archaeology and a hunt for "treasures" both real and imagined.

As if money were not an issue, he jumped in with both feet and raised funds for his archeology pursuits by charming people into believing that the treasures he unearthed were authentic. The ease with which he uncovered these artifacts was astonishing; however, to this day, I have no idea whether any of them were artifacts or not, but that dream was crushed the day he died. Vincent, of course, was on the scene several times in Panama, always departing with some of those very "treasures" in hand.

Greg's obsession with Vincent was so overwhelming that he was unable to stay away from the relationship long enough to be with me and share what ended up being the happiest day of my life, my wedding to Paul. It was the final knife that he stuck in my heart in December 2004.

Paul and I had made the decision to marry, and we wanted Greg and his family to be part of our happiness. One of my closest friends gave me the best wedding present anyone could have imagined. She bought Greg, his then girlfriend, and the baby round-trip tickets to fly from Panama to South Africa for our wedding.

We had planned everything around their arrival and were ecstatic to have them celebrate this special day with us. In fact, Greg was going to give me away.

They arrived just before Thanksgiving and were to stay for six weeks until after our wedding, which we thought would give them a magical vacation. From the moment they arrived, his combative nature took over, haunting nearly every moment of the day. His obsession to have Vincent in his life drove them to leave after only two weeks and less than a month before our wedding.

The blowup was well orchestrated by Greg but came as a total surprise to me.

He was argumentative, distant, and sullen, and made sure to be doing something else every night when we sat down for dinner. His behavior was disruptive and as always his sense of entitlement shined through his harsh exterior. I was totally frustrated and upset and finally asked if they were homesick and would like to leave early.

"Yes," he replied angrily. "I don't want to stay here any longer. You made me go to Panama to keep me away from the one person who ever really loved me . . . my grandmother."

I was in shock and disbelief at his words and frankly at a loss as to what to say. I stormed into the house seething with anger, even though it was a relief of sorts to hear because secretly, I was worried his anger would end up ruining our wedding. A day later they left in a cloud of disbelief, some sadness and tears, and the knowledge that the Universe had prevented more drama.

After the smoke and the tears cleared, it was revealed that they had not gone home to Panama, but rather flown directly to his grandmother's mansion in Beverly Hills for what turned out to be a well-planned pit stop. It seemed that Greg had been phoning his father in Colorado for days from our home, making arrangements to meet him. It felt like an assassination. I had been ambushed, betrayed, and deprived of that moment of perceived happiness of Greg walking me down the aisle.

Greg had arrived at his grandmother's house armed with a story that would make the most hardened person weep. In his "rendition," they had struggled and saved to pay for the airline tickets and hotels to come to our wedding, only to have us throw them out after only two weeks. It was a total lie, but the deception worked like a charm.

They ended up with a stash of money compliments of Grandma, sympathy over their alleged agonizing trip to our wedding, and new airline tickets to fly back to Panama. All in all, it was a resounding success, at least in their eyes.

In spite of the drama of their unforeseen exit, our fairy tale wedding went off without a hitch, or a tiny ring bearer. In the end, we were far better off with their premature but dramatic exit.

On some level, I never really forgave him for his behavior, and for his self-involvement and selfishness. On perhaps the most special day of my life, my only real wedding, to my soulmate, and Greg's self-centered, entitled behavior nearly destroyed it. Because of his all-consuming need for Vincent's love, Greg had stolen something very precious away from me on that special day.

That something was him, walking me down the aisle to marry my soulmate. It was having my grandson there to witness the magic. This day could never be repeated, and he left this world without even acknowledging the pain he caused me and without ever really knowing who I was or the amazing adventures I had experienced in my life.

The next time that I saw Greg was 2011 after his illness had taken hold once again and he was in a downward spiral. In May of that year, we flew into Panama because his condition had worsened. Our trip took the better part of two days, but once there we made our way up the mountains to Boca del Toro where they were living. Before we left home, I made the decision to make a few slideshows of my safari adventures to show Greg. I had the nagging thought that he never knew anything about my global travels or, truthfully, me. In my mind he was far too busy hating me to take even a brief moment to know that special person called Mom. It was a shock to see him, so weakened by the return of the cancer and looking worn out from the impact of this deadly disease. I sat with him on the couch and began showing some of my safari adventures to him.

Sadly, after the second slideshow, he was too weak to watch anymore but went to bed shocked and surprised at who and what he had seen.

"You did that, Mom? You were there so close to that lion? OMG, that is amazing." It was like he saw me for the first time ever.

"Yes, honey, and there is so much more. I wish you could see the adventures that I have enjoyed over the years."

For that one moment I thought he could really see me. The who he never knew; the who that was his mother. I am so happy that at least he was able to get a small sense of who I was and who I am today before he left this earth.

We managed to get him into a hospital in Panama City, but even that was a struggle that took two full days. It also took Paul going to their home in the dead of night to babysit the children and make sure that they got to the airport in David on time. Greg never paid much attention to time and distance as there was always someone there to bail him out if and when he got into trouble. They actually missed the first scheduled flight since neither he nor his spouse figured in the hour-and-a-half trip from Boca to the airport. Even as chronic late boarders, the ones you see running for the door, they missed the plane by a mile, had to hit the reset button and return again the following day.

The eventual outcome of that trip was that Greg threw the oncologist out of the hospital room after claiming that he never had cancer and planned to sue UCLA, a laughable threat that never materialized. After we left and somewhere between sanity and insanity, he began using the services and products of what I would refer to as a "witch doctor" straight out of the jungles of Panama to treat his illness.

What followed was a series of pastes and teas that he applied and ingested, and a delusion that those products were drawing the cancerous growth out of his body. It was a fantasy that would have deadly consequences when his life suddenly ended less than a year later.

His death, like his life, was destined to be tumultuous, and he seemed to relish sparring with me no matter where he was or what he was doing. The only difference was that now he was married to the girlfriend, and they had three children with a fourth on the way That fact was part of their final deception, and I only learned of her pregnancy after Greg had lost his battle with the cancer he denied having.

True to form and following the playbook Greg had set in motion as a child, his wife turned the rage he left behind into a minefield for my benefit. There was no memorial or service honoring his life, which punished me but also his collection of close friends. She also managed to leave the door ajar for my ex-boyfriend Eric, the one I had struggled to remove from my life years earlier. I suppose her motto might have been this quote from Buddha: "Holding onto anger is like drinking poison and expecting the other person to die." I didn't and wouldn't allow this misdirected poison to permeate my life.

Midnight and Fantasies

The year was 1980. It was a beautiful, crisp November day and I was in New York City on business for a fashion industry show. The leaves were turning lovely shades of yellow, orange, and red, and a veneer of excitement hung in the air. I was walking up Fifth Avenue to my appointment, when I suddenly burst out singing, "Start spreading the news, I'm leaving today, I want to be a part of it, New York, New York." I was feeling joyful, elated, excited, and suddenly thought that this could be my new home. Luckily, it was a springlike day and not the reality of a late fall or winter or my life would have been totally different indeed.

I had tired of California and what I viewed as the monotony of day in and day out great weather. The earthquakes had me teetering on the edge a lot of the time, as I had endured at least seven of them since my birth. They were intense, sudden, without warning, and the duration, although short, seemed like an eternity. Walls crumbled, statues flew across the room slamming into doors, ceilings collapsed, and people died. Cars fell into holes that opened in the streets, and it was terrifying, to say the least. I had decided on the spur of the moment, as luck would have it, that New York was where I should and would be. That seemingly spontaneous decision was to change the course of my life and the lives of others. I had been in the fashion business for nearly a decade in California and it was becoming tedious at best. Vendors who looked to me to sell their products were slow to pay or disappeared totally when payday came around. I was also getting divorced from Ira and felt a sense of wanderlust.

Every month was a struggle that I endured, one way or the other. The tensions made me want to get the hell out of dodge and head east, where the weather seemed more interesting, at least in theory. There I was, that almost springlike day in November in New York City, strolling down Fifth Avenue, singing "New York, New York." Life was good—no, it was great. I had fallen in love with the city, the vibrancy, the nightlife, the people, and suddenly California seemed tame and boring. *Of course, my business is there, but so what? Am I really going to allow that to stop me from moving? Am I really going to stay put just because of my business?* I wondered out loud how I could allow any business to dictate where I would live or what I would do with my life? I realized that I couldn't live like that.

Was I going to stay in one place and not experience the world just because I had built this successful fashion business? I wondered over and over out loud, and after a long and arduous conversation with myself, the answer was NO! I was going to move and that was the end of the story, case closed.

New York never looked so good. I was almost single again, young at heart, and ready for a change in my life. So, I did what any intelligent, thinking, mature person would do! I picked up *The Village Voice*, scoured through it, and that very day I rented an apartment in Greenwich Village. By the end of the week, I had also secured a showroom on Fifth Avenue that was to be home to my fashion accessories business. I was still torn about continuing with it, and ended up many months later letting it go, but this seemingly rash decision offered me choices. The business side of my brain said I needed to make money and enjoy my life, and my creative side wanted to seclude myself in my new apartment and write another *Gone with the Wind*.

I returned to California with wings on my shoes and a smile on my face, and immediately put my showroom up for sale. In anticipation of a major blowout, I waited a month before deciding to share the news with my soon-to-be ex-husband, Ira. We had made plans to have dinner at Trader Vic's in Beverly Hills on a Saturday night after my return. I was late to dinner and extremely nervous by the time I arrived, questioning my every move.

Had I made the right decision? We were still sleeping together even though we were separated, because it was safe, and he was readily available. I thought he was still monogamous, but time would tell a different story.

As I sped out of the driveway to meet him that night, I ran over a homeless stray cat and became physically ill. I sat there crying like a baby, as I had never so much as hit a bird in my life, and here I had mowed down a helpless cat. Now I was really late. I finally arrived at Trader Vic's, and by then he was strumming the table with his fingers, on his second mai tai and feeling no pain. That was until I announced that I was moving from Los Angeles to New York, and that there would be no more late-night, post-divorce sexcapades. He was stunned, angry, surprised, and confused, and all of those emotions converged at the same time over some mai tais.

At the same time, I was thankful that I had finally come clean after six weeks of suffering with my news and a signed lease. I was compelled to be in New York City, lock, stock, and barrel, within the month. I was moving and there was no turning back.

Over the next few weeks, my showroom was sold, and I had packed up all my belongings. Two months later, I was living in my New York apartment with a doorman, an elevator, a few used brick walls, and Greenwich Village right outside my front door. Greg refused to move with me and ended up living with his uncle for a time and then on his own in an apartment paid for by his grandmother.

I was in my element, at last. I had some money in the bank, thankfully, as I was no longer working. Ira and I had sold the house in Los Angeles, and he finally sent me my share of the profits. It practically took an act of Congress to get it done, considering how upset he was at me.

But at the end of the day, I was free to be me and do exactly what I wanted. What I wanted at that moment was to write. So, day after day I sat, lined yellow legal pad in hand, in front of the single window next to the used brick wall in my living room, working on the great American novel. It was February 1980, and I was happy, at least for the moment, even though I didn't know a soul.

My great American novel phase lasted all of ten months before I looked at my bank account and determined that I needed to change my thinking and make some money. So, I did what I usually did when a challenge presented itself, I opened up a newspaper and checked out the classifieds.

There it was boldly screaming at me from the "Help Wanted" section of the *New York Times*. The thing that first caught my eye was "Want to Make $75,000 a Year?" You bet I do, I replied to myself. I phoned immediately, made an appointment for an interview, and several mornings later found myself on Wall Street dressed to kill in business attire.

The company traded stocks and futures, getting people to invest in their ability to make money. The firm was 100 percent men and were I to be hired, I would have the dubious distinction of being the first and only woman there. My job would be to raise a minimum of $5,000 as an investment from a total stranger in order to open an account. My tools were a telephone and a great story, coupled with my innate charm and sexy voice. Basically, it was cold-calling, something I hated more than bad breath and mosquitos. It was, in fact, my least favorite thing in the whole world because it opened the door to rejection.

I decided to use my favorite tool to help me through this challenge. On one hand I needed and wanted to make money, and on the other hand I hated doing the very job that would bring me the money. I weighed the options: Did I need the money more than I hated cold-calling? The answer at that moment was yes, and so I took the job. I used that technique quite frequently in the daily challenges that faced me and that face most people. From the very smallest challenge to serious ones like money and employment. It worked every time, and I use it today to open or close doors as required. I always remember that any decision is for that moment in time, and when I was faced with leaving the Wall Street job and heading over to the nightclub to get it finished, I chose the club as that was more important than making money.

I was hired and jumped in with both feet, smiling and dialing my way to more and more money. I was given a desk directly in front of the huge whiteboard that served to embarrass those who had not performed each day. The names of the top performers were handwritten on the board along with the money they had raised that day, thereby forcing those not canonized to work harder.

Each week I was given a handful of customer names and phone numbers to call. These potential customers had at some point asked for information on stocks and futures, never expecting to be contacted by someone as determined as me. So began my successful, though short-lived, foray into the financial marketplace. As usual, I maintained the mindset that I could do anything even if I had never done it before as long as I had passion and commitment and believed I could do it.

I weighed my options: my need for money to pay the bills against my dislike of cold-calling and the need for money won out. I frequently used that thought process to make difficult decisions. Weighing my dislike of something against any benefit it might offer. It really works!

Despite the fact that I hated cold-calling, I was actually quite good at it. I spent a lot of my time at the company with my name at the top of the whiteboard, regularly raising the $5,000 minimum investment from each customer that I spoke to, and actually brought in $125,000 from one investor. I was rocking and bringing in more than enough money to ease my financial concerns. My tenure there ended nine months later, when the principals of the company were arrested for trading violations and ended up spending some time in Club Fed. I went on to work for a second firm, which lasted only a matter of weeks before I quit to get the nightclub up and running. But I am getting ahead of myself.

Upon arriving in the city, I met some interesting men here and there, and bedded at least a few of them, here and there. I have long since forgotten their names and faces, but I do remember that at least one or two of them pleased me sexually.

I recall that one bore the same name as my dearly departed father, but he wasn't the one who made my toes curl. Not that he was a turn-off, but rather he was just a fleeting recollection.

Another had a name like James or Bill or Steven, and he and I regularly had sex in all positions known, and some unknown, at least to me. Some were no doubt illegal, or at least frowned upon, and some I would never repeat again with anyone. None of these liaisons was destined to be long-lasting. Rather, they were encounters that lasted for a night, a week, a month, and one, even a few months, but far from forever. It was during this period of wanton near rebellion, that I met this oddly strange, eccentric, but interesting guy named Raymond who lived in a loft next door. I would see him regularly, a wave, a smile, just the basic recognition that one is still alive and in New York City. He appeared to be super-glued to a massive harlequin Great Dane named Conan, after the barbarian, and could usually be found on roller skates with chopsticks in hand eating Chinese food out of a take-out container. It was quite the sight even for the Village and of course grabbed my attention more than once.

He was, without question, a brash departure from any person, alive or dead, that I had ever dated before, and perhaps that was the attraction. The fact that we were diametrically opposed in character and appearance initially led to a friendship. That uncanny friendship continued over a period of several months before we moved into an odd, yet fascinating sexual relationship, one that tested the boundaries of my innate knowledge of right and wrong almost daily.

His bizarre, eccentric, even dark personality made him someone who seemed to have no boundaries, or at the very least boundaries that were far more relaxed than mine. The relationship was perverse, sensual, sexual, edgy, and experimental. It walked the fine lines of drug abuse and danced along the edges of S&M. It was frightening and exciting at the same time.

I lived many of my fantasies inside the walls of this relationship. I also ended up marrying him, twice, even though once was more than enough. The second time was in Las Vegas just to solidify our first union, which took place in Florence, Italy, complete with a horse-drawn carriage and a Palazzo ceremony.

One night, early on in this sexually charged relationship phase, there was a knock at my door, and I assumed it was Raymond. After all, I lived in a secured building with a doorman. Without thinking, I opened the door and suddenly I was grabbed and a hood was placed over my head. It all happened so quickly that I had no chance to react or to scream or do anything.

The silence of the attack exploded in my ears. I was led to the living room and bound to the wooden stairs that led up to a small loft. I called out to Raymond, but there was no response.

I was blinded by the hood but continued to call out his name and was greeted by silence. For the first and only time perhaps in my life, I was scared. *Who the hell was in my home? What was happening and why?* I was mentally moving between terror and disbelief. This must be Raymond that I let inside, but he refused to speak. I couldn't see and the silence terrified me far more than words might have.

I'm feeling cold and I'm scared to death. What the hell had I done? Who had I opened the door to? Who is breathing into my ear and caressing my face with his hand? Who the hell is this? What the hell does he want? Silence! I could feel my clothing being cut from my body, and I heard the thundering sound of my buttons falling to the wooden floor.

"Raymond, is that you?" I questioned in a terror-filled voice. "Raymond, stop fooling around and say something please," I pleaded with my captor.

I was surrounded by silence and could hear my fear in the near-empty room. After what seemed like hours, I was cut loose, half naked, and moved into the bedroom, still hooded.

I could feel a rock-hard dick pressing against my leg. It was oozing cum that dripped onto my knee. It felt sticky. I continued crying out to my mysterious captor, but he failed to reply. Then my pussy was pried open and the full weight of the intruder fell onto my body. I tried to scream but no words came out of my mouth. I tried to say stop, you're hurting me, but again, nothing but silence.

He moved quickly, expertly, and then he came with an unrehearsed but noisy moan. He rose rapidly, leaving me naked and afraid on the bedroom floor, and left without a word, slamming the door behind him.

I had been raped or made love to or raped. I was confused. In my heart, I knew it was Raymond. It was strangely exciting and frightening at the same time. My captor had said nothing. It had to be Raymond, or was it? Who else could it be? I lay there stunned, in total disbelief and silence, waiting, for what I didn't know.

I got up and made my way to the bathroom to clean up and get dressed. I was weak and nearly legless from the trauma. A few minutes passed or maybe it was an hour, maybe more. I totally lost track of time. Another knock on the door. This time I peered out through the tiny hole and it was Raymond. He came in acting as if he had no idea what I was talking about and spent the next hour coyly refusing to admit that he was my intruder.

As certain as I was that it had been him and that he had spent days planning his attack, this surprise sexual encounter, he played the "dumb" card.

"I have absolutely no idea what you are talking about. What happened? Did someone attack you?"

"Yes, but that someone was you. You were here, weren't you? It was you . . . wasn't it?" I was weak and traumatized, confused and angered, but he continued to deny having been in the apartment earlier that day.

Over the years, he never came clean, but I knew, at least I thought I knew that it was him. At the same time, I prayed that I was right. I mean, who else could it have been? I never found out. Raymond was just strange enough to intrigue my sexual senses and wild enough to carry them out in real life. Although I had no idea about this on the way in, I was to find that out later in our relationship. We would lay on a mat in the loft and fantasize about sexual encounters with other women, and with other men.

One night we went to Studio 54, and after ingesting some downers and wildly gyrating to the ear-pounding music, picked up a young, good-looking Russian guy, who I will call Mr. X, since I didn't get his name.

We returned to his apartment and proceeded to have sex. This was not making love, this was plain, unadulterated sex, for sex sake. For a couple of hours, he and I got lost having hot sex, while Raymond watched and masturbated. Then the three of us lay naked on the bed, our limbs knitted together, our bodies in exploration mode. Later, I watched as Mr. X licked and sucked Raymond's cock into a rock-like hardness that was unlike anything I had ever witnessed before.

It was raw, exciting, insane, dangerously stupid, but wonderful as well. I never repeated that night again, even though I used the fantasy many times to bring myself to an earth-shattering climax. I found out quickly that the idea of being fucked by two men at once was not particularly appealing to me, and that I would have preferred two women instead.

Our fantasies were often perverse, and most of the time the fantasy was far better than the reality. One night Raymond and I ingested some pills and then went to an infamous New York City swing club, Plato's Retreat. The club was well-known around the world and has since ceased to operate, but then it was in full swing, pardon the pun. Raymond shed his clothing from the waist down and proceeded to wander around the club with his limp dick hanging out. It didn't take long before a couple approached us.

They were gorgeous. He was tall and tanned, and she was an Israeli sabra, dark and sexy. We made our way to a room alone. Naked and swimming from the drugs, we began a sexual encounter that included Lila's husband Daniel and I, and then Lila and me. All the while, Raymond sat on the sidelines, naked and masturbating.

He couldn't get into Lila for some unknown reason, and instead, decided to get into himself. I suppose it turned him on watching me having sex with a stranger, and then watching the stranger's wife suck on my hot, wet, cum-filled pussy. This turned out to be just the beginning.

Several weeks later, on a hot and sultry night, we repeated this sensuous fantasy in real time again at their home and it was magical. There were more naked bodies in attendance that time, but it was much the same, with Raymond watching from the sidelines as Lila and I got it on, and then hunky Daniel and I having sex on the floor directly in front of him. It was hot and wild, and Raymond never took his eyes off of us. He still wasn't turned on by her at all, or anyone else in attendance, but luckily I was. This was not my first female encounter nor my last.

The first was in London, one freezing cold December night, when I was about thirty-five, give or take a few years. I had fantasized long enough about having sex with another woman, and so, on a business trip with my gay male friend, I decided to make that a reality. I had gone to the Flamingo Club, a fiery hot, happening spot with half-naked bodies dancing wildly to ear-piercing disco. I started scouring the club of mainly gay and wildly out of control straight people for a potential female sex partner.

Suddenly, there she was, a five-foot-seven, busty, sex-charged blonde stripper. Carolina was right up my alley, at that moment in time, a bit on the hefty side, with huge tits and open to any and all comers, no pun intended. She made it clear she was hot for me and I replied in kind. We went back to the hotel, my gay friend disappeared for the night, and she and I fucked ourselves nearly to death.

It was interesting and fun, and yes, it was an event I repeated over and over again during the next decade, more or less. I suppose I have always thought of myself as bisexual, with the caveat that I knew who I was sexually. I enjoyed having sex with men, or a beautiful, sexy woman who was also into men, and who was preferably straight.

After Carolina, there were numerous other excursions over the edge with women who were straight, some that I knew well. It just seemed to happen as an extension of our friendship but brought us to a more intimate place where we could express that love we had for each other in a different way.

While it may sound strange, it actually worked, at least at that moment in time. It was in some ways bizarre, yet fascinating, that we stepped over the boundaries of friendship into a brief sexual encounter, then never discussed it again. We just moved on, as friends but even closer in some ways.

Then there was the anonymous woman I interacted with online in a women-seeking-women website and later met as she was transiting through New York. I booked into a hotel in the city, and we met for lunch as if we were old and dear friends. During our lunch, there was an almost arm's-length sense to any thoughts of sexual encounters; however, that changed as lunch came to an end. My new friend asked to see my room. In the elevator, she reached over and touched my breasts. Once inside the trendy, tiny, box-like room, we made crazy love, literally falling off the bed and onto the floor twice, entangled in our nakedness. It was wild, risky, and wonderful, and I never saw or spoke to her again. It was truly anonymous, and at that moment I loved it.

I have never regretted my forays into the world of experimentation. I always thought it just fortified my knowledge that I was totally at ease with who I was and my sexuality.

I know I am an incredible, sexy woman who loves men, but also can appreciate sex with a woman. I have never fancied myself with a masculine woman, and all of the women that I have been with were and are sexy and beautiful, most of them straight and not masculine in any way. Truthfully, that has never appealed to me.

Years ago, I had traveled around to a number of different states trying to set up a concert for a well-known performer, Devine, who was idolized by the gay community. I would go into lesbian bars to pass out flyers in New Orleans, Los Angeles, Puerto Rico, New York, and was always ogled by the variety of lesbian women, most of whom were very butch.

I couldn't wait to get out of those places, although I was always polite and nice. I never understood why a woman would be interested in sex with another woman who looked and acted like a man. I enjoy and appreciate beautiful, sexy women who are straight but curious, if you will.

Once, however, I did make love to a woman who was gay, and it happened in a closet in Los Angeles. That was a wild and unforgettable experience. She was someone that I knew relatively well, was very attractive, and looked like Candice Bergen. One day we just happened to be in my new apartment in West Hollywood, and there was no furniture in it yet. There was, however, a lovely, carpeted closet, some extremely good coke, compliments of my former night club in New York, and the two of us. The next thing we knew, we were making love on the closet floor.

Exciting and risky for sure, but worth every moment. Interestingly enough, my relationships with the women that I have been intimate with have never changed other than to continue being only great friends. There is only one exception and that one is worth talking about, with the names changed for my safety and hers.

It was during my years in the nightclub business in New York City, and the friend was one I had known for many years through the fashion business.

Long after our interlude, I discovered, much to my surprise and horror, that her husband's family was "connected," and I mean that in the most literal sense, at the very top to one of the most powerful crime families in America. In retrospect, it was no surprise that she needed to distance herself from me totally, and that I needed to change the names of all parties.

It all happened quite by accident, not by design. My friend, for the sake of discretion I will call her Joanna, and I had known each other through business for years and decided to go out of town for a short holiday.

We flew to Puerto Rico for what was to be a long weekend. Shortly after our arrival, we decided for some unknown reason to buy some weed. I was in a relationship with Raymond at the time and lived in the Village in New York City. I never really liked weed, as it took me from control to no control, and I would literally consume every edible thing in sight, so I didn't really smoke. But this weekend, we decided to have a go at it. As we were getting freshened up and ready to go out for dinner, Joanna invited me into the shower. At the time I was a bit high and didn't give it much thought. In retrospect, I wondered if this was her first experience. Our naked bodies rubbed against each other in the shower as we soaped up. Soon, we were on the bed making love for hours, dinner was all but forgotten, at least for that moment in time.

We were so into each other that we quickly lost the concept of time and suddenly our weekend away was heading into a week, and I had to make a call extending our trip another few days, We were starved for each other's bodies and spent the days making love, oblivious to almost everything else.

Our senses opened up and we craved even more excitement, and so, on our way back to New York, we made a plan to surprise Raymond with a special fantasy, the two of us. Joanna checked into a hotel, and we planned to have him meet us under the pretense of going out to dinner. When he arrived, we were in bed, naked, and had left the door unlocked. Before you could say threesome, he was naked, his dick hard as a rock, and he had joined us in bed. Clearly, he was into her in a way he had not been in previous sexual encounters. It so happened that this was precisely when things went to hell in a handbasket. Here we were living our fantasy, or so I thought, but Raymond was not interested in masturbating on the sidelines watching she and I get it on.

Sometimes it is said that the fantasy can be better than the reality, and in this case that was true. My dear friend and lover Joanna was a gorgeous, sexy woman, and Raymond got so into her that he all but forgot about me. His hard dick was slipping in and out of her wet pussy while I lay next to them waiting to have Joanna lick and suck my pussy, which was our intention from the beginning. At least that was what I thought.

At the end of the day, the fantasy proved far better than the reality, as Joanna and I drifted apart, probably because her husband would have killed us both had he known. Raymond and I had moved away from each other as well, since I was hurt and angry, and never really forgave him for the way he handled that day.

That incident nearly proved to be the swan song of our delving into the netherworld of sexual escapades, although we did continue on just a little. We had an interesting encounter at our night club one night while we were closed. We had picked up a young, questionably straight male from a hugely popular underground club in the city, and went back to our club, which was shut at the time. We sat in one of the little living rooms downstairs and

I watched as this young, hot guy, Trey, we will call him, sucked Raymond off. It was a scene that I replayed over and over again. I must admit I enjoyed the fantasy of a hot man sucking another hot man off. Interestingly enough my sexual curiosity in women waned when I met my soulmate, Paul, and since then, he has been the focus of my attentions.

QUEEN OF THE NIGHT

My relationship with Raymond moved from the initial stages of lust to one of comfort and sexual experimentation. His problem was that he couldn't get out of his own way. I got weary of his constant chatter about inventions he thought of, or wished he had thought of, until that fateful day in January 1981.

Raymond was going on and on about opening a night club, a place based on the perverse world we were dipping our toes into. A place where "anything" could happen. It was the early '80s and cocaine was the drug of choice, and we dealt with our lack of reality regularly.

We were crossing Fifth Avenue when it hit me. This was not going to be just another idea that ended up in the round file. I was a doer, an adventurer, I made things happen. I would make this happen. I would get the money together to get the club up and running. I would call it Bolero after Ravel's famous piece of music, and so I began my search for the perfect spot for our "outside the box" club. After some initial searching, I located a space in the heart of the city, a townhouse on the east side on 27th, negotiated the lease, and raised the necessary money to get the project off the ground.

I was always able to sell, that was my forte, so I sold the idea of a trendy nightclub where "anything could happen" to a few interested and interesting investors. I created a slick, provocative ad campaign that featured two gorgeous women and one hot man. His tuxedo was in place, other than a tie that was askew, and the women hanging over him were dressed in plunging evening attire. The ad read, "Bolero, a place where anything can happen." What I didn't know at that time was the tagline probably should have been different, as I never saw anything out of line happen, but then my definition of that was always slightly skewed. Maybe plenty happened, but it just didn't raise my red flags.

Theoretically, Raymond was in charge of construction, a task he should have been up for but wasn't, and at the end of the day, he failed miserably.

I was working at the second company on Wall Street at that time and suddenly realized that if I didn't get myself over to the club, nothing was ever going to get finished. At the end of the day, time was money, and we needed to get open then not a month from then.

Raymond could talk a good game about inventing something, but when it came to actually putting it together, he just couldn't get out of his own way. Basically, he just wasn't tough enough. He was a dreamer at best and out of touch with reality at worst. I had to make a major decision. Either I was going to stay on Wall Street and make more money or I was going over to the club and getting it opened. I weighed the choices.

And so it happened, at the end of another day at the new company I started working at on Wall Street, I screamed in desperation into the phone,

"Turn over a paint can, I'm coming to the club." The money lost, the club won.

One hour later, I had quit my job and was sitting on a large metal can in a vacant space shouting at the workmen who were swarming around like ants. Once I turned the can over and started getting tough, it took about a month to get the club up and running properly.

Next, I had to hire the perfect PR person so that we could get our name into the papers. We found a fantastic guy named John Carmen, who also represented the amazing Devine, and he got us in front of the right people at the right time.

Then, suddenly, I was "Queen of the Night." The spotlight was on me, and the people were arriving in droves to the special parties we were hosting every night.

Bolero was nearly an overnight sensation, a happening before its time. What began as a well-situated townhouse on East 27th street exploded into a happening because of our imaginative ideas and money. On opening night Bolero presented complete with a butler at the door and gorgeous antiques in the entry way/living room.

The elevator that now graced the living room looked real, vibrating just enough after the metal doors closed to make you a believer. You were, for all intents, going up, going down, or somewhere in between, a fact that lirally freaked out some of our celebrity customers, like Debbie Harry aka Blondie.

When the vibrations stopped, the doors magically reopened onto a stainless-steel dance floor surrounded by speakers and ear-pounding noise created by our awesome DJ.

In the back of this huge, open space were custom couches and seats situated top and bottom, offering some semblance of quiet, but even more important, a bird's-eye view of the dance floor and all the happenings.

Overhanging the dance floor was a private VIP room that sported one-way glass and afforded celebrities the privacy that they demanded. A long, heavily carved bar with a television hanging precipitously above all but took over the adjoining room, along with a small boutique area with sleek seating, where we served drinks and desserts.

But the pièce de résistance, the compelling area of interest for many of the guests, was the downstairs, which was carefully guarded by security at each staircase.

There, ten small living rooms dotted the hallway. Our vision created them complete with sliding metal "drapes" to provide total privacy, if required or desired. Each "living room" had a built-in seat that was covered with a futon-like mat that opened out to make the entire floor a seating or reclining spot, as one wished. At the far end of the hallway, across from the lavish unisex restrooms, was a door leading to the locked, oversized Jacuzzi. This private area housed a twelve-foot Jacuzzi, towel boy, plenty of towels, lockers, and a changing area so that guests could slip out of all or part of their clothing, place them neatly in a locker, then retreat to the warm water in complete privacy, with or without the company of either sex.

This was totally private and available by reservation only. Amusingly enough, those who initially screamed the loudest that their friends or clients would never, ever go to a club with a Jacuzzi ended up being the first to reserve it! After we were well into the construction, I met with a major PR personality who was in fact the one behind Studio at the time. She made it clear that none of her friends would ever be caught dead in a Jacuzzi in a nightclub.

This was despite the fact that I had been watching some of her "friends" the previous months as they "partied" in the back rooms of Studio and Xenon and that gave me the idea in the first place. In any case, erring on the side of good business, we made the area private and by reservation only, and it worked like a charm. It was in fact a beautiful area for a private party and could have led to some interesting sexual escapades, but of course, I knew nothing about what went on behind closed doors, except when I was personally in the Jacuzzi.

The very first to reserve this private space was the staff at *Interview*, the late, great Andy Warhol's magazine. The door to the "fun zone" was always locked, and I had the only key. If someone left the room, the door would lock behind them out of privacy concerns, and someone either needed to be on the other side to open it again or I would open it.

On one particular night, I made my way downstairs, a routine check to make sure everything was in order. I was walking slowly past the occupied living rooms when from the bowels of the darkened hallway I heard, "Psst, psst." I looked around and to my shock, I saw Andy flush against the wall next to the restrooms. He was nothing if not immediately recognizable, his skin the palest of white topped by a large gathering of white hair.

"I locked myself out," he whispered.

I immediately opened the door and let him back inside. I couldn't help but find it a bit amusing that here was one of the world's most famous artists, most recognizable for sure, locked out of the Jacuzzi at our club.

I never forgot that moment as it is indelibly imprinted on my mind. Andy was a very unique and interesting man, and I enjoyed knowing him, even though, for the most part, it was an arm's-length relationship. I used to go to the Factory and spend time there with the staff, and also at the Underground club that Andy owned.

It was always a unique and fabulous experience, and I became quite close with the *Interview* magazine cover designer Richard.

We spent many an amazing night with Richard, and an assortment of unusual personalities, at a wild club called Crisco's, which was in the heart of the Meatpacking District. Each night was more memorable than the one before and provided me with many incredible life experiences. One had to enter Crisco's with an open mind and acceptance for the unknown, bordering on bizarre. It was to this particular club that I took my son Greg when he visited me at the age of eighteen.

The club was "the" place to be and to be seen. Gorgeous models streamed through the doors, along with Eurotrash, celebrities, and a few wild and crazy Club Kids, along with the requisite number of smoldering hot, gay men.

We knew that to have a successful New York night club, one needed a great mix of people, of all types, shapes, sizes, genders, colors, and ages. One night a well-known man about town named Russell, who had an older, very wealthy male lover, arrived at Bolero in a pair of leather chaps with nothing on underneath.

As luck would have it, this particular night we had a scattering of politicians in attendance, including a New York state senator, who also happened to be on the state liquor board and a congressman.

There was Russell chatting them up facing forward, and then he turned around to greet someone, and the expression on their faces as they stared at his bare ass hanging out of a pair of leather chaps was priceless, magical, and memorable. I tried not to laugh.

Our liquor license seemed destined to remain at the bottom of the pile at the board. At one point we took the entire package, twelve-inches thick of paperwork, to renowned attorney Roy Cohn only to discover weeks later that our package of documents had disappeared. Sometime later it "fell" into the hands of one of the five mob families. How that happened we never discovered.

However, it was clear that they had intimate knowledge of every document submitted to the liquor board. Despite this little blip, we did get our liquor license eventually. We also hired Russell to be at the door welcoming our customers. A win-win!

Days faded into nights, and then back into days again as we medicated ourselves with white powder, willingly provided by youthful purveyors of drugs. For a price, we could obliterate the bad days and make them into amazing days. We were rocking! Early each morning, after we did the count to ensure the bartenders hadn't cheated us, we would make our way to one of the after-hours underground clubs and continue the debauchery until we could hardly move.

There was AM/PM, Crisco Disco, Berlin, and Mineshaft, a hot gay spot we would go to some nights. Each club was a bit different in its decadence. There were movies of women with horses and containers with pigs in formaldehyde. There were mounds of coke and hot Dalí muses who looked like gorgeous, captivating women but were really men.

Nearly unforgettable was one incredible night when Greg was in New York City. It was his eighteenth birthday, so we brought him to New York to revel in some adult pleasures. Our first stop was the Underground, Andy's hot club, where he began dancing wildly with some gorgeous chick, then suddenly recoiled when he realized that the object of his attention was really a man. It was impossible to argue the fact that she checked all the boxes and looked sultry and stunning.

To us the mistake was amusing and understandable, but he was crushed and embarrassed beyond words. His masculinity, or his perception of that, had been demolished. In his mind, here he was making moves on what looked like a woman but in truth was a man. How could he live this down? To us, it was just another night in the New York City nightlife scene and just another happening.

In reality, he lived in California, and this was New York City where you could get anything, anytime, anywhere, for any price. No one really cared, and it was all in his mind. Unfortunately, none of us realized at the time, but this would be the prelude to one of the darkest times in all our lives.

After we got him back on track, we headed to Crisco Disco, an edgy, mind-blowing gay club in the then-ghostly area of the Meatpacking District. In the early '80s in that area, there was very little else happening, other than meatpacking plants and slaughterhouses. I had spent many an evening there partying with Richard from *Interview* magazine. This truly was a hot spot where anything could happen and did. It began as you stood on the sidewalk outside an innocuous door on a darkened street. A sliding panel would open, and eyes would peer out and give the once-over to whoever was waiting. It was like the speakeasies of the Prohibition period. Acceptance came by way of the door swinging open and guests going through metal detectors.

The first room you entered was the bar, crawling with every imaginable, unique, and unusual person, straight, gay, trans, or unknown. In the next room you could buy anyone you wanted, literally.

The room after that was where you could buy anything you wanted, purportedly to use with the anyone you picked up in the first room. If you made it past these enticements, you landed upstairs in the private room inhabited mainly by those who arrived by limo. The Salvador Dalì muses, both genders, but all looking like hot women, the drug dealers, the drug users, the hangers-on, the celebrities, the wannabes, and an assortment of other fascinating, albeit, curious guests.

Drugs traded hands in the bathroom like water flowing from a fountain. One night Raymond and I were upstairs and this gorgeous, captivating woman sat down on a bench between us. I watched as she put her hand on Ray's leg and actually found myself getting a bit jealous. I was sitting so close to her I could hear her breathing, but I saw no signs that she was anything but a sultry, hot woman.

It was only later that evening that Richard pointed her out, saying "she" was actually a "he" and was one of Dalì's muses. That was just an example of what Crisco's was like, and why it was clearly out of Greg's comfort zone. I think it was precisely that edginess that made it so exciting for me to frequent. That night we made it through the metal detectors and were summarily paraded into the bar area.

How quickly Greg forgot the incident a few hours earlier at the Underground. There he was draped around the bar, flaunting his hot eighteen-year-old body, muscles bulging.

Then he spotted a gorgeous young thing with a lithe body and a face like a Botticelli angel. Her blonde hair fell softly around her shoulders, and her legs went on for days, rendering her nearly as tall as he was. He swooped in and began to chat her up. It was only after he had hung over her for nearly an hour that he realized, once again, the angel was not a woman.

The realization struck another devastating blow to his ego. Head bowed, he made his way back to where we were drinking and announced that he wanted to go home immediately. I promptly called up our driver who was waiting in our car, a James Young Silver Wraith limo, and sent Mr. "I Know Everything" back to the apartment alone. In retrospect one would have thought Greg might have been a bit more cautious in his meanderings into the world of the unknown years later. But sadly, for all concerned, he was still the impetuous eighteen-year-old know-it-all even then.

His stay with me was short-lived, and within a week or so he headed back to California, still the "know-it-all" who embarrassingly knew very little about the "real" nightlife scene in New York City or, as it turned out, anyplace else. We never discussed that night again, and I knew better than to ever bring it up.

Bolero was slightly ahead of its time on all fronts. It had the intimacy of a small club, but the excitement, mystery, and celebrity of a Studio 54. There was no moon with a spoon flying over it, but the private Jacuzzi and intimate living rooms, along with the eclectic mix of partiers, celebrities, models, Eurotrash, and hot gay men made this the place to be. One afternoon, a well-known television host squired me to a riverside restaurant in the city.

A few drinks later, as he drank champagne out of my high-heeled Manolo Blahnik shoes, he requested that I remove my panties and give them to him. I refused, but we laughed and drank, and he pressed me to allow him to do one of his Lifestyle shows from our Jacuzzi. Again, I replied in the negative. We wanted publicity, of course, just not that kind.

Opening night at Bolero was a scene of chaos, congestion, and celebrity, as some fifteen hundred people oozed through the velvet ropes, past the butler, left their coats at the coatroom, and took the elevator ride to nowhere. We were flying high! That was until the wee hours of the morning when we realized how wrong we were. The club was still completely filled with partiers, oblivious to the hour and full of alcohol and drugs. A young, uninvited man appeared at the door trying to get past Russell, who was our "doorman." Visibly upset and angry, he began threatening to blow us up, literally, if we ever had an event like that again. Here we were exercising our right to party in New York City, being mortally threatened by some thug in the middle of the night. The "thug" turned out to be the son of the right hand of a major Mafia figure who had an illegal gambling club in close proximity to us. His desire for anonymity and the quiet of an undiscovered tomb was formidable, and a street teeming with limousines and raucous club people was not what the doctor or the Mafia ordered. Toning things down was not really what we had in mind, but we made a valiant attempt anyway.

Over the next months, there was the requisite amount of drama, drugs, and death, including a Park Avenue doctor named Peter who early on appeared to try to extort us before mysteriously dying of "natural causes" a few weeks later.

He had arrived at the club with a group of friends and turned his jacket over to our coat-check girl, who was very street smart. She carefully checked all the guests' pockets and made sure nothing of value was left, before giving them a coat-check ticket. It was a cautionary move on our part to avoid any "misunderstandings." When he went to leave, he claimed that $5,000 had been in the pocket of his jacket and was now missing.

Of course, given the circumstances, I made a call to our lawyers alerting them to a possible extortion attempt. Several weeks later, his untimely passing was announced in the news media. It was listed as a heart attack and death by natural causes, but given his youthful age of thirty-nine, as well as the circumstances surrounding his visit to our club, I always wondered but never questioned what really happened.

There was the unforgettable night when a well-known, very wild female celebrity/singer who I won't name climbed from the back seat of our limo, through the glass dividers, and dropped onto our driver's lap. Try as she might, she couldn't seem to unzip his pants.

ANGELS IN SIN

The magic of my nightclub made it a trendy place that was slightly ahead of its' time. From the moment the butler opened the door to greet guests, to the beautiful, stainless-steel dance floor, the VIP room with one way glass, the reservation only jacuzzi and the elevator that did not go anywhere, Bolero was the definition of pure magic.

Celebrities filled the rooms, while disco music entertained and artists like the incredible Mary Wilson, Grace Jones, Robin Leach, Andy Warhol and the Village People's Randy Jones, were just some of the stunning guests at the non-stop party. The nights at Bolero were spellbinding and are memorable to this day.

BERNARD JAY

345 WEST 55th STREET   SUITE 6H   NEW YORK, N.Y. 10019
Phone: (212) 586-3807
PERSONAL MANAGEMENT   THEATRE PRODUCTION

Ms Georgene Summers
Bolero
119 East 27th Street
New York
N.Y.10016   March 2nd 1981

Dear Georgene

A brief note to thank you most sincerely for your
excellent hospitality last Saturday night at Bolero.
I think you have created just what New York needs
and you have every reason to expect tremendous success.
Anyway, with you both there, how can you fail?

I'm sorry we won't be here for your opening, but
Divine and I would like to wish you a great evening
on the 12th and we both look forward to seeing you -
and perhaps "taking the plunge" - on our return.

Much love,

ANGELS IN SIN

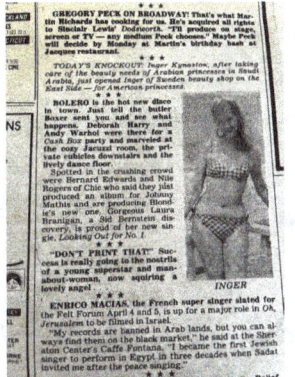

INGER

film, Blond Ambition, *next month.* ★ ★ ★

GET READY for Gotham's most exclusive club. The ultra chic Bolero makes its debut next month, complete with disco, video room, buffet, grotto with pool, cabaret and more if you want it. Since you're such a thoroughbred that only a chauffeur can bring you there, you'll call the club to fetch you in a white Rolls-Royce. Your membership card (assuming you pass muster) will show a number, no name, just like a Swiss bank account. Everything's secret. If you're lucky enough to gain entry, you'll put on a mask and revel in utter anonymity.

er directing duties after firing HOW- and Jane says a stickler he shot nes before he was

DAVIS is skyhigh over his romance LISA GERARD. fluffed the lines to meone You Love e song to her dur- as Vegas Hilton ence gave him a ding ovation.

d from Hollywood y KATHRINE e former beauty n, will send men's oaring when her

new comedy series Border Pals makes its debut on NBC soon.

The extraordinary Ripley's Believe It Or Not has been turned into a new weekly TV series by JACK HALEY. And he has already spent 15 days traveling halfway around the world with on-camera host JACK PALANCE for the special that kicks off the series run in May.

Sexy redhead GEORGINA SUMMERS' New York disco Bolero features a whirlpool grotto where patrons can freshen up from a night of dancing before heading to their offices. A chauffeur- driven Rolls-Royce even picks up and delivers guests.

Ignore those marriage breakup

reports about bea ABETH TAYLOR an WARNER. The coup to each other. So mu showers her dressi flowers after every tle Foxes performa gave her a full-leng one night.

One Sunday each ly married BARBI millionaire husba GRADOW invite a showbusiness frie Pasadena mansion we were graciously the most recent ga

Old friends CAR MEL SIMON and GONER were just celebrities on hand toasts as a 20-piec provided the backg

After rehearsin Academy Awards ROBERT REDFI volved in a high-sp he tried to flee Redford ducked ou Chandler pavilion his Porsche Turbo the shutterbugs co ture. But, undaun carrying photogr him all the way Hotel. The next da a burly bodyguard and his wife LOL

The day after was hit with "palimony" suit b girlfriend NANC the ex-Beatle fle new love BAR Ringo's publicist the country, Nan

stay home off his feet.

Disco goes Jacuzzi

Newest disco gimmick: "the Jacuzzi room," a black-tiled, locked chamber, which accomodates only 12 fun-seekers (bathing suits available but not necessary) at Bolero. It's the newest nightspot for the idle rich, which opened over the weekend in a brownstone at 119 E. 27 St. Phone number: unlisted (that's considered chic in some circles). Membership: $500 a year, plus $20 per visit. Lifetime memberships: $10,000—but that includes transportation to & from home, in Bolero's Rolls Royce. The opening night crowd included plenty of bankers and businessmen; median age, 45.

Exclusive gold metal numbered VIP card and numbered Member card. The gold card is the one that ended up in the hands of the Mafia family that was intent on taking my club.

This was after a wild night of disco and drugs had fueled us into the next morning. Two days later she ran into our driver on University Place and didn't even recognize him.

There were appearances from well-known celebrities like the late, great Mary Wilson of The Supremes, who we celebrated one evening along with the amazing and outrageous Grace Jones, and the wild and fantastic Randy Jones of the Village People. Here was one cowboy I couldn't get enough of. The singing went on for hours as gorgeous people cheered from the sidelines, some no doubt high on coke or other designer drugs.

The nights went on, one into the other, and many mornings I could be found half naked with a celebrity or two in the Jacuzzi, just chilling out from the night before and enjoying the relaxation at the end of a wild night.

We rarely stayed home for dinner, but rather would head out someplace trendy and fabulous every night before going to the club. In New York City there are fantastic restaurants at every corner and every block in between, and we enjoyed them all.

There were the great nights and the good nights, and then there were the ones that were filled with dread, where you wondered if you would wake up the next morning. On those nights it was like being in a terrifying mob movie, but one where you couldn't just change the channel. Emotionally I moved between terrified and a bravado that came out of nowhere to embolden me into a cartoon character from a Wonder Woman movie.

Then there were the threats, veiled and overt, especially after it was discovered that the illegal gambling club across the street had been sanctioned by another of the five families and was, as they say, untouchable. Somehow or another that fact had escaped the powers that had sanctioned our club in the first place. We were told to close or suffer extreme consequences. It was frightening, but we stood our ground. Our answer to the challenge was to have fewer guests at the club for our private VIP parties and to make sure the limos parked around the corner after dropping their clients off.

Then there were the "meetings." How could I forget those meetings? They were held in off-the-beaten-path restaurants, where a cluster of "guests" dined on what I termed the "lobster dinner," while the head "mafioso" sat somberly, not eating, just listening and waiting.

Once everyone was totally stuffed, filled to a near breaking point with food and drink, and a bit sleepy, he would spring into action slamming his hand on the table, shouting orders.

At each of these meetings, there seemed to be an oversized, dangerous-looking dog that parked himself between the table and the restroom, so there was virtually no escape from him, or the cast of characters seated around me.

At times, the "host" was so upset that glasses literally flew up in the air as his fists slammed onto the table. This should have scared me to death, but in fact, the white powder I was consuming made me feel invincible much of the time. Looking back, I could have made a fatal mistake at any moment, but thankfully I didn't, and my strength during those terrifying times has helped me every day of my life since.

One month turned into another, then another, and soon a year had passed and there were still some dark forces impacting our ownership of the club. There came a time months later when it was clear that we had to sell. That decision was brought to center stage by the continuing drama from powerful forces around us. They were squeezing us, trying to crush us, forcing us to move to make room for another, more invisible type of operation. I was flying high on the drugs and the euphoria of being the "Queen of the Night" and on some level, I didn't want it to end. On another, the end couldn't come quickly enough. We closed the club temporarily.

One night I sat in a theater on Broadway watching *Dreamgirls* starring Jennifer Hudson and methodically planning how I was going to exact revenge upon my tormentors.

The plan was so diabolical that looking back I have a hard time thinking that I was the one who cobbled it together. It included a vicious guard dog, a gun, and me as Wonder Woman, the fearless superhero.

My plan never came to pass, but in my mind, I thought that if I was going to die, I would at least take a few of them with me in the process. It was if nothing else a bold and just this side of insane thought.

Over the next few months, I would secretly stow my fur baby, Ashley, in a soft suitcase, board a train for Long Island, and leave, quietly spending days at a house I had secretly rented. No one knew where I was and for a time that worked perfectly. We closed, we opened, we closed again.

Our liquor license finally came through under the oddest of circumstances. The paperwork filed with the state liquor authority by our then lawyers labeled us a Supper Club, which meant we had entertainment. The term "Supper Club" was sprinkled generously throughout the entire application. Clearly that hadn't worked and our license was subsequently denied by one of the senior decision-makers on the board. Instinctively I knew it was always more about who you knew, rather than what you did or where you were located. Then we changed lawyers, and he changed the application.

Without so much as a flinch or a pause, he announced to the board that the clerk who typed the application had made an error and the club was actually a *Super* Club, not a Supper Club. What that meant was there would be no regular or scheduled entertainment. It sounded shocking, astounding, and amazing even to me, but within a few days the entire application was changed to reflect Super Club, not Supper Club. That, coupled with the change in law firms, was about to provide us with the miracle of a liquor license. Maybe it wasn't a miracle in the traditional sense of the word, but at the very least, it was the miracle of an intervention by some very "powerful forces." The same senior decision-maker at the state liquor board who vehemently denied us our license as a Supper Club stepped up to sing our praises and approve our license as a Super Club. Go figure! New lawyers, new application, it was a new day for sure! We were on a roll, once again.

True to form and unwavering in our commitment, we opened in a grand way, again, ruffling the feathers of the illegal club that sat practically on our doorstep. The parties, the models, the limos lined up to drop off the celebrities, the hot gay contingent, the half-dressed Club Kids, the Eurotrash, and the "wannabes." We were on fire, and we went for it big time, at least for as long as it lasted, even as demands continued to mount for us to get out of dodge.

At one point our phones were being tapped and the weight of the stress on us was unrelenting. There came a time months later when it was clear that we had to sell. That decision was brought to center stage by the continuing drama from powerful forces around us. Since selling seemed like a good idea, I reached out to our lawyers and suddenly several groups of potential buyers appeared ready to open talks with us.

They seemed to materialize like magic, but really, it was just some fancy sleight of hand. One group consisted of legitimate nightclub owners who were active in places like Florida, Chicago, and New Jersey, and had been around the block, so to speak. They had no illusions about what might lie in store for them and no apprehensions or concerns; in fact, later they went on to buy Studio 54. Then there was the businessman we had unearthed, who owned roller-skating rinks in the five boroughs. He was an African American man who fell in love with our operation and wanted to buy it.

Last, but certainly not least, were the "thugs," dressed like low-life mobsters in a B-rated movie starring Al Pacino as Scarface. There they were resplendent in their black shirts, white ties, and this, "I'm gonna break your legs" attitude that made me shake my head in disbelief more than once.

One night, as we stood inside the empty club having a moment, I actually said, "Hey, you know with your connections and my looks, we could go places."

Inside I was laughing uncontrollably, on the outside I should have been scared to death because this guy was someone to be terrified of. On some level, I know that I was, but I refused to allow that emotion to surface. My internal laughter covered up the fear that hid beneath my calm exterior.

In some perverted way, I was amused by it all but should have steered clear of making humor out of what was, without question, a deadly situation. Breaking legs was just a beginning, and these guys were as dangerous as they come. At the end of the day, it goes without saying that this turned out to be a very precarious situation. The club buyers were sent by our lawyers but, as it turned out, so were the guys in the black shirts that I had mocked.

Unbeknownst to us, neither group had any interest in dealing with our buyer because he was Black and, in their minds, unpredictable, so they put a plan in place, one that was carefully hidden from us. We scheduled a meeting at the club with all three potential buyers. There we were awkwardly seated around a table at the club as they began bidding against our buyer. They continued on until the price got too rich and he walked away. Then they picked up their proverbial toys and walked away too, leaving us with the rent, forty-two employees, liquor bills, utility bills, and more to pay.

It was a fascinating, clever negotiating tactic often used by these dark powers. It was an inside look at a mob way of negotiation. You are put behind the financial eight ball and then they just sit and wait. One quickly learns that when dealing with nefarious forces by any name, they have certain advantages over mere mortals. They have time, they have money—unlimited amounts of both—so you are always at a disadvantage.

I never forgot hearing about a restaurant in Little Italy that the "Mafia" wanted for a social club. I was in New York hard at work on our club at the time. The restaurant wasn't for sale, but a lawyer for the mob approached the owner and made him an offer. The lawyer offered around $500,000 as I recall, far below the actual value of the location. Of course, the owner said absolutely not. A month or so passed and one morning the owner arrived at work to find the inside of his restaurant vandalized and covered with green paint.

To say he was angry and upset would be an understatement, but he didn't really give much thought as to the who or the why. Crime happens everywhere, he mused, and this was New York City. He filed an insurance claim and moved on, although the restaurant had to close for a time. Once it was all repaired and up and running, it was vandalized again, and once more the owner filed for insurance and kept everything running. It still had not occurred to him that it was related in any way to the "offer" he had refused. The third time it happened the insurance company canceled his policy, and for a time, he was unable to find insurance. Desperate, he ended up calling the lawyer to see if that offer was still on the table.

"I'm really sorry, but my client already found something else. It isn't a secret that you have had your share of vandalism at the restaurant. Frankly, that isn't very good for business. I might be able to get them to come back to the table, but the price is going to be a lot lower for sure. You let me know, okay?"

A short time later the lawyer made contact again with a second offer.

"I've got an offer from my client. He said the location is being targeted by vandals and the best he can do is $250,000. Personally, given your circumstances, I think you should grab it. People are talking about all the problems you are having and frankly no one wants to get involved."

"Not a chance, no way. I would have to be nuts to sell for that price."

A few more months passed, with the restaurant plagued by several more bouts of vandalism. There were calls back and forth between the restaurant owner and the lawyer. At last, the lawyer came back with words of empathy and compassion and an offer of $100,000.

"You must be kidding! There is no point in selling at that price. I will just stay put and hang onto it. Thank you very much but no thanks."

He may have refused again, but the game of cat and mouse was nearly over. By now the restaurant had been closed for repairs for more than two months, which equated to hundreds of thousands of dollars in lost revenue and business. That, combined with the regular monthly bills like rent, increased insurance, employees, and utilities, finally made him "rethink" his position. At the end of this losing game, he reluctantly turned the space over to the lawyer and his client in return for payment of the outstanding debts. To get exactly what they wanted it only took an abundance of time, money, and the willingness to do whatever was necessary to basically take the place.

It was almost déjà vu for us. After initially entertaining the idea that the club would be sold, we were now sitting without any buyers but with bills piling up day after day, just like the guy with the restaurant. Rent was due, employees needed to be paid, and we were closed, and somewhat reluctant to go against anyone and everyone. All that time, however, I kept one thing in my mind that helped me go from day to day. This was America and no one, not anyone, could just take your business away. As ridiculous as that might sound given the circumstances, I held onto that belief.

I remained determined to keep that in the forefront of my mind at all times, right, wrong, or indifferent, no matter what. Then one morning, I had an outside-the-box thought. Early on in the business, I met a man named Frank who had an illegal gambling club in the city that was frequented by people like Sinatra, Jilly, and other well-known celebrities.

I figured that he, unlike many others, would know some extremely well-connected people that might be able to help us get out of the situation we now found ourselves in. I reached out to him, and he agreed to meet me at a popular spot on Fifth Avenue that Saturday afternoon. He was joined by a guy who was one of the originators of a product sold in head shops in the '80 s called pseudocaine. It was finally replaced with the real thing, although it did make your lips and tongue numb.

Frank had been at the club before and was aware of the presence of many "made guys" hanging around, so he was not surprised when I asked him for some help.

He agreed and had one of his contacts reach out to me a few days later. The person who contacted me was extremely powerful and the son of the head of one of the five families. He was so high up the "food chain" that he had no idea who the low-level thugs were that we had been dealing with. For safety's sake, I will call him "Jack," not his real name, however. A few days later he called and made an arrangement to come to the club.

He arrived that day along with another man who had recently been released from prison. "Jack's" appearance belied the dangerous world that he lived in. He was good-looking, very businesslike, with a nice demeanor and, in fact, was involved in both the fashion and music businesses on both coasts. The guy with him clearly came from the school of hard knocks and looked every bit the movie version of a "made" guy.

They surveyed the club, we chatted, I prayed my nervousness was in check, and he agreed to discuss the situation with his father and father-in-law.

I felt an icy chill as they made their way out the door and turned toward Lexington Avenue, where a car was waiting. Both his father and father-in-law were the heads of one of the five families. Their reach was massive, their influence and raw power formidable, and I knew that going in. There was no turning back now; I was in for the count.

This entire nightmare had been created because the right hand didn't know what the left hand was up to, and now we were infringing, so to speak, on the profits and losses of an already established gambling club on our street.

Our presence was unwanted and creating conflict in a tightly knit group that resolves any sort of conflict violently. It was a dangerous game, and we were now right in the middle and, in a sense, fighting to stay alive. Later that night he called.

"Sorry, but there is nothing that I can do. My family is already involved with your club. Heavily involved. I wish I could help, but they've got the VIP cards already."

It was suddenly very clear that his family already had their hands on our club, and they were the ones ordering us to close our doors or face the consequences. The slick, numbered VIP cards that we had given to our initial "contacts" made their way up the chain of command and into the hands of "Jack's" father.

That night when he phoned, I don't know what I was thinking when I responded to his inability to help.

"Thank you for everything and I really appreciate your help, but we are going to continue fighting on our own, in our own backyard."

"Understood. I'll get back to you," he replied dryly. The line went dead.

It turned out I couldn't have said anything that would have resonated better. I don't know whether it was dumb luck or just my own innate sense of survival that gave me the right words to say. Perhaps that, coupled with the unwitting "tip" that I had received in Rome years earlier from the retired DEA contact that made the difference for me and the outcome. I just remembered to play a better game of chess. A few days passed, and he called again to say he was impressed with us and the club and that he had gone higher up the ladder.

Unbeknownst to me, he had gone to the elders about our club to find out what, if anything, could be done. It was then that he asked me what we wanted financially, and I told him in a very matter-of-fact way.

Then I added something, a request that amazes me even now. "I don't ever want to have to look over my shoulder. I want to walk away a stand-up kind of guy."

I must have been watching too many movies, but I had heard that so often in the context of safety in the face of danger that it just popped out.

"Done. You'll hear from me."

With that, the conversation ended.

How my request was going to magically be granted, I had no idea, but I had to believe that he had the power and the authority to make this entire thing materialize, so to speak. Somehow, I instinctively knew that I would never have to look over my shoulder, for any reason. I hung up the phone, nervously shook a bit, and waited to see what was going to transpire.

Apparently, he had been more than a little impressed with me, enough so that he actually wanted me to work for him. He offered me a job, something to do with gold, and that blew my mind even more. *OMG, it's what I dream about every night. Working for the mob!*

It was an offer I knew that I shouldn't refuse, but I couldn't accept, so I politely declined. My knees were shaking just a bit as I thanked him and said no. Frankly, I had seen and heard enough for a lifetime. Three days later, our lawyer called and gave us the great "news." The club buyers, who a month earlier had walked away and left us holding the proverbial bills, returned and made us an offer. Remarkably, the offer was exactly what I had told "Jack" three nights earlier that I wanted. The club was subsequently purchased for that exact price. Soon after a gay spot was slotted in its place, and I walked away feeling secure that I had achieved "stand-up guy" status as well.

There was a bit of last-minute drama after the sale, when the new buyers began to make cosmetic and structural changes without having yet paid the full amount for the club.

Since that was not allowed until the full price had been paid and was part of our negotiated contract, we did what any law-abiding people would do, and we sued them.

It would have been easy to be intimidated and step back fearfully, but this was a legitimate deal that could and would stand the test of a courtroom, and we had to treat it as such. They paid immediately and continued with their cosmetic work on the space, unhampered.

Some months later the new buyers were called out about something by the owner of the building. He was a well-established real estate magnate with over forty-four properties in the city as part of his portfolio and the district attorney as a close friend. Obviously, he had no idea who he was dealing with, and over the next few days all of his properties were cited by the fire department for violations of one kind or another.

I went through a lot of traumatic experiences during this time, and frankly I could have lived without most of them. I thanked my lucky stars that I survived what could have been, and should have been, a disaster but today has given me the strength to confront anything and anyone that comes my way. The pervasive influence of the Mafia showed itself in so many ways during and after my nightclub days.

I am somewhat immune to it now because I see its dark underbelly and how it has transformed to meld with society in a more acceptable manner.

It has, for all intents and purposes, morphed into regular businesses new and old. While the days of a "made guy" threatening a business if they failed to pay to play are still around, the black hand has gotten more subtle and the reach far wider, a fact that I saw for myself.

One day early on in my stint in the nightclub business, I was on an elevator in New York City with our accountant who worked for the mob. We wanted to use him just so there was never any hint of impropriety. The last thing I would ever do is take one cent from these guys. They are known for slamming fingers in cash registers if a bartender steals a drink. The accountant was my contact for all things related to money, safety, and the club.

He had just returned from out of state after working with one of his clients who happened to be a well-known Fortune 500 company. So, our accountant and the mob's accountant was also the accountant for this massive Fortune 500 company. That spoke volumes and still does.

With the club now sold and the money paid, I'd had enough of New York to last me a lifetime, so I moved back to Los Angeles, with Raymond following suit eventually. A few affairs initiated by me, some cross-dressing drama initiated by Raymond, which surprised and embarrassed me, and I endured another two years of punishment in the confines of the marriage.

Finally, with a modicum of drama we divorced and quickly ended all contact. We had been through the wars and endured enough drama, fear, and anxiety to last a lifetime. We were done, with the club and each other. He went his way, I went mine, and other than a few rumblings from Venice Beach when he appeared in public, I lost contact for good and forever.

ANOTHER DAY, ANOTHER CLIFF!

The drama of the nightclub was behind me, but the remnants were still there front and center. Some people might have labeled me crazy; others might have ventured the opinion that I was a foolhardy risk-taker with no sense of danger. Truthfully, neither one would be even close to correct. Although it might not have seemed so, I had played a hand, taken a calculated risk, like any gambler worth his salt, and my risk had paid off. Right or wrong, I trusted "Jack's" words, and from that day forward, I never looked over my shoulder. I know some would say I was board certified, but that decision proved to be the right one. I played by the rules in the game of life that I was living at that time. I didn't deviate, and at the end of the day I won, whatever that means. To me it meant never having to look over my shoulder with anxiety, fear, or apprehension. That was winning in my book. Years earlier, I sat at a dinner table with the father of one of Greg's former girlfriends. She was special to me. I always looked at her as the daughter I never had and was secretly glad she never married him. She didn't deserve the drama that was part of the equation with Greg. Her father was a DEA agent who had retired and was living in Italy when he and I met. What really blew my mind was that he worked drug enforcement in Rome, regularly putting away Mafia bosses, and then he retired there. I didn't know it then, but this was to be a life-changing moment for me.

I was alone on vacation in Italy when her father invited me to dinner at his home, which was outside of Rome. It was exciting, as this was a fabulous opportunity to have dinner with "locals." Our conversation flowed smoothly, and I enjoyed meeting him and his new wife.

After dinner, we were sitting around relaxing and continuing our conversation when my curiosity got the best of me.

"Why did you decide to retire in Rome after spending so many years putting Mafia bosses in jail here?"

He smiled and his eyes glistened.

"They have a set of rules and I always played by their rules, I just played a better game."

Those words went directly into my soul and never left, only to be unearthed during my days as Queen of the Night. Only then, when they were most needed, did they emerge and essentially direct me in a manner that undoubtedly would save my life. With that information tucked away, I decided on some subconscious level to "play a better game and stay in my own backyard." No doubt that decision helped bring an acceptable conclusion to drama that had nearly consumed the club and me.

Contracts had been signed, money was in hand, and a few months later I got on a plane in New York, left all my possessions at the apartment, and flew to Los Angeles. I was older, wiser, and still breathing, albeit a bit heavily at times, and I had a mountain of information stored in the back of my mind. Much of it I had only seen in movies or read in books, and the rest of it was, at times, far more than I needed to know.

After that experience, I literally blanked out some of the information, but in a positive way. To this day, I have never mentioned the names of any of the players in this drama, practicing amnesia for my own well-being.

Several months later, Raymond piled my possessions into a truck and drove across country to meet me. While waiting for him to arrive, I had a brief but steamy affair with a very hot guy named Bill who I met on the plane on my way to Los Angeles. Months later, the affair had ended, and so did my marriage to Raymond, although not at the same time.

Our relationship became even more strained after our move to the West Coast, although the intensity of the nightclub trauma had already done grave damage. A few months into being in Los Angeles with Raymond, I took a breath and reevaluated my life. It was then, after some soul searching, that I moved alone from our apartment in Claremont, forty miles south of Los Angeles, to one in West Hollywood. I decided to put my skills in the fashion business to work and got a job as a showroom girl at the California Mart. It was quite the step down for me, working for someone, but at the time I needed money to live apart from Raymond, and that was my first priority.

Hard to believe, but this was one time when my exceptional skills were a detriment. I applied for the position, but nothing happened. I called over and over, day after day, and still nothing. It turned out that the owners believed I was too qualified for the job. In keeping with my beliefs that there is a solution to every problem, I continued to call and sell the one product that they needed, me. Sales were my forte and so no surprise that an abundance of calls later, I got the job!

This new company that I was working for had five duty-free shops in Hong Kong and the licenses to sell some major world-class handbag lines globally. Never one to rest on my laurels or step back like a shrinking violet, I had to be me, no matter the consequences. I had only been there for three weeks when a large parcel filled with handbags arrived. Of course, I unpacked and examined them and was left stunned and shocked.

Fashion accessories had been my forte for over a decade, and I made a great deal of money in the business. At one time or another, I sold my lines to every major department and specialty store in the country, from Federated to Neiman Marcus and Contempo Casuals to Mervyns and The Limited, and even traveled to the Far East to design fashion accessories for my own line. Consequently, I knew what was salable and what wasn't.

The bags were an anomaly, at least to me. They were made of a very trendy rubber-like material, but the styling was as old-fashioned as my grandmother's corset. I couldn't believe my eyes.

There was a dated Boston bag, and a Hobo bag among the group, and those were the most current. Surely this was a joke, and I was being tested.

When the owner arrived at the showroom that morning, he excitedly asked, "How do you like the new handbags?"

"They look like they were designed by a blind person. I could do a lot better than that," I replied dryly.

OMG, what had I done? I had never designed a handbag in my life and didn't know the difference between a gusset and a grommet.

But I also didn't know that I couldn't design a better handbag, so I jumped right in and made myself a target. It never occurred to me that three weeks could have been the duration of my employment at that company.

Moments later I was summoned into his office and slid into a chair directly across from his piercing gaze.

"So, what are you suggesting?"

I took a deep breath. "I need to take a few weeks off and I will bring you some amazing handbag designs."

After a few hours of back-and-forth dialogue, I was given the go ahead and three weeks off over the Christmas holidays to create a handbag line that **would** sell.

I hadn't a clue what to do, but I soldiered on because what choice had I left myself at that point? After all, it was my big mouth that had gotten me into this dilemma in the first place.

So, when that day was over, I breathed a sigh of relief, left the showroom, and went to my first stop, the local stationery supply store. There I purchased some oversized sheets of white art paper, some art pencils, Letraset (how else could I show the lovely snakeskin I envisioned?), and other supplies. Over the next few weeks, I pored over fashion magazines for new ideas; I drew, sketched, and carefully attached Letraset as designs onto my drawings.

When the smoke finally cleared, I had created a dozen gorgeous, one-dimensional handbags on oversized white art paper and could hardly wait to put them on display.

In my eyes I didn't see one dimension, I saw designer handbags, ala Carlos Falchi, Ferragamo, and Chloe displayed in stores across the country.

I returned to work three weeks later, my portfolio filled with drawings, anxious to display them to anyone. Once again, I found myself seated directly across from the owner, his gaze nearly piercing my soul. One by one I pulled the drawings out of my oversized black portfolio and proudly focused on each one, verbally emphasizing its beauty and details.

"See the beautiful snakeskin detailing around the front on this bag and look at how the lines of the bag flow."

One by one I slid the drawings across his desk and into his hands. His expression told a story of satisfaction, even glee.

"These are beautiful. I do love the details and the use of the snakeskin. I love them."

I had already decided what I wanted to do with the line, how I intended to get the samples produced, and once he asked me, "What do you see happening now with this collection?" I just blurted it out.

"I want to go to Italy, and I want a seventy-five-hundred-dollar bonus for the line."

"Are you kidding?" was the immediate response as his gaze turned to a glare.

Undaunted, I rose up slightly in the chair and started to make my case.

"If I let these drawings go without me, you are going to end up with another rubber handbag line that won't sell. I want to be there to oversee everything, to make sure that they are produced exactly the way we want them, the way we see them, the way they will sell."

The conversation continued back and forth for what seemed like an eternity. I began putting my designs back into the portfolio, determined not to give in or give up. The sticking point was my going to Italy, but I was adamant about that. My strong suit has always been sales, and I knew I could sell myself better than anything. After a great deal of negotiating, we reached a compromise of sorts. He agreed that I could go to Italy and would receive a bonus of $3,500.

Done! A week later I landed at Rome Fiumicino Airport, took the train to Florence, and was picked up by Franco, the company's contact in Italy. He escorted me to my hotel, The Excelsior, and made arrangements to pick me up the following morning. Little did I realize that I had a Judas in my camp who was ready, willing, and able to betray me for less than a few pieces of eight. Over the next two days, I worked diligently on my designs in the factory alongside Franco, even though I still had no clue about construction and was just winging it both days.

At one point he asked if I wanted a gusset or a bottom in each of my one-dimensional handbags. As a novice I had no idea, so I said no, expecting him to correct any manufacturing errors that I made. After all, I "designed" the handbags and expected him to deal with the construction part. He did in his own special way, but I still didn't get it.

The following day I made my way back to the factory to view my completed collection, only to find that they looked like oversized mailing envelopes. True to my drawings, the handbags were one-dimensional, flat as pancakes, and unable to hold more than a piece of paper and a pen, if that. It was only then that I discovered, much to my horror, that Franco was the "designer" of the infamous rubber handbag line that had arrived at the showroom the previous month. I was shocked and horrified.

OMG, what the hell was I going to do now? I was screwed! I had been royally used, manipulated, betrayed, and deceived. He must have known how badly I critiqued his rubber handbags, and this was payback! He clearly hadn't thought this through. Franco was the Judas, and now I had some serious decisions to make.

With only a few more days left in my trip, I had to do something fast. I have always been a survivor and a person capable of thinking outside the box when faced with challenges. It was then that I decided to give him two choices, one good for everyone and one not so good for him. When he arrived to pick me up that morning, I led him to the lobby seating so we could talk.

"Franco, we have a problem. I designed a collection of beautiful handbags, however, I don't understand construction and depended upon you for help. You failed to do that and now I have two choices. I can either return to the states without the collection and tell the owners how you sabotaged me. They will be out six thousand dollars and probably won't be very happy."

I winced a bit at the suggestion and continued.

"Or you take me to the appropriate handbag manufacturer, one who can make the samples I need, and I will take the collection back with me and say nothing to anyone about this misunderstanding. It's your choice."

Moments later, we were on our way to the proper factory, and by the following afternoon, I had my samples with bottoms or gussets as required, and they looked amazing. I had a lesson in handbag construction. I had quickly learned the difference between a gusset and a bottom, and the need for one or the other in a handbag. The collection went on to be sold in major department and specialty stores throughout the country, and I even knocked the line off in Korea and sold it with different leather and without the snakeskin trim, to other less expensive departments in the major stores.

Fortunately for me and many happy customers, I didn't allow the fact that I had never designed a handbag stop me from trying. I also didn't allow Franco to vengefully interfere and destroy the project. I stood up for myself and the collection and won big time.

There were several life lessons here, not the least of which was "just go for it." You don't know that you can't do something unless you don't try to do it then you fail for sure. The other lesson was never let anyone sabotage you or your work. I could have just left defeated and gone home without a collection, but I stood my ground. I weighed the harm that would be done to the company and to Franco. Then I gave him some choices, and everyone ended up winning.

A few months later, the owner asked me to give myself a title.

I didn't hesitate. "Director of Design and Development" was my reply.

I went on to have a sales force in New York, Florida, Texas, San Francisco, Chicago, and Los Angeles and got a commission override on all the sales that they made. In the space of less than three months, I went from making $1,500 a month to over $8,000 a month just because I said yes instead of no. It didn't matter that I had never designed a handbag before; I said yes, and I won because of it.

This was not the first time I jumped off a cliff without a net, and it would not be the last.

A day that I shall never forget as I am greeted by First Lady Hillary Clinton at a private cocktail party at the White House for seventy-five guests. That day President Clinton joined us for a short time before meeting with visiting President Yassar Arafat.

The Presidential Inaugural Committee
requests the honor of your presence
to attend and participate
in the
Inauguration of
William Jefferson Clinton
as
President of the United States of America
and
Albert Gore, Jr.
as
Vice President of the United States of America
on Monday, the twentieth of January
one thousand nine hundred and ninety-seven
in the City of Washington

My invitation to the Inauguration of President Bill Clinton. This is an honor that I will treasure always. I also had the privilege of attending several other events in honor of First Lady Hillary and President Bill Clinton. More magical moments to cherish.

In the late 1990s I found myself without consulting work once again and was happy about it from a certain standpoint. I always believed in the power of manifesting whatever I wanted, verbally and in writing. I had long since tired of working and decided that it was time for me to be taken care of. One morning I woke to a bright and sunny day and made my way outside.

"I am tired of working and I want someone to take care of me financially," I declared to the Universe.

It was a powerful statement, and as an independent woman it was one that I only declared once in my life. A few weeks passed when suddenly some friends volunteered to introduce me to someone they knew. I quickly discovered that he was a legend in his business circle.

He was twenty-five years older than me and wealthy beyond words. His company owned the rights in a number of states to sell liquor to restaurants, liquor stores, and any other venue wanting alcohol. It was a billion-dollar industry and he owned it all. His name was Al.

He was quite a fascinating person, a bit cantankerous, a risk-taker and gambler, who thought little of losing tens of thousands of dollars on the Craps tables in Las Vegas. He lived a high life transiting from coast to coast with gorgeous homes, servants, and expensive cars at each end. He was a shrewd businessman, a good card player, hard-charging negotiator, and a rather stern father. He was also a no-nonsense kind of guy who put up with little to no bullshit and called everything as he saw it, even if it was out of line. At his age, he didn't really care if it offended or angered, he said it anyway and took a position that shouted, "get over it." He fell in like with me, and for the next two-and-a-half years I had an amazing life in so many ways.

During the time we were together, we traveled first class, went on fabulous cruises on the Seabourn and Sea Goddess, and met dignitaries from around the world. He was an extremely charitable man who gave generously to those projects that were dear to him.

One year we traveled to Israel where he donated hundreds of thousands of dollars to build a memorial wall at Shaare Zedek

Medical Center in Jerusalem, and I had the distinct pleasure to meet privately with the then secretary of defense, Benjamin Netanyahu.

It was mesmerizing to be seated in a private room with a handful of dignitaries listening to him speak. I also greeted the Ethiopian jews who came by the planeload to Jerusalem.

It was magical seeing these beautiful Black people speaking Hebrew and wearing shirts with Jewish symbols on them. They were truly some of the most beautiful people I have ever seen, with sculpted features and a skin tone that looked as if it had been painted by an artist.

I was fascinated, and day after day I took their pictures, returning to the hotel where they were staying to gift them with a copy of their photograph. Most had never seen a picture of themselves.

I had what one might call a charmed life with Al in so many ways, but as reality set in I knew that I was sacrificing far too much of me in exchange. It became difficult to deal with, at least for someone so fiercely independent like me. It's been said many times before, be careful what you wish for. For several years, I had everything that I thought I wanted. All my bills were paid, I had a generous allowance, an apartment in Beverly Hills, expensive jewelry, fabulous trips, luxurious cars, and a gorgeous wardrobe, but somewhere along the way, I had sacrificed myself.

I lost my right to a freedom I had enjoyed and counted on, without restrictions, for most of my life. No more sushi dinners alone, no more twenty-six-mile bike rides on the oceanfront, no more dressing in jeans for a casual night out. No more private phone conversations, because he always managed to stay on the extension phone far longer than necessary. No more casual anything. We lived as if the Queen was arriving momentarily, dressing at night for our forays to fabulous, chic, trendy restaurants with friends.

I was, for all intents and purposes, a prisoner of my own making. Every night, except for one night a week, we were either on a dais at a costly charitable event, with me decked out in a killer custom gown, or at a hugely popular, expensive restaurant dressed to the nines joining three or four other couples for dinner. There was no "me" time at all left in my life.

I had gained financial freedom but lost myself in the process. He had two daughters who spent an inordinate amount of time hating on me, because in their mind I was too young for their father. He used to say that he had ties older than me. While that may have been true, I took great care of him, and I suppose on some level they did appreciate it. In spite of our crazy lifestyle, I had him home before nine at night and made sure he took his meds and ate right. While we were together, I built two businesses and hold two patents for fitness- and health-related products. It wasn't easy, but I was nothing if not determined. One of my business ventures supported me for the next twenty-plus years. Again, I just went for it and made it work.

We traveled a lot, fabulous cruises on ships with hundreds, not thousands of people; we partied in Venice, saw the Northern Lights in Norway, clubbed it in London, and were honored in Israel. We sailed around the Greek Islands, and I explored some of them on foot because Al didn't want me renting a motorbike. I made my way alone into Southern Israel and covered myself with the rejuvenating mud from the Dead Sea. At one point I was covered with mud from head to toe, my blonde hair perfectly styled, shocking against the coal black of the Dead Sea mud.

I had my own suite of rooms on both coasts, in Century City and Atlanta, and always had a wad of $100 bills in my wallet, all thanks to Al. Conversely, I was on call every day to do precisely what he wanted, where and when he wanted it, without regard to what I might have planned. It made no difference what appointments or meetings I might have set up, his wishes superseded any of that.

It was always much the same.

"Pick me up at six, sugar," he would say in a gravelly voice. He always called me sugar. There were no arguments to be had, I just picked him up at six.

One night we were dining alone at one of his favorite restaurants in Beverly Hills discussing his desire to gift me with a nearly brand-new Jaguar convertible. He wanted to ship it from his home in Atlanta to our home in Century City. The practical me knew there was no such thing as a gift without strings, and so I said I wanted to buy the car. In his raspy voice he then proceeded to tell me all of the reasons why I shouldn't do that because the company would pay for everything, including insurance, license fees, gas.

To which I replied, "Thank you but I still would like to buy it and have it in my name."

"You're a schmuck," he bellowed in his raspy voice.

"Excuse me?" I was shocked and livid but said nothing more, hiding my emotional distress. I was seething because no one had ever spoken to me like that. I never forgot that insult and never really forgave him. When I finally left, that was the single most important incident that propelled me out of the relationship. No one was going to call me a "schmuck."

Life had been good, at least I thought it was for several years, until the weight of my longing to be me outweighed the lavish lifestyle I enjoyed. One day I just had enough. The word "schmuck" was still ringing in my ears.

Then the proverbial straw happened. All I wanted to do that Sunday was put on a pair of jeans, grab my bike, and ride along the beach from Santa Monica to Manhattan Beach. Instead, I ended up at his country club having lunch with him and a stellar cast of well-known comedians. I suppose to anyone else that would have made their day, but I wasn't anyone else. I was me, and I had a host of other dreams. By the time lunch was over and I had been "dismissed," the day was gone and so were my dreams of bike riding along the beach. That night I sat alone in my room in the dark and took an "autopsy of my soul." It wasn't a pretty picture. I had always been true to myself and now I was giving me up for what amounted in my mind to a few pieces of eight.

What did that say about me, about my values, about my life, about what my life had become? It spoke volumes, not about who I was, but who I was becoming. I had to change things no matter what, and I had to do it then not later.

A few days passed and we were dining alone for a change at Spago, a trendy, chic restaurant in Los Angeles owned by stellar chef Wolfgang Puck, and suddenly, over the main course of pasta, I announced that I was leaving. At first, he acted as if he didn't hear me and then he moved into the "I can't believe my ears" mode.

Seated directly behind us was the famous comedian Carol Channing, who was busy making her table roar with laughter. Our table was silent except for the sound of his shock He stared vacantly at me. "You must be crazy. You are crazy. Why would you do that?" he mumbled.

How could I express that by being with him, in this relationship of lavish excess, I was losing myself. How could I tell him that I would rather go on a twenty-six-mile bike ride along the ocean on Sunday morning than to be dining at the country club with a bunch of high-profile comedians? How could I explain to this incredibly wealthy man that I would rather don a pair of jeans on a Friday night and head to the local sushi bar for dinner than go to Spago or Chasen's or another five-star restaurant all dolled up to the nines? I couldn't! I was speechless, a first for me for sure. I was frozen in time, unable to express my innermost emotions.

Here we were, the two of us, alone at Spago, dining on the best lobster pappardelle ever, surrounded by celebrities, and I was breaking up with him. How could I? Was I board certified? It was what I asked the Universe to give me! It was what I wanted, what any fully competent young woman would jump at. What was I thinking? Surely a ride on the beach on a bike isn't more important than my well-being. He had done so much for me financially. My credit cards were paid off, I had a fabulous monthly allowance and a suite at both homes. I had a Jaguar convertible that he gave me with all of the expenses paid for, and an investment in a motor park. I traveled first class, sat on the dais at charity functions, and dined at the finest restaurants. I must be totally insane to walk away from all of this, for a bike ride on the beach or a sushi dinner in a pair of jeans.

But there was one thing I would be gaining in all of this, and no amount of money could give that to me. I had done a lot of soul searching, and to save myself, I had no choice but to give up that life. I needed to get back to being me, to doing what I wanted to do, without reservation or compromise. I needed to be true to myself and my values, and I knew deep down inside that I wasn't.

But I am nothing if not pragmatic, and there was something else that was quite important to me. Important enough to make me step back, hit the pause button for my intended departure, and wait. Months earlier, Al loaned me $100,000 to start a skincare business. I had already used some of that money to put a small line of skincare products together, but I had two other projects that I believed were going to be even more lucrative. So, I decided to wait before making any moves. It turned out to be the right and perfect decision.

One of my new projects involved two fitness inventions that I had patents pending on. One was a piece of fitness equipment, and the other an instant tooth whitening and breath-freshening spray, both of which I ended up licensing to a major television marketer.

The second project had not revealed itself to me yet, so I conversed with the Universe, stood atop a mountain, so to speak, and announced. "I want to make five-thousand-dollars-plus a month and live wherever I want, and only need a computer and a fax."

One minute it was nothing more than a wish shouted into the Universe, but I already knew how well wishing out loud worked. Then suddenly there it was, the answer, appearing almost like magic, for my retirement. The phone sex business! Let's face it, sex sells. It makes no difference where you are, what the weather is like, or what is happening in the world of finance.

Phone sex sells because people are lonely and want to talk with someone, and sometimes, anyone will do. At the time, I had a very close gay friend and I initially thought gay phone sex was a great idea, and it was, just not for me. I pored over the sex ads in half a dozen adult magazines, calling customer service lines trying to dig deeply enough to get to the companies behind the lines and finally I hit the motherlode—a publicly traded company that had sex on its roster. Imagine that! I set up a meeting with the powers that be, and after what seemed like an eternity but was really just a matter of a week or so, Avanti Communications was born.

After our initial meeting, my work really began. There I sat staring blankly at a jumbled list of 800 numbers and started to spell what I thought was sexy real estate. I selected the hottest images and crafted the ads with a local agency. Before I knew it, I had a dozen great phone lines and an IP business, providing adult chat services to global callers. By the time the dust settled, I had fifty-five phone lines that spelled hot and sexy names. Real estate was our name for it, and my ads got the phones ringing. They were raw and exciting, and enticed customers with their smoldering visual appeal. I was up against a ton of other ads from companies with very deep pockets and I still held my own in an arena in which again I had absolutely no experience.

It was the onset of this business, and I did it all, from checking out lists of 800 numbers to see what they could or would spell, to writing ad copy and selecting those raw, sexy images for the ads. I even designed some of the sexually charged ads. I was up to my proverbial ass in alligators and naked women for the first six months. I had never done it before, but I jumped right in determined that I could do it. A life lesson presenting itself.

There were deadlines and lead times that were months in advance and $15,000 monthly for the ads. Then there was zero revenue, loads of stress, and a boyfriend named Al who had absolutely no idea what I was up to. The lead times meant that I would pay in January for an issue that arrived on the stands in May.

Every month I had to make the choice to run the ads again at $15,000 a shot or stop running them, without knowing at that moment if they had generated any revenue. In short, you didn't know until the fourth month if the three months of ads you had already placed were working or not.

If you didn't blindly proceed with month four and the ads were working, you lost an entire month or more going forward. I was running on empty.

Finally, more than four months after the first ad was placed, a magazine hit the stands and my hottest line did $42! *Forty-two dollars, are you kidding me? OMG, what to do now?* I struggled. Should I run the following month or knock it on the head? I had no time to decide as the deadlines were upon me for the next month. Do or die. What the hell was I to do now? It was daunting, to say the least, but true to form I jumped off the cliff without a net and decided to stick it out and run the ads that following month.

As I held my breath, the second magazine hit the stands and made more money than $42, although not enough to retire on. The die had been cast, and month after month the revenues increased.

My phone sex business was born, and over the next twenty-plus years it supported me very nicely. In what was a highly competitive arena, I made money and never looked back. I had created the perfect life, a business that operated twenty-four, seven, 365 days a year. Once again, I had reached out to the Universe and had manifested my dreams. I could live anywhere in the world that I wanted, and all I needed was a computer and a fax machine. As the years went on, I didn't even need the fax as the computer took care of everything.

Over the next two decades, I selected the hot images, designed the ads, placed them in glossy adult magazines with copy that ensured the phone would ring twenty-four hours a day, 365 days a year. Holidays, Christmas, Thanksgiving, Easter, New Year's Day, the phones were rife with callers, happy to pay to chat with their "dream girl," even though that girl might have been a nightmare. Some callers were just lonely, married, single, divorced, widowed, it made no difference, they just needed someone to talk to.

At times I listened in, and I quickly learned that you can be alone and lonely and still be in a relationship. So many people live their lives exactly like that.

The competition was fierce even then, because the companies that had the girls and a million dollars in phone equipment were actually marketing their own competing lines. It was like having the fox in the henhouse. Over the years, as business leaned more and more into the internet, those same companies had to find ways to capture their lost revenue, and they did so by helping themselves to ours. Ours being the companies that they were serving.

Day after day I monitored the figures, watching as my income grew and grew, until I was bringing in far more than the original $5,000, I had asked the Universe for. I lived through the hell of having the service bureaus continuously cheat me out of revenue, much like bartenders who fill up empty premium liquor bottles with the cheapest liquor available, then sell shots of the "premium" and pocket the difference.

They became skilled at finding ways to take revenue by unearthing a back door into your system, in a sense. One of the methods they employed was to redirect calls in the middle of the night from my lines to their lines using their computer. When one method ceased to garner the desired results, they found another, and then another. Like the Mafia, they had plenty of time, nearly endless amounts of money, and the ability to wait you out. But over the years I lived, loved, traveled, spent money, and was able to live anywhere in the world I wanted, hence my move to Africa. Then, a few years ago, they made me an offer that they knew I couldn't refuse. Actually, I could have but didn't, because it was futile at the time.

Had I refused they would have just found more ways to take all of my revenue. So, I made the decision and sold the lines, walked away from the business, and didn't look back, not even to check what the lines were doing until a year ago.

Then, recently my curiosity piqued, and I phoned my hottest line, only to find the same exact promo was there. My words were there, luring people to put their credit cards into the system and spend $6.99 a minute to talk to their "dream girl." Everything that I had put into play some twenty years earlier was still being used and making money, for them.

I was upset and angry, but in my heart, I knew there was no choice other than the one I had made. I worked with different service bureaus over the years, and they were all the same, skilled in ways to legally appropriate your revenue into their coffers. No telling where I would be today if I hadn't sold, but then again that would be wasted time and energy. It is what it is, and the time is now to pursue other avenues. I had a great run of more than twenty years, made a lot of money, and lived my life to the fullest never sacrificing my values to make more money. Another door had opened, and it was time for me to walk through it. I did it before and I damn well could do it again. One thing that always stood out in the forefront of my mind was when to walk away and shut the door behind me. I had done it before under far more dangerous, deadly circumstances, and I would do it again and come out the winner.

DON'T STOP THE MUSIC

Nothing is easy, everything requires time, money, hard work, commitment, and passion, and there are successes and failures along the way. One can only hope that the failures are not too devastating, and that you recover quickly, pick yourself up, brush yourself off, and move on to another idea. Sometimes, for reasons unknown, people are dragged down into the oblivion of darkness that is depression. It is devastating, often dealt with by using pills and booze, but often it isn't dealt with at all, leaving the person literally gasping for breath and not understanding exactly why.

While it is easy to get into a state of depression, sometimes it is hard to understand it in another and nearly impossible to get out of, depending on the circumstances. One can seemingly have everything the world has to offer—money, family, gorgeous home, health—and be so deep into depression that they can't see the light of day at all and survive only in darkness. Sometimes we stand helplessly by as someone we know and love falls into that pit of depression and stays there, hiding behind a facade of success.

Years ago, I lost a good friend to the effects of depression in precisely that manner. She was a strong woman, a warrior, at least that was how I saw her. On the surface, she had everything one might long for. There was plenty of money, she was living in Newport Beach, California, in a seventeen-thousand-square-foot mansion and was beautiful inside and out. She was a gorgeous, successful woman with a new boyfriend who was a doctor. Her life seemed to be perfection on steroids, until darkness closed in that night. It was late one evening when the call came in. I was living in the Hamptons and a dear friend phoned to give me some news.

Our friend, the beautiful warrior, had taken her life in a most dramatic and compelling way. Her wealth failed to stop her decision to hang herself from the balcony at her Newport mansion. She was found by her then boyfriend, a fact that I am certain devastated him beyond mere grief, and I can't imagine what happened to him as a result.

Depression can be a funny thing. One day you think you're fine and coping with all the stress life throws at you, and the next day you can barely drag yourself out of bed. Everyone experiences dark days every so often, but it is what you do to overcome them that counts.

There have been days when I felt the world was closing in, and I wondered if there was any reason whatsoever to go on. Sometimes I want to scream out loud, loud enough for someone, anyone, to hear my cries. Sometimes, I hide those cries and pretend they don't really exist. I don't want to upset anyone close to me with my sadness. There are always herds of elephants to eat, and I am forever quoting a favorite saying: "How do you eat an elephant? One bite at a time and don't start with the tail." I have eaten herds of elephants in my life. Sometimes, many herds in one moment, other times, they are spread over a week, a month, a year. But it is those times when the herds try to trample you with their presence that I have found myself in the darkest of moments and unable to share my pain with anyone.

There have been times over the decades of my life when I thought the best course of action for me might be an elephant gun in a plastic Dexter-type chamber, somewhere far, far away.

It is now, as a consequence of the death of my dear friend who chose that route, that I am reminded of my own demons, my own darkness, and realize that there are always choices, options if you will. Only you can step back, step outside, and make the choice that is right for you and for those you love.

Option one is to fade into the darkness of your depression and end it all, taking those who cherish you down that dark hole. Option two is to suffer and struggle then seek counseling that might pull you from the depths of despair, at least in time to unload the elephant gun. Option three is to speak to someone you trust and work through your feelings, coming out with a better understanding on the other side. My dear friend chose option one, not the messy but effective elephant gun, but rather a noose, and a step over the palatial balustrade surrounding her Newport Beach second-story hallway. She, who seemingly had it all, had fallen into the abyss of darkness created by depression left to its own devices. A dangerous decision for sure. I always choose option three, just saying.

While it was shocking and devastating to all who loved her, it was an effective solution, leaving her bruised and bloated but intact and not in pieces all over the living room floor. My friend, I will call her Andrea to protect her memory, had enjoyed a charmed life with jets and expensive jewelry at her disposal on a daily basis. Her marriage was somewhat of a sham, and the children from that union were mildly out of control.

Her husband enjoyed a double life, carrying on a duplicitous relationship with another woman, and as it turned out, he was responsible for even more mouths to feed on the West Coast. When that shocking revelation finally came to the surface, Andrea threatened bodily injury, both to herself and her cheating husband, neither of which was very effective. He continued his philandering, finally carrying it onto the public stage by way of a brief appearance on a well-known reality show.

That was, in effect, the straw that broke Andrea's back, and she filed for divorce, citing mental and emotional cruelty.

In her fragile state, she thought she couldn't make ends meet in the massive home she rented in Newport, California, for $200,000 a year, which was a lot more than the annual salary of many people! She knew there would be a battle royale for support money from her soon-to-be ex-husband, as the children were grown by then.

To effectively add insult to injury, the new man in her life was barely able to meet his own obligations, much less hers. Her standing in society as a philanthropist had already spiraled down, due to mandatory pre-divorce cuts in spending. Tragically, her answer was to take a swan dive from the balcony. End of story, her story that is. I shudder to think of the emotional devastation she left in the wake of her tragic and preventable death.

I have thought about her time and time again and wondered what that moment was like. The moment she made that decision, to take her life in such a dramatic way. Was there a moment when she questioned that choice? Did she have second thoughts as she was free-falling from the second floor? None of us will ever know. Was there anything we could have done? Had we missed important signals, or had she failed to provide them to us? She was a beautiful, very special woman who left us suddenly and without warning. I wondered, was there a moment in one of our conversations when she did cry out, and I failed to hear her? Maybe the sounds in my own head were too loud, or maybe I was just too busy, or tuned into my own elephants. In hindsight, maybe there were a lot of warning signs, and we all were far too busy to see them. The thought haunts me to this day.

I hope that isn't going to happen in my life. If I am ever depressed, or feeling hopeless, will I reach out again to someone I trust?

Will I have second or third thoughts, and will someone, anyone close to me, recognize that I am calling out and need their love, their compassion, their understanding, their intervention? My very life on earth might depend upon them listening to me, hearing me, understanding my cries for help. I think we may have all failed to pay attention when Andrea needed us the most. For that, I will be forever remorseful.

The thought of her crying out and of her cries falling silent on the ears of her friends and family hurts my heart deeply. Sometimes I find myself sitting in a darkened room listening for the sound of her voice, but nothing is there.

One night I woke with a start after hearing the piercing scream of a woman's voice. I knew in my heart it was Andrea as she fell from the second floor of her home. I believe I will be haunted by her death for the remainder of my life. I will always be left with the silence of her cries for help and the silence that was returned to her by our failure to listen. I will always wonder if I could have done something to stop her, and that will serve to make me pay closer attention, listen to the cries, real and imagined, from those I love.

A SOLITARY JOURNEY INTO MYSELF

I had been dreaming of Africa for what seemed like a lifetime. The fantasy of going on safari, seeing the wild animals up close and personal was something that never left my thoughts. I was doing well in my business, was single without any significant other structuring my life for me, and so in 1996 I decided to go on safari. The only thing at that time that was significant was that nothing was significant. I had finished with the nightclub business and with Raymond, both of which left me wiser in ways that I didn't really need, but with my eyes wide open to what I had endured.

I was living a beautiful life in East Hampton, New York, in a four-bedroom home I had purchased when it was being built, so I had the last say and I said plenty. A stainless-steel banister led to a guest room upstairs away from my bedroom, providing maximum privacy. I turned the other two bedrooms into a den and office. A safari theme of cheetah and zebra was hand-painted on the wall around the kitchen windows, and I looked out past the wildlife onto lovely trees and the deer that fed on my plants. I loved watching them trim the bushes in the front of my home.

Everything was open and the ceilings reached to the skies. I was home for the first time in a very long time, at least that was how I felt! Sadly, my mother didn't live long enough to see my magnificent home, but I thought of her regularly, and part of her is resting in the garden around the pool. She was like a mermaid in the water and loved it so much, swimming every chance she got. It was 1996 and a very good year, despite the fact that my left knee was killing me and I knew that I needed surgery. No doubt this was partly a result of the double spiral fracture I suffered in a skiing accident years before, but still, I was walking, running, and planning a massive first trip on safari to Africa. As it turned out, I would be alone with just my guide. Whatever my fascination with Africa had been and continues to be, this would be the first of my incredible adventures into the African bush.

I was to go on with my quest to fill my life with wild animals and to experience the unusual, the bizarre, the untamed, and the risky in 1999, 2002, and again in 2007 after I married Paul. These were just the longer safaris, three to six weeks, and I managed to sandwich in some shorter week-long ones in South Africa, Zambia, and Namibia as well. I also enjoyed a couple of elephant safaris, riding on the back of an enormous bull as we searched for other wildlife.

As an independent, self-motivated woman, I refused to allow anything to stop me, even when a New York doctor did an arthroscopic surgery on my knee in early '96 and told me I needed a full on, all-hands-on-deck, total knee replacement.

"When do I need this?"

"When the pain gets so great that you cannot stand it any longer," he quipped as if this were some bad joke. Well, I had a fully paid for safari to go on in '96 and I wasn't about to let a little thing like that stop me. It took another sixteen years and a second arthroscopic surgery later before I finally went under the knife.

Once I had made the decision to go to Africa on safari and paid the money, the countdown to my actual trip made days seem like weeks and minutes like hours. I hadn't really planned to be totally alone on safari. That decision was actually made for me. The first part of my magical trip was in Botswana with a couple, the Penstones, who had been referred to me by friends in DC. She was the cook, and he was the guide, and they took their guests through three reserves.

A family of five was to be joining me but three weeks before our scheduled trip they canceled. It was a stroke of good luck I was to realize later, and no one took their place. Because the couple was taking a large group to Victoria Falls before returning to their base in Maun, they agreed to take me from Victoria Falls in Zimbabwe to Maun Botswana for the same price.

At last, the day finally arrived, and I boarded the TWA Flight to Greece, as I was making a stop there to visit the family of some friends of mine. The magic of Greece was not lost on me, even though I contracted a massive cold on my flight over.

I was sick as a dog and felt like I had been run through a wood chipper. But there was no way that anything was going to sabotage my trip, and so I grabbed more Kleenex and some nose drops and soldiered on. Looking back on those weeks I can only say how thankful I was for my journaling, something I have done during each of my longer safaris. Today, I am reminded of many things sadly forgotten, lost in darkness, or just part of a conglomeration of thoughts that prevailed one on top of the other, in the recesses of my mind.

Weeks inside a tent in the middle of the bush, with only the sounds of wild animals echoing through my mind, was magical. I know that, because today I can almost feel the energy through my words, of the elephant, as he brushed by my tent, or the vibrations on the canvas wall from the roar of that lion, or the unmistakable, near deafening sounds of the hippos in the water near our camp. Then there was the piercing hum of swarms of tsetse flies as they hovered over our vehicle.

During one trip those miserable creatures bit me more than forty-three times over the next week and caused me to make an emergency trip to the closest hotel in the Serengeti, which was over an hour and a half away from our campsite.

It turned out that I had an allergic reaction to their bites and ended up getting an injection and some pills from the doctor at the hotel. I also ended up with huge red blotches all over my body, including one on my left breast that stayed inflamed, a bright shade of reddish purple, for months after I had returned from the bush. Once it disappeared, a hot shower would revive it just to remind me of the tsetse fly attack.

Journaling also reminded me of the Maasai warriors as they descended into the crater early one morning. I can almost feel the reverberating sounds of those two warriors and their cattle and goats as they came over the top of the Ngorongoro Crater. A stunning sight that I ended up capturing with my camera. Five almost endless minutes that I shot image after image as they made their way onto the floor of the crater. It was only as they got closer that I realized I only had two bags of wrapped lemon candies with me to negotiate for the rights to take those pictures.

It was understood that the Maasai would expect compensation for the images I was taking of them. Then, suddenly almost silently, they were directly in front of us, and Hagai, my guide, began to negotiate in Swahili for the rights to my photos. As it turned out, the wrapped lemon candies went over well, and while there were some critical decisions for the young Maasai warriors to make, all in all the candy was a hit. One of the young Maasai was holding a newborn goat that was still covered with afterbirth.

I captured him on my camera as he struggled with the decision of whether to put the baby goat down and unwrap the candy or continue to hold the baby and not open the candy. I remain unsure to this day what that final decision was.

Journaling brought back the magical feeling I experienced soaring through the skies in a hot air balloon, then landing in the middle of a herd of wildebeest and zebra. We dined that morning on foods that I had never tasted and foods that I hardly ever wanted to taste, like eggs, but how fantastic they were in the mist of the Maasai Mara, just after dawn. I remember the thrill of helicoptering over Victoria Falls and watching double rainbows dance along the thundering waters. I remember that lone baboon who attacked me at the marketplace in Zimbabwe, nearly making me drop my camera, and of walking miles from Victoria Falls over the border to Zambia to get America dollars from an ATM so that I could buy a stone statue I call the "Model" from a shop in town.

The banks had been closed by then ruler Robert Mugabe, who controlled the entire nation with intimidation, violence, and an army of plainclothes thugs who patrolled the streets. They even posed as money changers hoping to arrest anyone trying to score a better exchange rate on the streets.

My journaled words bore witness to the magic of the Milky Way, as it blanketed the coal black, starless sky. I had been camped alongside the Zambezi River at the time. OMG, what a sight and now I am able to see it again through my words.

I can almost see the three-foot tree monitor lizard that pretended to be a log one afternoon and the deep blue color of the Okavango Delta as the wind pushed it from side to side making tiny waves.

All those magical moments were brought to life once again through the words in my handwritten journals. Each journal was written by the light of a kerosene lamp in the dead of night, in the silence of the bush. Sometimes almost illegible but nonetheless canonized that moment, and I remain so thankful that I completed this task four times. I am fortunate that I kept a journal each year of those safaris so that I can remind myself in real time today what I was feeling during the magic. Prepare to share the magic of my first safari in 1996 with me, my words become your vision of what those days and nights in the bush were like. My thoughts in real time, my strengths, weaknesses, courage, fears at times, you are there with me the entire journey.

THE SOLITARY JOURNEY

1996
MY JOURNAL IN REAL TIME

> NOTE: The following is my exact journal as it was written by the light of a kerosene lamp in a tent. Nothing has been changed except for grammar or punctuation as the reality of the journal must be maintained. The year is 1996: my first safari.

I returned to New York, from my first safari, on September 6, 1996, feeling an attitude of great gratitude that I was fortunate enough to experience the magic that is Africa. It is with this feeling that I share so much of myself and my trip in this next chapter, where the daily musings of my adventures are canonized here from the journal that I kept each day writing by kerosene lamp in the darkness in my tent. I titled it The Solitary Journey.

How I longed to have a farm at the foot of the Ngong Hills in Africa. Meryl's words but my dreams as well. Then I could say "shoo shoo, it's my Limoges." Childhood fantasies rarely realized. Children dreaming foolish dreams of wild cats that curled up beside you on overstuffed chairs, and big black panthers in the backyard tethered to trees with tiny leather leashes.

The African dream has been running in my blood ever since I was a small girl. At last, that dream is a reality and Africa is within my grasp. In a few days, I shall embark on the adventure of my lifetime. Always the adventurer, slightly inflexible at this point in my life, I have chosen to make a trip alone into the regions of Africa on safari. Dreams of panthers all but shattered, I now see spots in my dreams.

TUESDAY, AUGUST 6, 1996

And so it begins. The adventure of my life. Actually, a lifetime in the making, six months in the actual planning. Today I felt very disconnected. It was almost like I was free-falling from a plane and waiting in vain for my chute to open. The boys were noticeably distraught yesterday when I left. Winno didn't stay with me in the morning when I readied myself. I missed his bulging eyes and snoring. In the middle of the night, Dakota was sitting at the end of the bed staring. He walked the edge of the bed to my arms and snuggled. His cat-like demeanor only offers this behavior in the morning. He suspects that I'm leaving.

The suitcases do it every time. Now I embark on the adventure—alone. Slightly nervous, but all is great. When I disembark in Athens, I will be number five for the purposes of Clemis and Carol's pickup. How sweet! They are shepherding me in Athens! Wednesday means great moussaka. Mom, I feel your presence here with me. Please, don't leave me. I need to spend some quality time with you, now, today. After all, I miss you, I see you, easily, You are here.

Aside: My knee is like a giant toothache that has captivated my entire muscle structure. Fine beginning. I am propped up with airline pillows. Two Relafan, four wines. Too many hours to go. Better take some magic melatonin.

Sleep, airline style. My body has been transposed into a series of pretzels carelessly strewn about. Thoughts of Flight 800 permeate my mind. Did they feed them first, fill them with liquor? Was it sudden? My mind races with the anticipation of what lies ahead.

WEDNESDAY, AUGUST 7, 1996

Athens, Greece

It seems as if age takes a toll. My body is tired. Each cell yearns for sleep. Years ago, I didn't need a rest when I traveled. No jet lag. Today my pores ache! That knee is throbbing. Oh well, I can't let that deter me. I'm off on an adventure of a lifetime. Down the Yellow Brick Road in my ruby socks, once I've had a few winks.

The other day I used the term "disconnected" while describing my feelings. Today I found myself feeling the same. The flight over seemed like I had an almost desperate desire to verbally connect with people. To speak to others, know them, have them relate, be interested in me. Standing before the mirror in my hotel room on this first day, I yearn to hear the voice of one I love. Who might that be? To see my dogs. Already? Surely this does not mean I don't wish to travel alone. I've felt this way before, it seems, but I have never examined it so microscopically.

Tallis, Clemis' nephew, called. He waited at the airport for two hours. Oh well. He said that everyone commented on the number five he was holding. Everyone except me, who obviously failed to see it. Today we went for lunch. Tonight, we will go to the sea for a meal of fresh fish. Tomorrow, I have asked to go and visit Clemis' 85-year-old mother and 87-year-old dad in Nafpaktos, a seaport village about two and a half hours from Athens. I thought of my mom in a loving light. Tallis' mother lives there too. The Acropolis for the second or is it the third time pales before this opportunity

Thursday, August 8, 1996

Athens, Greece, 4:00 a.m.

So much for sleep. I can't anymore. My body cried for repair yesterday. This morning I feel nearly human once more. Sitting in bed munching on a tootsie roll, horrifying thought, but I need to wake up all cells early. From now on my mornings need to begin very early with game drives, and end early in the evening. So, wake up and get ready.

My leg is challenging my ability to sleep. I think I may have found a comfortable spot. I climbed the mountain in Machu Picchu with this malady, so why not Kilimanjaro. Only joking, but perhaps not. In a few hours we leave to visit Mother Clemis.

Lunch in Nafpaktos with Helen and Bob Lascaris and Voula, Tallis' mother and Nikos, his brother. We sat, wind gently shifting the blue waves, eating by the sea. I met Ima, Tallis' girlfriend! Tonight, I sleep. The trip just begins tomorrow.

Tonight, I dined on the rooftop of the hotel. The hill on which the Acropolis stands was lit like a jewel against the dusky gray sky. On either side a ruin spiraled up toward the heavens. I sat and people watched as streams of vacant-eyed couples dribbled by. I blessed my aloneness instead of compromise . . . Indeed! The adventure begins.

Friday, August 9, 1996

Athens, Greece

Morning begins several steps out of sync. The zipper on my carry-on bag (new) has a big chunk out of the center, lost teeth. Not fixable! Safety pins respond to the mini emergency. Also, I have contracted a cold, Redoxon and Biaxin. Ten hours on the plane with no nose spray. What a bummer! Oh well. I will knock this out by tomorrow. I will not be disabled or derailed by a mere cold! We land in Joberg in less than 2 hours.

Sidwell picked me up. I am going to Soweto with he and his wife and then to a birthday party. Sidwell and Aaron met me at the airport. They have been friends for over 35 years. On the way to my hotel they told me of their life in Africa before Mandela became president. They shared stories of studying by candlelight, no electricity until a mere ten years ago. No running water! Working all day, studying all night. Documents required in order to move about. Black buses, white buses, black restaurants, white restaurants. I wouldn't have come here then.

Saturday, August 10, 1996

Joburg, late night

I didn't sleep at all last night. I have this nasty cold. I feel as though I have been made into roadkill. I do know that this too shall pass. Today on my outing to Soweto, I saw hopelessness. Johannesburg is indeed a city of contrast. Soweto with its divided sections. Indian, Colored and Black, settlements of clapboard lean-tos with trash all over. Unemployment is rampant. The old government deprived the blacks of all rights but conversely gave rights to the Indians. Contrasting this unbelievable situation are the wealthy South Africans. It is truly amazing. The US dollar goes far enough here to allow a fantastic lifestyle. I think we are so very limited in our experiences. Last night I enjoyed a fabulous meal of seafood with Bill Harris and his wife, Theresa. I had such a horrid cold and was so very sick. They were just great and took me to the local pharmacy, filling me full of African medication. Thank God for them. I stocked up on Kleenex, Vitamin C, cough drops, and the like for my sojourn into the bush tomorrow.

Sunday, August 11, 1996

On my way to Zimbabwe. God was good to me. I could have been seated next to some computer nerd or a lady with a baby. Instead, I got some Italian stud and what I think was his lover. So, I guess that's where all the great-looking guys are these days. He reminded me of Mace.

Arrived at Iiana Lodge. My arrival was unheralded by any particular event or events, save for the gaggle of banded mongoose that paraded past my windows. I announced the sighting in my "first postcards from the bush," as my first animal siting. As the days went on it hardly seemed worth an honorable mention as sightings go.

If I had one wish at this particular moment, it would be that I didn't feel so sick. But the good news is that I will not give in to this sickness or let it hurt my trip in any way. I settled into my room as a large family of baboons sauntered by. Several approached my window fearlessly. I'm brave, but quickly closed my window.

Walked to the open marketplace with all its excitement. There I bought a pair of masks and several stone pieces, one of which I promptly dropped. The people of Zimbabwe are very friendly, polite, and helpful. I am overdosing on Biaxin and vitamins so that I can feel better.

At 3:30 p.m. I was picked up for my helicopter ride. Boarding the six-seater I donned a mic and earphones, just like a real pilot. We lifted off and soared like a giant bird towards Victoria Falls. Now, I experienced my first real animal sightings, though even these would certainly pale as my trip continued.

From our birdlike vantage point I could see tiny figures of elephant herds, zebra, and a raft of hippos lazing in the Zambezi River, and giraffes, babies, and moms. They appeared taller than tall, even from the air. Hard to shoot from the copter, although I made a valiant attempt, as my hand and the camera shook. The blades from the copter cut through the air sharply as we headed towards one of the wonders of the world, Victoria Falls. My first thoughts were, my God, what an amazing sight. My body was frozen as I watched a rainbow dance across the entire width of the Falls. Its thundering girth poured into a narrow rocky gorge, causing the water to rise like smoke and create an almost surreal picture. The mist hangs like a cloud over the rocks, while brilliantly colored rainbows shift from side to side in a magical dance: I feel unbelievably fortunate. What a gift to have given myself. I shall pray that my overall health improves tomorrow. The silence of an African night. Lights are automatically turning on and off outside. Each moment, I get up from my bed to peek out and see who or what is there. So far the only presence was a lone warthog. Scary site.

Monday, August 12, 1996

Victoria Falls, Zimbabwe

How I love Africa! It is truly a paradise. The feeling one has when standing in an open-air vehicle, watching the zebra stare you down or the sable dine on grass. It is truly amazing. I decided to jump right in and go on my first game drive. I arranged for it through the liana. I left early, by someone's standards, that is. Early, as my trip progressed, was 6:00 a.m. Early here at this moment in time is 8:30 a.m.

I took the catbird seat in an open-air Land Cruiser and off we went. During the first hour I spotted kudu, kori bustard, zebra, sable and a few cute warthogs. Africa is a place I will return to. The parched dry heat of the African sun is not a deterrent to every minute being filled with a new experience. Standing in the open vehicle, the hot sun beating down on me . . . no hat of course . . . the wind whipping across my face and hair as I watched zebra and sable grazing on the open grasslands.

I returned to the liana, spent but still feeling incredible. Kim gave me a homemade sandbag so that I could stabilize my camera. Unfortunately, hands shake while shooting. What a Godsend! Kim was going back to Dallas, Texas, after spending three weeks in this paradise. She was lamenting about her return. I know that I will be feeling the same. I returned to the marketplace once again. There is so very much to see, so much that I want. I think it is a pity that I only have two hands. I bought some wonderful Passport masks! Decided that I wanted to get a special gift for someone. The definition of a gift is something that the other person will want, that you give freely, no strings and no expectations.

Passport masks are all one of a kind, depicting the different tribes. They were made in a village in West Africa called, I believe, Grodin. The warriors wear them on their arm to tell all what tribe they belong to. Since I fell in love with the masks I bought eight of them, each one unique to itself.

I stopped at the liana to pick up my camera and head to Victoria Falls on foot. Of course, as the Queen of bad directions, I went a mile or so in the dust out of my way. It was worth it though! Every speck of dust I swallowed.

A wonder of nature! The mist rising up like clouds to spray my parched face. Water thundering from every direction into a narrow gorge like a hungry open mouth below. Double rainbows, one following the same pathway between two sheer rocks, glistening with fine mist. I shot over and over until the film ran out. Breathtaking sight. On the way back to the lodge, a family of baboons were lunching by the road. As I stooped and shot a photo of one baboon sitting in the street with his feet on the curb in some water, he turned and headed towards me.

I moved out of his way as quickly as lightning. This is not the zoo. There are no fences, wires, or gates between you and lions, cheetah, elephant, giraffe, hippo, crocodile. Nothing is between you and the animals, not even your Calvins. This is day two. I dread the last day already as I know I am not going to want to leave here.

Clive picked me up in a smartly appointed Land Cruiser that screamed Kandahar Safaris from both sides. I was number one in what I was told would be a party of ten. A family of six (horror of horrors), a couple, and perhaps salvation, a single guy. Well, there is a God. At first, I was wondering what cruel trick of fate this was. A family of six indeed! Screaming kids, four of them no doubt? Oh, what had I done to deserve this?

We picked up the couple, they hailed from Canada and were very nice. Then we made our second stop and the family jumped on. A lawyer from London, his wife and four incredibly well-traveled children. The youngest, Sarah, was about 8 or 9 and had absolutely no fear at all. Then the single guy swung onto the Land Cruiser. Allah is good. A forty-two-year-old, single actor named Robert, from Hollywood, can you believe? Just finished shooting a picture in Sun City. Oh well, it was a tough job, but someone had to draw duty. So, our happy group motored down the dusty road towards the campsite, which was set up alongside the Zambezi River.

While motoring along, we had the dubious distinction of being charged by a young male elephant who was quite irritated that we had stopped to watch him and the rest of the herd dine on some branches. We thought little of it until a few minutes later when we looked behind us and saw the elephant running after our vehicle. What a sight.

We also saw our first lion hiding in the tall grass with her two cubs. As the African sun began to sink into the night, I was overwhelmed by Africa and its beauty.

The campsite consists of several tents, a bath tent (that is a bush shower), and a medical toilet tent. A dining table has been placed with lovely candles in the center. By the time we arrived, the group that was preparing to depart had already been seated for dinner. We just slid in and shared our stories of being charged by an elephant with a much more seasoned group.

Robert walked me back to my tent, which I refused to share, gave me some fleeting instructions on keeping warm, and left. Unfortunately, I had no idea that a sleeping bag was on top of my bed and therefore I nearly froze to death alongside the river that fateful night. All night I wondered what would be done if I ended up with pneumonia on this trip. I reasoned that it would be easier to treat than a plain old cold. The sounds of Africa gently wafted in the backdrop of the rushing river. I couldn't sleep at all. Hippos cried out for their babies, snorting as they made their way up the riverbanks to graze on the grass, birds sang, calling to their families; an eternity of nighttime surrounded me.

The African sky at night is a blanket filled with stars. So many stars that the entire sky appears almost white. The thick and luscious Milky Way forms a wide pathway that cuts across the sky like a machete. The severe black background of night held diamonds by the millions for us to gaze upon for hours on end. It was overwhelming. All I could think about was canoeing in the morning. I had no preconceived idea about what to expect, but I wasn't expecting what I got. Therein, my newest phrase: Expect the unexpected and never expect anything. Absolutely two phrases in sync.

Tuesday, August 13, 1996

Canoe Safari, 7:00 a.m.

Today is the dugout canoe Safari. I'm really not sure what that is. I sort of have this vision of Venice, with a ruggedly handsome Adonis rowing me down some peaceful river. The hippos were snorting in the background of the beautiful Zambezi as off we go to the mouth of the river. Well, imagine my surprise when I am handed a smart little purple lifejacket and a canoe paddle and given instructions on how I am canoeing 26 miles. Yes, you heard correctly, 26 miles! Just as I was recovering from that shock, I heard the word rapids. They were sandwiched in between a sentence that began, "The first two rapids come one right after the other." First two! I couldn't believe my ears. First two? I repeated the words again like someone incapable of a basic understanding of the English language. Those words were followed by "After the second rapid take care to veer to the left as there is a large rock in the center." Rock in the center. Veer to the left. I was still reeling from the word RAPIDS.

My head was pounding. The heat of the morning sun was beating down on my bare, uncapped head. The combination of the malaria medication and the antibiotics were making me very sick. On top of that, I hadn't signed up for a 26-mile canoe trip over rapids, with me as the canoe person. Whoa, hold everything, stop the presses, I need a time-out.

I looked around and carefully weighed my options. I could cry like a sniveling princess and whine and wail that I could not, would not, should not ruin my hands by using that canoe paddle. But then here was this eight-year-old jumping into the canoe in front of me. Oh my word, how humiliating! Then there was my canoe partner, Robert. Oh, how would this act look! I could never live it down. Besides, the options were slim to none. There wasn't even a car to take me back to the campsite. That left walking or swimming, both of which I vetoed immediately.

With that in mind I donned my purple vest, grabbed up the paddle, and took my place in the front of the canoe, with Robert seated behind me. David, you are right, this is a dangerous trip! In practice mode, with my canoe paddle in hand but hardly comfortable, when Robert yells, "hippo!" Clive screams for us to paddle and by the look on his face he means "for your life." This it turns out is exactly what we were doing, paddling for our lives.

You see, the hippo was at the shore and spotted us. A human sighting! Since hippos feel threatened when they are not in deep water, their sole purpose becomes getting to deep water. Anything between them and deep water can be in deep trouble. The hippo submerged, to rise again somewhere in the river. While paddling for my life, I took an enormous chunk of skin out of my right hand. Sad but true, this medical emergency occurred during the first ten minutes of my canoeing. By the time we had outrun and outmaneuvered the hippo, I had nearly forgotten how frightened I was of the R word ... Rapids.

As Robert screamed for me to paddle, I used my feet as anchors on the inside of this little rubber boat and slammed the paddles into the water as we were tossed around like rag dolls. It was all I could do to remember that we needed to veer to the left, to avoid being squashed like two bugs against the large boulder that loomed out of the white water. Rapid number three was the worst. It was during this foray that I nearly parted with my Armani glasses, as the boat leaped towards the heavens, abusing our bodies on the way down. During rapids four and five, I succumbed to pressure from Robert and gave him my glasses to hold for safekeeping.

I can't say that I was displeased when Clive announced the finish of the final rapid and called for smooth canoeing from that point forward. Unfortunately, he failed to mention the new wrinkle in our smooth sailing trip. Hippos and crocodiles ... hippos and crocodiles. So, as we made our way blissfully down the river, suddenly, right in front of our boats, were both species amply represented. A 14' crocodile sunbathing about 20' from the shore in the water and a raft of hippos, about 30' from the crocodile. We dragged the boats out of the water and stood, watching. I suggested that we walk the boats past the crocodile and hippos. I thought that was the best approach given all the facts. Clive said, "Back in the water." WHAT? This is insanity! No way! So, back in the water went our boat. Clive instructed us to stay close to the shore. Oh no, I thought, I don't want to stay close to the shore, I'd much rather just canoe right out to the middle and get eaten by a crocodile! Sure, I'll stay by the shore. How about on the shore, like on the land? What about that Clive, old boy? Oh well. Robert seemed very certain about all of it so I gave up control, grabbed onto some brush along the water, and prayed silently. The thought that crossed my mind at that moment was that I was too old for this, I should be home gardening. I detached from that thought immediately. We made it! Further down the river we stopped for lunch. I fell asleep on the side of one of the canoes. Not the most comfortable place, but when every cell of one's body is exhausted then anyplace becomes comfortable. We pushed off into the river once again, only another ten more miles to go. I couldn't believe it. Ten miles, it might as well have been 10,000 miles!

My fingers were bloody, and throbbing. The bandages had fallen off, exposing a large raw area nearly a ½" deep. My nose was stuffed, my head was pounding like someone was inside with a jackhammer, trying in vain to get out. But I trudged forward. Suddenly, about 200 meters in front of our boat, a male elephant strolled into the water.

Clive called to us to stop canoeing. By this point in our trip we looked like a finely tuned, precision Olympic team. Stroke, stroke, stroke. We stopped, but our boat continued to drift. It wafted and waned until we came to rest a few feet from the elephant, who was now up to his proverbial ears in water. We sat quietly as he surveyed his territory and then just walked around us as if we were nonexistent.

Truly a day of sighs of relief. It was dark when we paddled into the campsite. The sounds of silence were deafening. My hands were bloody and cut, my body exhausted beyond mere physical tiredness; the entire surface of my skin ached; but I did it. I didn't think I could do it, but I did it! Bully for me! In order to fully understand the experience of today and of Africa in general, I think it is important to understand and accept that every day, every moment, one is at risk. At risk from the elements, the hot African sun which parches and dries you, the animals which at best are very unpredictable. Each day is a new experience because one can never be certain of what will happen, ever. A guide with years of experience cannot second-guess a hippo or a lion.

You can only do what you may and hope that your experience guides you correctly. If not, you die or are hurt according to the law. You may be viewing a herd of elephant from 100' one day and all seems fine. They could be playing in the water or bathing or feeding. One day a young male decides to assert himself and charges. One never knows. This is not the E ride at Disneyland where the guide whips out a rifle and shoots a fake hippo.

The sounds of hippos emerge from the river. The power of the bubbles, the rush of the water, little ears wiggling. There you are in a two-person rubber canoe, in the middle of the Zambezi River and the hippos suddenly disappear.

There could be a raft of 10 or 12 hippos, and they just might reappear right under your canoe. Hippos cause more carnage than any other animal in Africa. What a comforting thought that is!

Africa lets you know its power, its ability to control absolutely. Africa is the dominator in all ways. The country and its inhabitants own you and your life. If you leave Africa, it is because Africa has allowed you to leave.

WEDNESDAY, AUGUST 14, 1996

Still on the river

Awoke this morning feeling great. The early morning sun danced along the waters of the river. The deafening sound of water rushing over rocks filled my night's sleep. I was serene. Small birds sang sweetly to one another.

We headed back towards Victoria Falls so that Patrick could pick me up. The rest of the group, without the Canadian couple, stayed on the river. I couldn't have canoed another inch.

I did some last-minute shopping before Patrick picked me up. He looks the part of the consummate adventurer, beard and safari hat, rugged looking. Heather was already in camp waiting for us. We drove into Botswana, passing two Passport Control centers where hordes of tourists spilled out onto the ground ready for their "safari." The hot African sun beats down as Patrick drives us into the Chobe Game Reserve in Botswana. The fine silt holds onto my face. I feel as if I need water all over my body. We see a herd of elephants bathing in the mud. Fifty or so hippos lay in a pod on the shore. I can't believe how they amble up roads to munch the grass. Sometimes they travel up to three miles at night! Frightening thought, coming upon a hippo in the dark. He's on his way to the water and you are on your way from the water. You are now between a hippo and safety. The rest is hippo lunacy.

Three giraffes nibble some leaves and a herd of sable dart from the watering hole across the highway. Dirt, dust, rocks, no road that's paved. Finally, we arrive in camp. The dining tent is lovely, all set for lunch with beautiful linen napkins, wine sits in a bottle on a tiny table.

My tent is sweet, and the bathroom has been placed right behind it. I feel the need for a shower. Hot water is placed in a large canister above the tented bush shower. I look up at the sky. Nothing between me and Africa now, just air. This is heaven. I went for an evening game drive. It was beyond belief. The light purple sky of an African sunset became the backdrop for a herd of elephants, eating and bathing in the Chobe river. I am one hour into the Reserve. Nothing here but dirt roads, rocks, and brush. No contact with anyone for the next ten days, except for Patrick and Heather.

Close encounter with a female lion. Soon, others were all around. My adrenaline is rushing. This is like nothing I have ever experienced. I have never felt like this in my life. What a rush. A wild dog begins to chase a pack of antelope. Wild dogs are very rare. This turns out to be the only one I will see on my trip. We leave the park in a hurry, as we need to get out before 6:30 p.m. A herd of cape buffalo is in the area. Perhaps they will visit us tonight.

Thursday, August 15, 1996

Chobe Game Reserve

The African night is a melody. A cacophony of the roar of lions, sweet, melodious birds calling out, the trumpeting of the elephant. A continuous flow. Looking up through the open netting of my tent at the blanket of stars that fill the midnight sky.

Something is in the camp. Some animal is near my tent. I dare not go to the loo for fear I shall meet a lion head on with only my flashlight and the African moon between us. So, I shall be very still until the morning. The sun is up in the sky in various hues of orange, purple, red. Unbelievable. We are going on a game drive.

Just returned from our 6:30 a.m. drive. Our campsite is in a remote area of Chobe Game Reserve. A dining tent in the middle, a kitchen tent, my tent with a loo, and a shower tent. It's awesome, being out in the middle of a Game Reserve. The only people I see, other than Heather, Patrick, and our staff, are when we are on a game drive and I have the misfortune of spotting a truckload of tourists.

The delicate balance of nature is amazing. I know it, but hardly think of it. Survival of the fittest. There can be no interference of any kind or in any way. It is legal to kill elephants in many African countries.

We have just finished breakfast and are waiting to refuel before heading out. I realize how little I enjoy traveling with other people. I suppose I have become a bit inflexible. I want to do what I want to do. I suppose I would make some allowance for a special person. Sharing the experience with oneself, truly experiencing that special moment totally and completely enables you to share with another. I can, therefore, share my African experience with anyone I choose. They will enjoy it through my total saturation of the moments.

Patrick has just strung up some wire and such. He is trying to get through to Maun by shortwave. Remote, yes, remote. The only people here, Patrick, Heather, myself, and the staff. The wind is blowing gently through the trees, leaves rustling, leaves taking flight then crash landing. The flaps on my tent slapping the sides. The sound of the wind and the noise of the truck as it refuels. Native tongue spoken here and there. A few birds in the backdrop and a resounding stillness. Quiet, the sound of my own breathing is all that I hear. The cut on my hand is not healing. I was injured canoeing and lost a chunk of skin off my right thumb. It hurts. I am using my new first aid kit bandages and such. At least my cold is better, although I still sound horrid. We are going to the Chobe Lodge to try and book the boat trip on the river today.

I have officially given up on doing anything with my hair. It was a nice thought but quite impossible. Last night in the bucket shower, I just wet it and today I poured water onto it, brushed it back slick with a tie on it, and covered it with a baseball cap. That certainly will have to do until I arrive back in Johannesburg, one week from Saturday.

I actually saw civilization today at Chobe Game Lodge. It must be something like the Mt. Kenya Safari Club, I think. Tourists all pressed, perfumed, and done, sitting in the bar having drinks watching the animals at the watering hole over a martini. The thought crossed my mind that I should cancel that. I'm not totally sure about all that Africa is, but it is not the Mt. Kenya Safari Club.

It's hot, parched, and dry. Green patches spring up around cool pools of water. Trees show their winter coats without leaves. Yes, hot as it is, it is winter here. We drive over rock and dirt roads, vehicle going airborne, equipment jumping for the sky. Nothing is paved, just potholes, dirt, silt. African soil, hot from the day's burning rays. Sun beating down, drying you out.

I'm surprised that any cold can survive this African sun for more than one day. But I'm not tired. I can't get enough of the animals. They are so majestic. A giraffe peeked over some tall shrubs, as I frantically snapped away. They are so very sweet, so very amusing. I will never tire of watching them. Each day is so very exciting. I can't say that I miss the office or work in the least.

It's evening. I am writing by kerosene lantern. The African winds are blowing gently across our site. Heather is in the open kitchen tent, cooking. The scents of her culinary delights fill the air. Something with prune and port. Creamed potatoes and homemade soup. As I took a bush *shower, the warm water running over my silt-covered body, I thought of how lucky I am to be here. I thought of how I would like to share this with someone special.*

This evening's game drive was astounding. I sighted my first zebra in Chobe. Two skittish zebras who were anxious to flee my camera's eye. I saw them twice today and got back-end views of them as they fled. Curious giraffe watched me watching them. I find all of that very amusing.

More often than not, as I focus on the animals, they stop, and all begin looking at me. I wonder what they are thinking. One becomes spoiled with the animals in Africa. The very first day in Zimbabwe, I marveled at my sighting of one warthog, a family of banded mongoose, and some baboons. I now pass with some degree of disregard herds of impala, unless a spectacular male or two are present.

Warthogs and baboons, save for the rather precocious one in the tree by himself today, are curious. He flashed me, as he sat in a tree with a fish eagle. Then he climbed to the top and balanced himself precariously on the dry branches above. We were nervous for him.

This evening's drive, we saw a pride of lions majestically posing on the side of the road. There were six, all tawny, fading nicely into the African sands. They yawned and moved with planned laziness. It appeared that they had eaten and were certainly sated for today. As I shot and shot pics of lion after lion, we discussed the plight of the seventh lion, who seemed to be missing. Could she be dead, wounded?

One had been in a fight with a buffalo earlier in the week. Suddenly she appeared, walked to an open spot and lay down. As my camera's eye was focused, one of the lions rose and assumed the stalking position. In the distance about 300 yards away, several impalas were dining on leaves. They did not sense danger. The lion moved swiftly and quietly to the trees behind the pride and disappeared. We waited. Impala dined and all was well.

Suddenly one of the lions rose, assumed the stalk position, and crept towards the dining Impala. I climbed back over the seat for a better view. Of course, at this very moment, my 36-roll film was at 35. I shot (photographically of course) a lion staring, pressed the rewind, the sound of it like a jackhammer in the stillness of Africa, and popped in a new roll. The lion moved to within 15' of the impala. He waited, I waited, binoculars focused. The rest of the pride looked on in an almost careless disregard.

Then an impala looked up, a female lion, one of the pride, walked carelessly behind the crouching male and strolled across the dirt road. She had cubs and they were waiting. The lion paused, the impala ran, and adrenaline stopped. All in a heartbeat. We returned to camp. As a side note, the stalker was the wounded lion. His wounds to the back right haunch were not serious.

FRIDAY, AUGUST 16, 1996

Chobe Game Reserve

Lying in my tent in the black African night, my two lamps have been darkened by the winds and the only light is from the stars and a dying campfire. The sound of owls and other assorted animals echo with a deafening pitch across the still Savanna. I can hear each leaf, as it rustles under the arms of the gentle winds. A grass fire burns in wild abandon on the Namibian horizon. I sleep, for at 6:00 a.m. we rise for the early morning drive. The tall dried grassy plains are still in the early morning sunrise. Slowly we moved over the rocky dirt pathways, eyes sharp, looking, watching for signs of wildlife.

There is nothing like waking up in a tent, in the middle of the bush to the sounds of silence or the roar of a lion. It is magical!

The majesty of a bull elephant playing in the water at sunset near my campsite.

ANGELS IN SIN

Magnificent female lion calling for her cub in
the Ngorongoro Crater In Tanzania.

Young female lion searching for prey

Two beautiful female lions nestled in the bush in the early morning hours in the Ngorongoro Crater in Tanzania,

A majestic Lion oversees his pride from the top of a huge rock formation. Lions often hide behind these rocks and one can never be too sure if you are going to meet one face to face if you venture behind. Maasai regularly interact with lions with only a spear by their side. It is a sight to behold the Maasai entering the crater with only a spear and some makeshift sandals on their feet.

Male lion is staking his claim to the kill of a baby buffalo earlier that morning. Two males and one female continued the battle for hours seeking occasional refuge under our vehicle. The standoff came with me flanked by three hundred Cape Buffalo, two male lions and a female under the car and about twenty hyena vying for the kill. The end for us came when the female leaped onto the hood of our vehicle, put her paws onto the windscreen and roared her disapproval. Hagai turned on the car, threw it into reverse and knocked her off the hood leaving a huge dent!

The female lion being chased by the angry Cape Buffalos back to the safety of our vehicle.

The weary female sleeps with one of her companions under our vehicle, after giving up the fight for the dead baby buffalo. This amazing sighting consumed a full morning that was filled with hours of on the edge excitement in the crater.

ANGELS IN SIN

A matched set of sleek cheetah that seemed to mimic each other with every move. These majestic animals are magical as they move effortlessly through the bush.

Another amazing day in the Ngorongoro crater watching a female lion relaxing in the branches of a tree. She seemed unphased by the captive audience below her. Lions in a tree are a rare sight unless they are tree-climbing lions which she was not.

Suddenly, to our right, down a bank by water, we saw her. A single female drinking water surrounded by her three cubs. The cubs were playful as two jumped the mother. Then as we watched from above, they began to play together tirelessly. The female and her brood crossed the road directly in front of us and on into the bush.

I have long since given up on my hair and nails. All my nails are broken. My hands are cut and scraped, my body bruised, my nose red and raw from blowing, and my hair, well, let's just say I stick my head under the shower, pull my hair back, and slap a baseball cap onto my head.

Later this morning we watched as a huge elephant herd crossed the river. They made their way onto the banks and crossed directly in front of our vehicle, single file. A baby put on a show for me, rolling around in a dust bowl, then getting stuck and needing help from its mother.

My film went out, again. I panicked, forgot how to rewind, and lost a Kodak moment. Later, I was redeemed when I spotted a group of three females and babies. Three of the babies were sleeping on the ground while Mom stood guard. This is a very unusual sighting. My camera worked perfectly. I remembered some declaration I had made prior to my heading for Africa. I think it was something about not wanting to get caught up with my camera and miss the experience. The camera captures the experience, so that you have it with you always.

Drove to Kasane for supplies today. This will be our afternoon drive as we are going on the Chobe River for animal viewing at 4:30 p.m. So here we go to post my cards, and we spot a large herd of hippos lying on the riverbanks lazily taking a sunbath. On the opposite shore, closest to us, several large elephants rolled in the mud then dusted off with sand. A baby elephant got stuck in the mud and struggled to get out. Suddenly from across the road, a lion walked to the water, then another crossed in front of our vehicle. They hunched over the water and drank while crocodiles sunned on the riverbank. The balance of nature, very delicate indeed.

We drove to the high road where the fresh kill of a baby elephant could be seen on the roadside below us. It had been killed earlier and dragged to a small clearing, where the three lions were feeding. They will return to feed when it cools down. In the meantime, they made their way past us, faces bloodied, to drink some water. On one hand I wanted to see them feed, on the other, the baby elephants are so cute, it made me a bit sad. One cannot interfere. Africa is the law. All things happen for reasons beyond our scope. We must accept the laws of nature.

We're going to lunch, then rest, I need that, then off to Chobe Lodge for the River Cruise. This morning I ran into the two Italians I had met at Victoria Falls on Wednesday, no, it was Monday morning. I can't get away with anything, anywhere. Frankly, I don't want to. The cruise was very touristy. Sunset was lovely. Italian contingent on board. Amazing how I put up walls against people, tourists, I wonder why.

Patrick and I met a girl, Mandy, from London. It turns out she is a stewardess for Mohammed *al Rashid, the mega zillionaire. He is now the ex-husband of the infamous Mouna, the late toast of New York. From his post as financial adviser to the Saudi King he surveys his 355' yacht, Gulfstream Jet, crew of four. Unfortunately, Mouna was a prisoner! She escaped. I think I would like to know her, if only to meet someone so strong of principles. Later I watched as two giraffe darted across the moonlit sky. Just took a shower, a bush shower. It is enclosed on three sides, a large can hangs overhead with a shower head and turn valve. The sky above is pitch in color and blanketed with stars. The African night is mild, and a slight breeze rustles the leaves in the trees above. A lion roars. Birds call out. I turn the valve and perfect warm water sprays onto my body. I stand there for what seems like forever, looking at the sky, thinking how lucky I am, contemplating what I should care about, where I should be right now. I feel so relaxed, I can't believe it. The water runs over my naked body.*

This is Africa. It is not the Mt. Kenya Safari Club or Chobe Game Lodge with tiled baths and CNN. I have that and all of its woes in New York. I came here to experience Africa, and I am. This experience called Africa. I have thought of nothing else, save the majesty of this trip. I worry, not about business and in effect to have thought precious little about it at all. I have really in all honesty given it and all around it except Mitch, only fleeting and meaningless thought since I arrived. I have however spent time imagining sharing the Africa I am seeing with someone special.

Saturday, August 17, 1996

40 miles of bad road Savuti style

It's 6:00 a.m. and we are breaking camp to move to Savuti Game Reserve. Last night, the stillness of the dark, star-studded sky was broken frequently by the roar of my lions and the trumpeting of the elephants.

I thought sadly of the baby elephant who became food for the lions, then let it go to the balance of nature. Birds all varieties are singing and calling. We are heading out for an early drive to check on our lions, then we begin our six hours to Savuti. I'm thinking a lot about relationships and what should be consistent with a healthy one.

I have made some decisions about what is important in the framework of a relationship. Any relationship. A Synergistic Relationship, to be exact. Synergistic is a word that David uses, and I have begun to like that word a lot, it says so much. So during this six hours of hard road, I define that relationship for me. The harmony of relationships, those common threads that weave a real relationship together.

To begin with, it needs to be a place where you can fully and freely express who and what you are at all times, safely. Second it should be a place where you are empowered, encouraged, enabled, and inspired to reach your highest potential for growth and greatness, live your life to the fullest, and realize all of your dreams. Third, it should be a sanctuary for appreciation, admiration, and respect. A feel-good place. Sounds like the right place for me to be. Sounds like I could use some work on number three with Mitch.

So our game viewing was not great, but the thought processes were stupendous. Just narrowly missed a lioness and cubs. This is not an exact science. I must learn an important animal lesson, patience. The Savanna is wide open and dotted with brush and tall nutria-colored grass. A perfect set of camouflage for all wild animals. Giraffes tucked between two trees; lions nestled behind tall grass. You stare at the horizon and suddenly a herd of elephants appears. You allow the eye to wander for a moment and like a Copperfield magic trick, the herd disappears as they drop into a tall, grass-filled gorge. Moments later, in another location they rise tall and proud like a herd of Phoenix, rising from the dry Savanna grasses.

We are on our way to Savuti. We are now traveling on a one-lane sand road. There is nothing between Kasane, the last outpost, and Savuti. We just passed the last village, a grouping of thatched-roof huts by the roadside. A traditional store with crafts in the middle, where I selected a woven basket-type bag. The silence of our campsite, with all its animal sounds, is loud by comparison. There is nothing out here save for a slight breeze and the distant, very distant, minor sound of a single vehicle of some sort. It is probably our truck with all the supplies. Other than that, we just ride the roller-coaster sand road for another two hours before we truck back into Chobe Game Park.

We are up to our asses in sand, in the middle of nowhere. This is the road to somewhere, although it looks like a road to nowhere. Suddenly, rising before us like a huge green dragon, is our supply truck. It's stuck in the sand. No accurate word on what is happening. If you do have the unfortunate luck to get stuck, the good news is that one or two cars travel this way each day. The truck has overheated and blown its water pump.

I am being summarily surrounded by Manapali flies. They are little, horrid flies and seem to be as abundant as the grasses of the Savanna. I have taken my tiny Calvin Klein shirt and placed it like a CK mosquito netting on top of my baseball cap, to keep the flies out of my eyes and ears. A truck is stuck now ahead of us so we must drive off the road, so to speak, and forage through the brush. This is literal. So, as we are driving through and over the brush and small trees following our supply truck, me swatting little flies, the fire extinguisher in the supply truck goes off and sends all of the staff scattering. All that behind us, we set up a picnic by a mud hole, about one hour from our final destination. I wanted adventure. I got adventure.

This is not for princesses or the faint of heart. It's nearly 4:00 p.m. and we are here. Every single inch of me is covered in a fine African dust. Savuti has no water. It had water at one time and several companies put up tented camps to accommodate tourists. Then the water dried up, so the Government fills three water holes to keep the animals and tourists coming. We went to one of the watering holes and saw four lions. I took great shots of them drinking. They were reflecting their strong tawny bodies in the water beneath them. Majestic creatures, I never tire of watching them. Our campsite is remote. I use this term and now qualify the word remote. Savuti is remote. Its accessibility is by an off-road sand-type stretch. It is 100 miles of this fine sand, deep at times, accessible only by four-wheel drive. So, getting here is not particularly easy.

There are three lodges, a term for set-up campsites in one case, Lloyds, or two other hotel-type accommodations. There are five private campsites like mine. Our site is at least seven to ten miles from anyone or anything. As I walk in our cleared site, the sound of the dry Savanna grass echoes miles to the next site of civilization no doubt. All one can hear are some birds, the staff chopping firewood, my breathing, and turning the pages in this book. Never have I known such silence except when I went into a retreat of silence, self-imposed, in Montecito, California. The fire smells pungent, and I can hardly wait to get into my bush shower and wash off this layer of sand.

The smells of Heather's cooking hit my nostrils like a speeding train. Suddenly I am ravenous. All thoughts of dirt and dust are gone, washed away by the fixation of one of Heather's great bush meals cooked over an open fire. For a moment, I imagine someone special, sitting here in khaki shorts, enjoying a glass of wine with me by the fire on this balmy African night. Our vehicles stand before me, no longer dusty, dirty hulls, they are giant black Cyclopes silhouetted against the navy-blue sky and lit by the Man in the Moon.

Sunday, August 18, 1996

Savuti

Africa is not for the faint of heart or weak of spirit. It challenges you every moment of every day. Never allow yourself to become complacent, because in that instant you will be jolted back to the reality of Africa's hold over you and its omnipotent power. You are merely a mortal in a world where the rules are no longer yours. I went to sleep last night with an upset stomach to the voice of Nana Mouskouri and I thought of David as I fell into a sleep. Awakened later by the trumpeting of elephants and a noise I later found out was a hyena fussing around in the kitchen. I had my spotlight on once or twice in the night but failed to turn anything up. Patrick is worried I might be dehydrated. That is another word for Medi-vac. So, I am drinking more water instantly! We spotted some giraffes, and I got some great shots of lions as a pride lazed about in some tall grass. Two males finally stepped out of the shadows and permitted me to canonize them on film. Regal and majestic, they crossed the road like the kings that they are.

Water is pumped into Savuti to three man-made watering holes. It's dry like desert and much, much more difficult terrain. Sand, deep at times, make your insides rock from even the shortest trip. Tracking leopard on this morning's game drive when I forgot Rule One about becoming complacent. Unfortunately, I did and got whacked in the face with a branch. It hit clean over my mouth, but luckily missed my nose which it surely would have broken. I applied a small plastic bottle of water . . . bottle and all, to the area.

The coolness helped and I trust I won't have the proverbial fat lip. Sighted a pack of jackal by a small watering hole. One of them caught a bird and ate it for the camera. Ever the sequence shooter I was able to get some interesting shots, I think.

Africa is changing me. I see it already in how I have been thinking and analyzing. I feel as though I will be less concerned about problems than ever before. Also, I have an attitude about honesty and forthrightness that I will use in this entire situation with David. If it's meant to be than surely it will be. There is a saying here in Africa . . . "AWA, Africa Wins Again." That is very true. You are the minority player here, humbled by the elements and animals, or you should be anyway. I am very proud of myself. This is really a major thing dealing with Africa, remote Africa, alone! People, men and women, can and do suffer so dramatically from the isolation and the danger that they cannot cope and must leave. After all, you are in a sense invading their turf. Anything can and does happen and there you are. You must sort things out in an orderly way. I have just defined Synergistic Relationships, which is the basis for what I must have to bake the cake called relationship.

Africa makes you think. It is about survival; it is about growth; it is about what is important, life and death. Africa really does take me back to basics. I have done more thinking of an analytical manner in these past days than I have done in years. I must have a Synergistic

Relationship first. This has absolutely nothing to do with harmony of a sexual nature or those other ingredients necessary for a good, solid relationship. These are the building blocks, the structure, the foundation. On top of this you add your structure, but it will not stand on sand. These tenets are the steel pylons for a relationship for me at this stage of my life.

Sightings of ostrich. Four stately birds this morning and two near the man-made water hole before lunch. Great! A family portrait of four baby giraffes and one mother all standing wide-eyed, long lashes curling up, under a tree. The land is so parched and dry one's breathing gets shallow. The heat is with us today in waves, although the nights and mornings have been a bit chilly. The other night I thought it was raining but it was the sound of insects' bodies slamming into my tent from the inside!

The air seems very thick this afternoon. Even the breeze isn't really moving it. I had my first wildebeest sighting and topi, which is called something else here in Botswana, that I have difficulty pronouncing. I am resting now until 4:30 p.m. when we go out again.

Tomorrow, we leave for Moremi. Lack of water in this area makes it very different. Few baby "anythings" are in Savuti. All male elephants. Male-dominated herds. Still no leopard or cheetah or rhino, but maybe in Tanzania.

Africa really makes me look at myself, at relationships. The word Synergistic applies to all relationships as we tend to place far too much emphasis on the sexual aspect. That can make it begin and can also destroy it. Sex subverts synergy because somehow, sex implies ownership. It should be a harmonious supplement to a Synergistic Relationship. Instead, people forget the synergy and begin to stake claim on the life of the other, smashing dreams and hopes, denying pleasures and subjugating that other person. As in the case of an old relationship, the deprivation of my dreams created fear and anger, and drove me away. I want David physically, as an extension of our total Synergistic Relationship.

The sunsets in Africa are fantastic. Tonight a herd of elephant were backlit by a purple African sky. They were perfectly silhouetted, a tree outlined behind, its branches reaching to Heaven. One large male took his trunk and pulled his ear forward to give it a scratch. Just goes to show the versatility of a good trunk. Tomorrow we break camp and go to Moremi.

It will be Monday evening or late day when we arrive. This will be my last leg with Heather and Patrick. They stick me on a plane to Kujana Lodge on Thursday. Saturday, I will go to Rosebank and sometime in between I will make contact with Mitch and with David. On Sunday, I head north to Nairobi.

Monday, August 19, 1996

Rough road to Moremi

We have broken camp and are doing my early morning drive looking for the lioness and her cubs. I find the nights here unusual. The contrast that is Africa.

Days hot, mornings and evenings a bit of a nip in the air. The deafening silence of night where few animals call to each other. A few lions and elephants can be heard. Now, birds call regularly. I noticed the animals at night were more vocal in Chobe.

I feel good but sound terrible. Last night we were visited by hyenas. In the midnight hours a pan turned over in the kitchen tent. I, flashlight in hand, head to the opening of my tent. There, less than 25' was a hyena, eyes glowing like red-hot coals. He ran off! This is the last leg of my trip with the Penstones. I shall miss them. This experience certainly does separate the men from the boys. Africa takes you and makes you look at yourself. It tames you. It is not tame, far from it, but it tames you. The heat of the African sun beating down through the open windows of the oversized four-wheel-drive vehicle. The whole vehicle is open to allow easy game viewing. A fine brown sand covers every part of your body. It slips over your clothes like a sheet. What you put on clean in the morning will certainly resemble "bag lady" clothes by sundown.

Africa gives so much to you. Not in the traditional, materialistic giving, but it gives you back yourself! That sense of purpose, revalued values, a look inside the outside to examine what's there. An Autopsy of your Soul. As you stand under the water, African sky above, it washes the sand from your body but leaves you with new thoughts, profound hopefully.

The trip to Moremi is long. One learns the art of patience here. Animals have patience, they must in order to live, to survive. So we made our way for nearly six hours over sand, one-lane deep sand, rocks, trees, through flood waters 1 ½' high in the Okavango Delta. Past zebra, giraffe, elephants, a chorus line of ostrich, wildebeest, and steenbok. No lions, but two flat tires.

During the entire trip you realize that it is what it is. No point in getting upset. This is it! Relax and use the time wisely. Don't waste it foolishly by being upset. So I thought of my relationships and the Synergy of them, or not! Enid and I are not Synergistic. I must correct this or cease the relationship.

Our campsite is in Paradise Pools, and it is paradise. On the Okavango River with reeds reaching for the Heavens. I can hear the staff breaking up the firewood now. Pods are falling from the trees. A herd of buffalo are loitering about ½ mile from here. That means Lions are near. There is NO ONE else around for many, many miles. I have not seen a store, petrol station nothing for days now, save for the tiny gift store in Savuti that had two postcards, a few T-shirts and hats, and is for the 16 guests who stay at the "lodge."

Remote is not a word I use lightly here. I did see Mandy for a second as we were making our way here. She was at the "airstrip," which is a cleared area for five-seater planes with two people inside. She was waiting for a plane to land. She is staying in Moremi at one of the camps, but I will not see her again. You are not allowed to drive anywhere after 6:30 p.m. or before 6:30 a.m. You could get eaten! Of course you could get eaten at other times of the day as well. This rule is obviously for the protection of everyone. There are no fences, no ropes, no boundaries here. Just open land filled with wild animals. Nothing disturbs the balance of nature. Animals kill other animals to live. Elephants knock trees over all the time. This is like the forest of twisted and broken limbs.

When a tree falls across a "road" (for purposes of this journal a road is made of sand or rock, five feet wide or less, and has large hills or valleys in it, along with gaping holes and sometimes water and trees or tree parts) no one moves the fallen tree. One just makes a new pathway through the sand and brush. I have a love affair going on with this place. Africa is in my blood, and I know that my life will never be the same again.

Tuesday, August 20, 1996

Moremi

All night the lions roared around camp. The hippos ambled about noisily, and I fell asleep to the sounds of Nana once again. I awoke for the early morning pickup at 2:00 a.m. to the symphony, a cacophonous melody of millions of frogs, assorted birds, hippos, and lions. I could hardly sleep, my excitement at waking and game driving was so great.

At 6:30 a.m. we left but couldn't find the lions straight off. We got very close to a large herd of cape buffalo. They are very aggressive and dangerous, and a wounded one will backtrack and ambush you. I could count the eyelashes on one of them. Saw a small pride of lions, two female and four cubs sleeping on an ant hill. The way the sun plays with their coats and glints off of their tawny bodies. I also spotted two lions walking into the bush by the "airstrip."

Truly, it is like seeing a needle in a haystack. Found several more aggressive hippos that were not lying in the sun or on the banks or just toasting in the water. These were stationed mouth to mouth, reed to reed. Zebras too, their beautifully marked bodies moving quickly as they darted across the road.

Giraffes, many of them, nibbling on the succulent leaves. A herd of wildebeest next to another herd of cape buffalo. A few crocs, water buck with their ring at their back. OMG, just another morning in the bush. We drove through watery marshes, as water seeped up into our truck. The dust is thick, and it is chilly this morning.

I am hopelessly addicted to Africa. My hair is a mess, hidden under a cap, and nails are totally broken off, hands cut and chapped, skin broken and dry. Clothes are dirty, no, more than dirty, filthy, I don't care. All I want to do is to see more animals. Even nine hours a day isn't enough. I am insatiable.

I do miss David, Mitch, Greg, and of course, my boys. But I have not had a moment of stress since I got here and I am not concerned about anything.

I do hope David feels about Africa as I do. Took the boat into what surely resembles the

Florida Everglades. Tall yellow reeds, narrow winding watery passageways threading around tiny crocodiles. A sighting of the rare sitatunga, a web-footed animal that looks like a small antelope with webbing between his hooves. This enables him to navigate the reeds. We cleared the channels and then pulled in at a remoter than remote spot. Patrick checked for lions and cape buffalo first. Several months earlier a cape buffalo had gored two of his clients a few miles from where we were picnicking. Seems the son wanted a close-up picture of the buffalo and the buffalo charged, goring him and the father who had jumped in to help. This was their very first day on safari. No good common sense at all at age 22. No animals in sight so we picnicked and then threaded our way back through the maze of water and reeds onto the truck.

Oh, on our way to the boat earlier we found ourselves stuck in marsh water in the truck. Took four people and many branches pushing, rocking, pulling, before we pulled free. So far, two flats and a stick in the mud. Here there were three separate leopard sightings today. Oh well, at least that means they are here. I am thinking of canceling the Mt. Kenya Safari Club night. Much effort for one night. A 2 ½ hour drive, then flight, then a bunch of tourists sipping martinis and looking out at a water hole to see wildlife. I mean you can go to the zoo for that. I don't think it is worth it.

It was parched and hot on the evening drive. Right away we had our third flat just as I sighted a bushbuck splashed in sunlight, square before my camera. I scrambled, he scrambled, boom the tire blew with some energy and then Patrick, as always, fixed it. I have lost my sunshield. I suppose it won't impact my photos.

WEDNESDAY, AUGUST 21, 1996

Moremi

I slept soundly for the first time, falling asleep to Nana. What romantic sounds, what a coincidence that Nina and Belafonte are David's favorite singers. Africa is the great teacher and also the great leveler. You are not in control in Africa. You must relinquish all controls and just go with the ebb and the flow. I am learning so much about life, every sighting, every encounter with an animal opens the door to an opportunity for a new experience. Each experience is different. This goes for people as well. Expect the unexpected, have no expectations. I am learning patience. Go with the flow. Examined the Synergism of my relationship with Mitch. How he enabled, encouraged, empowered, and inspired me to live this trip, my dream, and how much I appreciate, admire, and respect him. I must tell him this more often.

Today was windy and chilly. One animal sighting, so very sparse this morning. I thought about getting jaded and how I must experience all parts of Africa with equal enthusiasm. The sighting of wildlife is not an exact science. Each sighting is unique unto itself. A warthog intent on removing some unknown item from the ground ten feet from our truck provided me with a great photo opportunity this morning.

So, the African motto I have coined is "Expect the unexpected and never expect anything." So this afternoon, as I peeled off layers of clothing left from the windy morning, we sighted a three-foot tree monitor scurrying down a sandy road. He paused and pretended he was a log. I quickly saw that he was indeed a tree monitor pretending to be a log and snapped away.

Later we spotted Pavarotti, an errant but dangerous hippo who has staked out his munching territory right adjacent to the tiny store near the boat channels. There he was fat and sassy munching the grass down as we came to photograph him. Since hippos are either in water or in pods beached like giant tubs, seeing one ambulatory and dining was a treat.

We also suffered our fourth flat tire. I am now an old hand at this and lazily watched crocodiles bake on the side of the crocodile pools as Patrick changed the tire. We also sighted a lovely family of giraffes. The baby, who had injured one of his legs, was initially lying down. Then after giving us all angles of their glorious bodies and doing some glamour shots, they sauntered off to find more tasty morsels. The baby had quite a limp but showed no signs of being mauled by lions. I had spotted a small group of people with a Guide earlier, two women, gold earrings, pressed, creased outfits, smart pith helmets, hair recently done. Marvelous, they must have just arrived from the Mt. Kenya Safari Club, where they have spent a week sipping martinis from a veranda overlooking a strategically placed water hole. A few days in Botswana will change all that. Africa will level that quickly.

In the bush, the control is with Africa. One doesn't have the choice of giving up control or not. It is taken from you. It is slipped out of your hands like the reins of a wild horse. You cease to make choices. They are made for you. You are humbled. You are leveled. You do look at life differently than ever before. If you don't, it is only because you have isolated yourself in one of the "resorts" and have not really touched the soil or are so blinded with your own false sense of importance that you are unable or unwilling to open up to the power and magnificence that is Africa.

At dinner this evening . . . after a disappointing array of sightings, Africa had swallowed the animals today . . . I relearned never expect anything. We did have a very exciting, unnerving experience in the afternoon when, as we tooled along, forgetting my rule of expect the unexpected, there was a loud sound. Our vehicle screeched to a halt and to our right, a male elephant, ears flying in fright, bolted behind a large bush. It seems we had nearly hit him as he took an afternoon stroll. We could never figure out who was more frightened. At dinner, Heather and Patrick toasted me, my courage. It seems that many people on safari like this don't make it all the way. They get ill, think they are ill, pretend to be ill just to get out. They both said that everything else I am doing is going to be too tame and that I am tough! Well, bully for me!

Mom used to say that, well, bully for you, big deal. I certainly could have let myself down and quit. This cold has followed me every day. But that isn't me. Even Patrick thought I was going to have to be airlifted out of the bush but that was NEVER going to happen. I had waited far too long for this trip and nothing, NO THING, was going to stop me now. I am tough and if that is what it would take for me to finish every last moment of this amazing trip, that is what it would take.

Again, a cacophony of sounds, lions who magically reappeared at night still hiding, but very vocal. Hippos, oinking and sputtering. I imagined a pod of hippos ambling along the road at night and laughed. The wind was whipping up last night as it shouted goodbye. Leaves sounded like lions, and I was up and down all night looking to see something big. Nothing occurred. Today I fly to Kuganha for a few days. I had hoped to talk to David but there are no phones in the Okavango.

Thursday, August 22, 1996

Okavango

The Penstones had a vehicle breakdown, which was disabling. They needed to be towed. Bob from Camp Moremi had me shuttled to an airstrip for the short flight in a four-seater to Kuganha. My God, this is really a slice of Heaven. Betsy was right. I am sitting in my frame Chalet, looking out to the water. Birds fly in front of my netted windows. The silence I have known for nine days is no more, as I have entered civilization.

People's voices in the background. Although I must say the isolation of the bush does make you yearn for some human contact. In the bush, everything is on generator and battery, so hair dryer is out, no electricity, but a real shower is here. No moon and stars above but real running water in a sink and a real bed. The thatching of the Chalet, the reeds it is built of are charming. It is very romantic. How I should like to share this with David. A resident hippo lives behind the next Chalet, so I have been warned not to stray far from the camp and lodge. After being in the bush for nine or ten days, I wouldn't stray.

I went on a mokoro ride today. This is what I thought my canoe trip on the Zambezi River would be. A tall canoe man with a large pole, sort of like being in Venice. It's all couples here, save for me. It's really okay. It is very romantic, and I would love to be here with David. He is on my mind for very good reasons. This place is very peaceful.

I don't really want to do the game walks. It is a bit too tame after my experiences, but I did it today. I took a boat through tall reeds to a mokoro for a two or three mile walk among the tall grasses where lions and giraffes, elephants and lechwe frequent. Crazy you say, yes I agree.

Friday, August 23, 1996

Kuganha Lodge

Kuganha Lodge is just the perfect spot for the next few days. I need a rest. My body is thirsty for the hot shower and a real bed. It's amazing what we take for granted. No lights here during the day. The generator only operates at certain hours. I am sitting outside having just finished breakfast, believe it or not. I ate eggs! They tasted different!

The deep Blue water of the Delta ripples before me gently, as the wind pushes it from East to West and then whips around and moves it back, making tiny waves. There is a chill in the air, and I have layers, shirt upon shirt, topping the ensemble off with that sac jac that Steven gave me. It has come in handy.

Across the Delta as far as my eye can see are tall reeds, which provide excellent camouflage for the resident wildlife. This is a real departure from the isolation I have experienced over these past two weeks, although this morning I am the only one remaining here at the Lodge, except staff. The other guests have boarded motorboats and are going to birdwatch.

Since this is my vacation, I have decided that what I need is a day of rest and relaxation. Reading, writing, and reflection on what is important and what isn't. Tomorrow I leave here for Maun then Johannesburg then North to Nairobi for an entirely new set of experiences.

Last night, around 1:00 a.m. I heard a cry, the voice of emergency, the resident elephant . . . unwanted, of course, had breached the electric wire and was dining on trees by the dining area. Fitting indeed! This morning there were branches all over the ground and huge elephant tracks all around. I wish I had seen that.

Spending time alone, precious moments just listening with every cell, every pore, thinking. The quiet of your own breathing. An echo of your thoughts shattering the stillness of this Delta when all the guests are tucked away. It's been a long time since I have experienced this peace, this study of self.

I have been dining with two other couples, a German couple, Doris and Gaylord from Munich. She is young and very pretty with ice blue eyes and flaxen hair past her shoulders. Her skin is clear like fine porcelain, her body tight and lithe as an Impala. He is tall with a strong, forceful bone structure. His smile is dazzling, and he is quite good-looking. The other couple Sarah and Dennis are from New Zealand. She is slender, plain, with short brownish hair that is windblown. No makeup, but no support for that look, as plain works. He is an Investment Banker, and they have four children.

I have been thinking about David. I must say that I really have been interested in David since before I really knew him. I yearned to know him and when we met I sensed that our lives were intertwined. Perhaps that we had been together in another life. I feel very strongly about he and I making this work. I am very anxious to talk to him tomorrow. Truly I have missed him.

I decided to do the late day boat ride and game walk to Sausage Island with Gaylord and Dodes, not Doris. Camera bag in hand we boated first, spotting numerous crocs of assorted sizes, all the while wondering how we could have been in those channels yesterday in mokoros, which are flimsy, long canoes.

Out of the boat and on foot through the high, thick yellow reeds and pampas. We left our footprints, five sets in the African sun. Sausage Island is named so because of the Sausage Tree, a tree with pods, long and fat that hang down off the viney branch like sausages in the Italian style. Then we saw birds, more birds, beautiful birds, and I was trudging along fantasizing about making love to David and suddenly we see an elephant in the distance. Miles we trudge through tall, yellowing, dry reed, wild animal camouflage and then there he is no more than 150 feet in front of us. I climb a tall gray ant hill and photograph him. My adrenaline was pumped.

I was a little nervous because this was a young male, and they can be very aggressive and dangerous. We moved away, walking down wind so that he wouldn't smell us. Trekking around I took photos of Gaylord and Dodes as they walked in front of me through the high grass. I turned to Claire, the girl from the Gift Shop, and said how amusing it was that animals could be anywhere in the grasses and we are all walking it so casually.

The Guide, who was not armed, stopped and said something to Gaylord which he passed on to Dodes and then to me . . . Lion, he murmured. OMG, suddenly looming before us, no more than

100' away under a tree was a male lion. We all froze and were reminded not to move. I grabbed my binoculars and looked. There was this large male staring right at us.

I took my camera, focused, and couldn't shoot. It was so still that I was fearful that the beeping noise when the camera focused would be heard. Another head pops up from under the tree. My God, there they were, two male lions. I was frozen in time, unable to do anything. We stood riveted to the ground, trying not to breathe for fear they would come. One gets up, oh my God. He glances toward us, then runs the other way. A moment later, the second male follows. I shot my photo. They stood in the tall grass for what seemed like an eternity, watching us watching them. My heart was pounding like a jackhammer. Once they were lost in the tall grasses, we made our way back the two or three miles through the dense, tall reeds to our waiting boat.

ANGELS IN SIN

The elusive leopard majestically perched atop the tree gives me two beautiful views as he glanced to one side as if to ignore my presence, then stared directly at me for the perfect picture. The Serengeti is an amazing spot for wildlife for sure.

The matched set of cheetahs strike another pose in the Serengeti.

Hardly anything more scary than a charging rhino. This one skidded to a stop then calmly strolled over a few feet from our vehicle and took a giant pee Now that was a moment! Never expect anything and always expect the unexpected. This is a truth I have learned over years of safaris and the surprisingly unexpected behavior of the wildlife.

ANGELS IN SIN

One of the most incredible moments of my safari adventures was in the Ngorngoro Crater at 7 am one morning. I saw a cloud of dust approaching our vehicle as two Maasai warriors led a cluster of cattle and goats to graze in the crater. It is customary to give money to take pictures of the Maasai but all I had in the car were two bags of wrapped lemon candy, Hagai, a Maasai, said "keep shooting" and so I clicked off picture after picture as they approached. Once in range they were happy to have the candy, however one little Maasai boy had a dilemma. A baby goat was born as they crossed into the crater that morning. He was tenderly holding the goat, but what to do about the wrapped lemon candy. I call the picture "Decisions" as that is what he was faced with that morning. By the way, he unwrapped the candy with his teeth.

There is nothing quite as exciting as a tribal marketplace filled with Maasai women and fabrics that are stunningly colorful and beautifully designed.

This is the bush…miles and miles of brush and not a tourist in sight. Alone with just my Maasai guide as company in the middle of my private campsite in the Serengeti

Morning wakeup call from a magnificent bull elephant who is outside my tent as dawn breaks.

A lone hyena stares out from a bush in
the Maasai Mara in Kenya.

A female lion roars as she nurses her cub in the brush
in the Ngorngoro Crater in the early morning hours.

Saturday, August 24, 1996

Okavango

I am awake and ready, listening to Nana, "The White Rose of Athens." I am ready for a new Falling in Love Again. It has been played so very much. Darkness wraps itself around this lodge like a big black blanket. It wraps us tightly as if keeping all harm away. I can't wait to accelerate into Phase Two of my trip. Punctuated by tonight at the charming Rosebank, where I will have a hairdryer and a phone, two things I have not seen or heard in two weeks.

I guess now that I recognize we can do without anything like that, and all will really move forward. I would love to be surprised by David, but I won't be expecting anything. I want to talk to him but if I can't it will be as painful for us both.

The sounds of the hippo, Cassidy, as in Hopalong, resonated all night long. Have yet to see his fat body though. Transiting through Gaborone to Joburg, chaos, but controlled in Maun. One learns to let go, to release, no controls. I finally was able to get some Pula. The search started because I wanted to call Bill and Theresa about dinner and needed a phone card. To buy a phone card one needs cash, Pula or US dollars, neither of which I had, other than fifty-dollar bills, which would result in Botswana change, so I had to buy another cap. One can't have too many caps. Got the change in Pula and returned to buy the card, only to find they are busy with friends and will call me later. It's okay really.

I want to speak to David early, rearrange my luggage and such. I've grown used to being more solitary and making good creative use of my time. Somehow everything works like a finely tuned piece of machinery, even when something breaks everything works out okay. A sea of faces as unique as snowflakes, light and dark, and young in a mélange of polyester and cotton. No smells in the air, save for the dryness. I have stopped feeling the heat.

Sunday, August 25, 1996

I have languished in the time, the hours that I was on the phone with David. I reached him as soon as I came in the door of the hotel Saturday evening around 7:30 p.m. My body was tired, my clothing covered with fine African silt. My hair straight, dry, and flat under my DKNY black cap. But I needed to hear his voice.

We spoke for over an hour. I shared my fantasies of making love to him, he shared his desires to be with me in bed. There is no doubt that we are giving this relationship a go. I feel pleased. His daughter was sick, and David went to stay with her while his wife was at his other daughter's shower . . . she is getting married November 16. He left as soon as she returned amidst protests that he should stay. He phoned, trying to reach me for half an hour, and then we talked for another two hours. The feelings are there, the words are there, but unspoken for us both, as David said. There is so much to say but I am here halfway around the world, for the next two weeks. He did say that he would be fine if he had my support, good wishes, and love. I said you have all of that. He said I know, and it is mutual, I know that.

I have never been so "out there" before. Whatever David decides, we will be together. We have a history. I don't know what, but we both feel it. We are supposed to be together, and we will be. I don't know for how long, but I know we will be lovers. That will happen the next time we see each other. That is a given.

I am on my way to Nairobi now, a four-hour flight, then four-hour drive to Arusha, Tanzania. David and I are going to make this trip next year, I feel certain about that. No matter what, we will be together in Florida or here on my return. It's time for us to be close, to follow our hearts, to be intimate, to cover each other with warmth and love. The feelings are there for us both. We've been trying to keep things at a reasonable distance since April, but our emotions are too involved. I want to be close, to feel his warmth, to hold him, sleep with him, enable, empower, inspire him to achieve his greatest potential.

It is Sunday and I just landed in Nairobi, Kenya. No one is quite certain which carousel the bags are to arrive on.

All the monitors are now gaping holes surrounded by a metal frame. They look like open toothless mouths over each baggage beltway. One bears a sign: wet paint. I can't help but wonder where, as the belt is made of rubber, so no paint there. I wait. The front wheels on my airport cart suddenly collapse and I scurry to find another, climbing in and around boxes like a little mouse. A flight has arrived from Bombay with more luggage than three planes might have.

I wondered what they could be bringing in from Bombay. Mother Theresa is dying in some hospital. The very thought of that saddens and depresses me. Eighty-six years young on Tuesday and an angel on this earth.

Leonard was right, there with a sign that said Georgene, and soon we were off and on our way along a narrow road. I thought well of this road initially, as it was not sand or dirt, but tar. That was until we bottomed out on the first major pothole. I was delighted to watch the Maasai men, women, and children as they tended to the cattle, made their way from village to home, or stood by the roadside. They looked magnificent in their red plaid traditional Maasai garb and handcrafted jewelry. A vision to behold for me.

As the African sun set with its hues of yellow, purple, and red, the sky looked like a watercolor painting, the trees silhouetted like patchwork against the tawny backdrop of drying yellow cornfields. As it darkened, the three-quarter moon rose like a face in the sky, sending light down to the pitch-black streets.

I marveled as tiny figures, heads loaded with bags of commodities, made their way along the darkened dirt path or on the road. Cars sped along this two-car wide tar road, bright lights double barreling, or single lights shining, barely keeping their wheels on the road and out of the dirt and rock ditch that ran parallel to it. Wild bumping over potholes strewn like feed for hungry animals. Mr. Toad's Wild Ride.

The radio played interference with a faint backdrop of African music. The driver didn't notice. I thought of listening to Heaven and Paradise, when the radio station was flipping between weak channels, or just trying to hear, barely. The radio is now all interference, but the driver still doesn't know. The purple sky outlines the mountains on a canvas called the Universe. The driver shuts off the radio. I thought of David as we arrived at the Mountain Lodge. I thought I had stepped into Hansel and Gretel's cottage. Grounds that are like paradise with the scent of Jasmine and Camelia filling your nostrils. Green plants and flowers and stately sausage trees with vines that gnarled like withered tusks, and sausages that hung in Deli-type splendor.

There was a group of six splendid, vine-covered, thatched three little pigs huts with stone floors and a tiny stream running in front. Crickets chirping. I thought of David and I enjoying the romance of this amazing place.

Dinner in the glass dining room was wonderful. Tomorrow, I will be picked up at 8:00 a.m. and on to the Ngorongoro Crater. I love this place.

Monday, August 26, 1996, 7:00 a.m.

Arusha Tanzania Gibbs Farm

OMG, I opened the curtains in this cute, round little hut and there are beautiful flowers around, small, gorgeous green sloping hilly parts with big trees and to the left, a lake. God, what majesty to wake up to in the Morning. My little beds, two of them, also have an elaborate tie-back mosquito net overhead. It slides around, floor to ceiling, and surrounds you like a big cocoon. I left it tied back. I hear dogs howling. No hippos or lions here. Looking up, the entire pointed round roof is thatched. I think I am in a Hans Christian Andersen fairy tale. This is so cute. I can't tell you how much I love Africa. It is truly amazing.

Serene and beautiful, we dined at Gibbs Farm. A tiny, heavenly spot tucked inside magnificent flowers and trees on the top of a hill, overlooking a Coffee Plantation. The Lodge is charming and quaint and served us a delicious lunch and fabulous dinner. I also met Margot Maine and her husband Robert, no last name. She works for Sotheby's selling client art and he is a writer. I will call her when I return.

My new phrase seems to be "my God." I am in awe of this extraordinary place. It takes my breath away, and so my love affair with Africa has begun or rather is just escalating. Never in my life have I felt such overwhelming joy, such happiness, such excitement at being, doing, anything.

My entire being is alive with a joy I have known only on occasion in my life. I feel as though I just won the lottery. My body is alive with an energy. Africa and I have a relationship, a Synergistic one. I am sitting on a wooden rocker in a sunroom at Sopa (hello to Maasai men) Lodge on the rim of the Ngorongoro Crater.

It's 4:00 p.m. on Monday. The curved expanse of windows allows me a full, breathtaking view of the crater. A Maasai Chief greeted us at the door.

The drive here over dirt, rock, and an occasional tar road took us six hours The incredible landscape was dotted along the way with the colorful Maasai men, women, and children.

There are Kenyan Maasai and Tanzanian Maasai. Villages built by Kenyan Maasai are down several feet in a round circle with brush all around. This covers the outside of the circle, so that from a distance the tiny Maasai village appears to be only low-lying brush. The Maasai do not like to be photographed without permission, for which you will pay. At the Kenyan border, several Maasai women hawk curio art and have become an industry. As I am looking for a double-wide elephant hair bracelet for myself and David, I will make a point of stopping on my return.

Tanzania is an agricultural Paradise. Fields of honey-colored wheat stretch across gentle, sloping hills. The "Grevillea Robusta" is a tree planted to increase the fertility of the land, which is a rich terracotta color.

The trees are planted abundantly, and coffee grows underneath them. There are beautiful, full green plants with rich, red beans; rice delicious beyond any I have tasted; corn and a fruit called Custard Apples. It has a funny greenish outside shell and large black seeds in a fruit that is incredible and tastes like the sweetest combination of pear and apple imaginable. We also tried the red banana, a small, reddish banana that tastes like no banana I ever tasted.

I have made a life-changing decision. One should do that, which makes them happy. I have only recently discovered several areas of passion in my life. Things that I can do without regard to time or sacrificing. One is to write. I love my writing which is why I will retire and write within two years. The second, I know now, involves Africa. I must spend time here as I love it beyond words. I love the feeling, energy, country, splendor, animals, color, and art. I love the people, their warmth, their kindness, their truth.

I have begun by promising myself two months a year in Africa, two trips a year. I am working with Hagai, my Guide, to determine my first trip of one month. I think it will be June for the majesty of the wildebeest. February is when I would have to arrive for the full herd migration as two herds broke off. My only question is, can I wait until June. I have never felt like this. The dirt, rough roads, no electricity (a hairdryer here though, wow!). I don't feel any sense of sacrifice and I am willing, anxious to sacrifice to come here and spend time. Africa has forever changed my life. Some people love golf, tennis, others are card nuts. I am hopelessly addicted to Africa and happy about it. I hope David loves the Country like I do. If not, then mine will be a Solitary Journey indeed, as I will not give it up for anyone or anything. It is as passionate a pursuit as my writing.

TUESDAY, AUGUST 27, 1996

Ngorongoro Crater

We started our game drive at 6:30 a.m. this morning to the most magnificent sight I have ever seen. Clouds falling over into the crater like a spectacular 180-degree, 100-mile-wide waterfall. It was perfect They cascaded down the inside of the crater in a surreal fashion. Giant Acacia trees with their flat tops loomed in the distance.

This day proves to be the most incredible day I have had in three weeks of incredible days. First we sight three black rhino. I couldn't believe my eyes as they ambled along in the distance. Two adults and one baby. We waited with the patience of Job for them to come within a reasonable distance, so they would look like more than just smudges on landscape So, they laid down and disappeared into the landscape.

As we moved along I saw a group of rocks and thought a pit stop could be accomplished. This was just 100 yards from where we first spotted the rhinos. Moments later, a female lion appeared from behind the rocks and sitting on top were three tiny cubs. They were ever so cute. I watched as they followed their mother into the tall, tawny-colored grasses. Moments later, as we rounded a bend, three females appeared, walked out in front of us, and allowed us to tailgate them down the dirt road. A short time later we got a rare treat as six young males were gathered together in one place. At one point, one young male posed lazily, and I got so close I could count his eyelashes. I was less than ten feet away.

ANGELS IN SIN

Enormous hippo floating in the river. Hippos are responsible for more death than any other animal. They go underneath you and take a chunk out first and then the crocodiles finish you off. Scary stuff!

A gorgeous male lion hangs out under my vehicle. It was incredible to see how comfortable he was and how long he shared his beauty with me.

Up close and personal with a beautiful gecko.
He or she just made my day. Funny how little
things like that can make you light up!

ANGELS IN SIN

Dangerous crocodiles lurking on the sand by a river. The Maasai women collect water daily from rivers that are filled with these deadly creatures. They dip a plastic pot into the river risking their lives each time for water.

Mother giraffe stands guard over her baby, who is maybe just a month old, while surrounded with kudu and zebra in the bush near my campsite in the Maasai Mara.

A curious trio of Maasai boys stands by the roadside waiting for me to stop and interact with them, which I do. As is customary I give them some shillings in exchange for being able to take their pictures.

ANGELS IN SIN

The breathtaking colors of a Maasai marketplace complete with beautiful fabrics and amazing designs. I have many unbelievable pieces of fabric that I now use as cloths to cover my table, and they are unique and gorgeous. I have also had some made into napkins.

A herd of incredible elephants' baby in tow, parade past my campsite late one afternoon. Babies that are under a year old can still walk underneath the mother.

The same herd as they departed into the distance a few hours later. All of them in unison marching to the beat of their very own drum. They are so magical and their movements so quiet despite their enormous size.

We stopped for lunch under a fantastic fig tree whose branches grew up and down, and was several thousand years old. The massive trunk of this tree was probably over 150' all around. The limbs hung like vines reaching to the ground to form roots that made the trunk even bigger.

While I was attempting to eat my lunch, two guinea fowl became very curious, and at one point one male took the quiche right out of my hand. It was so funny. After lunch, we were treated to three young lion cubs, maybe eight months old, who were sleeping in a tree.

It was so unbelievable. The tree was broken and about five feet of it off the ground and 30' long, like a big, gnarly trunk. Then we spotted some more rhino and once again they eluded us. We began to track a male rhino who we thought would cross our path, but he went the opposite direction. While in pursuit, we came upon two female lions with three cubs in tow, right by the road. We watched them for what amounted to several rolls of film.

At one point, the two lionesses were using the shadows of two, four-wheel-drive vehicles as shade. Then they got up after the cubs had gone into hiding behind a bush. They were different ages, and one was only a few weeks old. The other two were maybe four or five weeks. The older cubs started following the females, but the little one wouldn't come out from the bush.

Then he came out just a little and cried and cried for someone to come back and get him. It was so sad yet so amazing to watch this little fellow. The females had already moved about 25 to 30' away, so the two older cubs started to come back to see the little one. Before they could venture back, the baby still crying and screaming, the mother got up and chastised one of the other cubs.

She then walked over to about ten feet from the baby who was still yelling and let out the growl of life. Like, she said, "Shut Up Now." The baby came running out, went to its mother, and rubbed up against her. No doubt saying, "Mommy, I was scared." It was super sweet and what a moment.

Then we found . . . get ready for it . . . FOUR Rhino, Three Adults and One Baby. We waited, me standing head and body out of the vehicle.

Finally, these incredible creatures ambled over and crossed right in front of our car. I kept saying, Oh My God, as the four prehistoric, nearly extinct animals crossed the road. My heart was pounding with excitement. I feel as if I have just won the lottery, but that is how I have felt since I arrived.

On our way back to the Lodge, we passed the female lions again. Both were sound asleep, one in the road looking almost dead, and the other upside down and sound asleep. The babies were hiding in the bush. The sun is setting, and the crater is serene. I wanted to photograph them. I gave candy and some barrettes to a few children. What a day, what an adventure.

THURSDAY, AUGUST 29, 1996

Ngorongoro Crater

I wrote nothing yesterday as I was under the weather and had 11 hours of travel, not feeling 100 percent, over roads that Baja vehicles would be tired of. Ruts, potholes, rivers of ruts, dirt, and rocks. Maasai children, young warriors with their wooden collars, and more ruts! Eleven hours to Nairobi. When I arrived at the Five-Star Norfolk Hotel, wishing like hell to talk to David, I couldn't get a line out. Disappointed and stressed! I finally got one and we spoke for a short time at his office. I then called him this morning at 7:00 a.m. He had dined with his daughter and showed her my cards. She read them and sent her regards. That felt really good.

Obviously, my cards are all inclusive with the words missing you. I shall buy some nice pieces of African jewelry for her or something else. He has told her about me, about us. He is also trying to get to the airport to meet me on Thursday

What a blessing that would be . . . three days, three nights, I can't wait. If he can't, I shall go to Florida the following weekend. I feel so close to him that I want to take this intimacy to its closest place. The Mara River Camp is great. I am going to pay $520 more to have my own car for two days. I refuse to buy a "pig in a poke" and end up with a gang of strangers who will ruin my game drives. Saturday, I go Hot Air Ballooning. I can tell already there is not going to be silence like I have had on the rest of my safari. On the *way in from the airstrip I saw three Cheetah lounging on several rocks.*

Their dark spots ablaze in the afternoon sun. Then on top of that, a magnificent leopard appeared from the bush, and as we approached camp, we spotted a female leopard with two tiny little cubs sitting in the tall grasses, in the pouring rain. If that isn't enough there is a one-week-old hippo in residence here.

Can't wait to see her or him. Tomorrow, I will go with Daniel and Sylvia who came to pick me up with Jeffrey today. They are from London. We leave at 6:30 a.m. for a day of game driving.

Friday, August 30, 1996

This morning started off with a bang. A mother cheetah and her two tiny babies were posing for us in the grasses. The mother was so unbelievably beautiful with dark spots against her cream skin. The babies had no spots but were little balls of fur with big eyes. So very cute. Then in the afternoon, I was feeling quite poorly and decided to nap. I am into a month of Africa, and everything is catching up with me.

I am ready to head home. The couple I am with in my vehicle are leaving tomorrow. Daniel and Sylvia from London. Very sweet people indeed, and I rose to the occasion and went gaming with them. I think I have done nearly 200 hours of game drives.

Today we sighted a leopard cub lying on a rock. What a sight! Its magnificence hit by the rays of sun as it dangled its body over several rocks. Then, when the tourist traffic became unbearable, we went elsewhere and found a pride of lions. Eight females with sixteen cubs of all ages. What a treat to watch them play as the African sun was setting on the horizon. The cubs were adorable.

A Tour Group, Abercrombie & Kent, got stuck in the mud. I didn't really want to help them. After all, I am here to see game not to dig out Tourists. I was quite put out frankly, but then one of their other Tour Vehicles, which was 100 yards from them, returned to assist.

In the evening, we all watched as Maasai women & warriors entertained us with traditional dances usually done for weddings and circumcisions. It was fantastic to watch.

The Maasai men spring into the air two or three feet straight up. After, I bought some lovely Maasai Jewelry. I will give a collar to David to give to his daughter, a little memento of a Maasai wedding ceremony. Tomorrow, I go hot air ballooning.

Saturday, August 31, 1996

Maasai Mara

So excited last night that I could hardly sleep. Today is my Hot Air Ballooning day.

Up in the blackest of black nights at 4:30 a.m. . . . sleep in my eyes. Threw on 20 layers of clothing.

I looked like the Pillsbury Doughboy! Picked up at 5:15 a.m. It was still dark but not dark enough to miss the large hippo, eyes shining, ambling to the water right in front of our vehicle. You don't argue with that! I was told that the road was rough, but at that early hour I was ill-prepared for vehicle rock climbing. I don't really think a road exists between the Mara River Club and Little Governor's Camp where my balloon lies flat awaiting my arrival.

I wasn't feeling 100 percent, so I lost my stomach three or four times over a road that qualified as 12 kilometers of the worst road I have ever seen. Not really seen but experienced.

We arrived, with me and my stomach thanking God, in the dark of the African morning. On arrival, I met two nice couples, June and Kenny and Phyllis and Herb from Brooklyn. They were really funny. I have invited them to my upcoming African Party.

So the balloons were laid out and then inflated and we climbed inside. There were 12 people going, six of us in my balloon. The Captain, a cute pilot named Mark, lit the fuel, a burst of flame zipped into the balloon, and we began to rise.

How magnificent to see the world as a bird. To fly free atop the trees. Around the World in Eighty Days *sprung to mind. Every few minutes the flame would shoot up again to take us higher as we soared into the now rising sun! Brilliant! From our vantage point we could see a small family of giraffes.*

They stopped and watched, as this curious bird of yellow, orange, red, blue, and green flew higher into the sky, making a funny noise. We must have looked very strange, like three big birds. The light played in the sky like dancers moving in and out of the clouds skillfully. Such beauty every place you look. What magnificence.

Landing is the fun part. First, you need to get rid of all items that could hit you in the face, like cameras, or binoculars.

Then you put all that paraphernalia under your feet, sit on the bench with your back to the landing and hold onto the ropes. You hit hard, you bounce, you drag like a ride in an amusement park.

Thrust up, up, and away over ant hills, aardvark Hills and the like, until the basket flips totally back, and you slide like a pancake to a stop. Then the bottom three climb out, then the top three.

It was interesting and exciting and worth every cent. Then there is the champagne breakfast of things I never eat but ate. You know, all that good stuff, bacon, with . . . whoa . . . 50 grams of fat. Baked beans, sauteed mushrooms, cheese . . . all before 10:00 a.m.!

Then we get into the vehicle for the drive back to camp. They already have the message that I dislike tourists with a passion. The ones who are loud, inconsiderate, who put "people" in pictures with lions behind the cars. Who cares?

So they gave me a private vehicle and driver back to camp. Very cool! We saw two male lions with an early morning kill. They were so full they couldn't move. They just rested and laid there, breathing hard! The road back was the same road, awful! Nineteen new people arrived today. I am not totally impossible. I wasn't going to go game driving today as I had to share, but the desk has carefully culled a cute couple. Ruth is very pretty and looks to be Thai or Vietnamese and her boyfriend/husband is Ian. They seem nice so I am going. I need a cat fix. Also I have realized that I think I can make money doing what I love to do. Eureka!

So what is that? Well, I love the zoo, I love wild animals, I love to write, and I love Africa. Africa has wild animals, so I am going to test my theory by putting an article together on this trip along with a few dozen excellent photos of what I have seen. This is not about money, it's about being true to me.

Imagine being able to come to Africa, photograph animals, write about it, write it off, and maybe even get paid. Now, I am tired and ready for some rest.

Sunday, September 1, 1996

So, today I have my own car.

This morning we found the herd of elephants that has the tiny baby. He is no more than a month old. He is so very uncoordinated that the other day he tripped over his own feet. Today, he was trying to pull up some grass but ended up putting a trunk full of air in his mouth. He is so cute. He tried so hard to get this branch up and to eat it like his mom, but he couldn't quite do it. He would pull it up then drop it. Then he tried to reach up to the trees like her. What a sight that was.

Today is a very important day. I received a present from a Maasai woman named Esther, I made a friend, a Maasai boy of 11 named Simuel, and at 54 years young finally realized what I want to do with the rest of my life. I have a Love Affair with Africa. I can film animals all day long and never tire of them. I have never felt so incredible in my life.

Africa is in my blood.

I am forming a company that will specialize in Wildlife Photography and African Art.

So I spent most of the morning watching the mother cheetah with her babies. At one point I dropped my Armani sunglasses, and they fell on the ground outside of my vehicle. The cubs were playing under our car and in two seconds one cub was out and had my glasses in its mouth. We opened the door and scared the babies away. I now have cheetah cub marks on my glasses. Lucky me!

Monday, September 2, 1996

It is the day before departure! Oh my, I don't think I can re-enter. Up at 5:00 a.m. This, Africa, is truly my passion. I went hunting for Cheetah, in a photographic sense only, and finally found her, with her cubs, majestic in her posturing for my photos.

The early morning sun rose splendidly over a herd of elephants.

Two babies are in the herd, not just one as I thought. Tried to get this amazing shot of mom and the two little ones, but both cameras failed to respond to me. Onward!

The cubs were really playful this morning and they played seesaw, (let's see who falls off first) on a piece of wood. They are a riot! I could have watched their antics for hours.

I have watched their antics for hours, as my film will confirm. It started to rain early today and what that becomes roadwise is what one refers to as a sinkhole of blacker than black tar like wet stuff, oozing around.

Vehicles slide and splatter this ink-black goo everywhere. Getting stuck is sort of the way it is here. "Hakuna Matata!" I met Jonathan Scott and Frans something, cannot spell his name, who are World Class Wildlife Photographers. I learned that I have much to learn. But I am really on course with what I am to do. I will be specializing in the unusual in photography and Museum-quality African antiquities. An office will be set up in our offices, a showroom. I cannot express how good it feels. I'm writing this in the dark. There is no light until 5:00 a.m. so my penmanship is pretty poor.

We exercised patience waiting for three hours as a leopard cub lay in the high grasses several hundred feet from me.

I was forced to be a policeman for the leopard because of the misconduct of drivers and tourists. I became a spokesperson, regulating traffic movement away from the cub.

As a result, the mother returned a few moments before the pre-African darkness hung over us and called the cub with a chirp. The baby jumped up over the brush and into the safety of its mother's body.

We had removed a thorny Acacia tree trying to get to the site and God rewarded us by giving me the baby and mom as they romped in a tree.

Later, he walked by me within feet of where our vehicle stood quietly, looked directly at me with those green marbled eyes and MEOWED! I was so excited trying to take photos that the unstamped card for David flew out of the open land cruiser and landed directly in front of the baby leopard. He continued to look at me and cry. Then he turned and began to stalk his mom, who was seated quietly, majestically on the top of an ant hill.

A vivid rainbow spanned the skies behind this duo as they roughhoused on the ant hill. The African sunset was stolen by dusk and the only people left filming were the BBC, the Guys, Mr. Wildlife and Frans Lanting. Only now do I realize just how amazing and incredible these two were and, lucky me, I met them.

Tuesday, September 3, 1996

I am wide awake at 5:00 a.m. Boy, do I love my Holiday! Animal fix is in order so off we go to find cheetah and babies, I hope. I just love traveling solo, every decision is a unilateral one, and in most cases when I look around at people in other cars, I find the thought of spending any time with them, quality time, horrific. They are really boring. It is much like a notch on the belt of a sex addict, I think. Armed with an Instamatic camera, they see one hippo, one elephant, a lion and a cheetah, take a picture and now they can go home and say they were on a safari.

Their clothing is always neatly pressed, right out of the Abercrombie catalog, not a hair out of place; starched and ready for lunch or dinner or fresh from breakfast, they gather like locusts in the vehicle, chatting it up with other tourists. Not for me, not now, not ever.

On my Game drive this morning I saw the lioness and her gorgeous male lion boyfriend. They walked following each other in majestic splendor.

We followed them at a respectful distance allowing them space to just be. Earlier this morning I spotted a lone male cape buffalo in a setting directly out of Central Casting.

A field of light grass topped with acres of dark, dark, forever green acacias, and a blue sky. The buffalo had a superb starling perched on his head. He munched his breakfast warily, watching us from one eye. At one point, I cautioned Francis to start the car as he looked as though he had had it with us. But then, nothing. Cape Buffalo's ambush and attack even if not provoked. Nana Mouskouri is practically worn out. I go to sleep listening to her rich, resonant sounds. Reminds me of David so very much. I shall speak to him from Nairobi tonight.

At 11:30 a.m. we are to visit a Maasai village. I have a little friend there, his name is Simuel. He is 11 years old. The village is typical Maasai, made of mud and wood. Tree are cut in round shapes and the huts are thatched. Ester was happy to see me. She is tall like a giraffe with one tooth in the front. She has invited me to her home. I enter into pitch darkness, a darkness I have never known before in my life. It was like being dropped into a vat of black ink. No light at all, not even from the morning sun. It was a wall of darkness. I hear Ester's voice asking for my hand. I reach to the right in the dark of her home and feel it. Grabbing on, she guides me over a log and right between more branches which I assume reach vertically toward the Heavens.

She pulls me down and I can see nothing. Ester lights a candle and now I can see the faint silhouettes of Denis Steve, Pilwa, Simuel seated on some bed-like item five feet in front of me and on the floor. My first thought was how amazing it was to get so many people in such a small space. Ester sat beside me on her bed and the boys, Steve and Denis, were on the children's bed. Ester has two or three sons and one daughter. Pilwa stood in the shadows and Simuel stood in the doorway I had just stumbled through.

They cook over a fire between the two beds. They eat all around this round structure, which is one room, no larger than my kitchen. They presented me with a "club" for Greg and bracelets for me over the next 15 to 20 minutes. The children seemed to need medical attention, although that would be the interpretation of a mother who cannot bear to see runny noses. Afterwards, we returned to the sun and outside. I discovered that Simuel and his brother were not in school because the parents can't afford to send them.

Tuition is 500 Shillings per term, a pittance. There are three terms per year around $25 to $30 per year. I made a commitment to give them money for the boys' schooling. In return, their father made a commitment for the debt to me and vowed to use the money for school. I will be back when the wildebeest return in March to be certain and to give them money for the next year. In the meantime, they will begin school immediately and will advise me by letter on their progress. I have also committed to send the boys baseball caps, four, books for Simuel and a watch for Ester. Later, I watched in amazement as Maasai women beaded jewelry. What a job, picking the beads with the pattern in their mind's eye!

What an experience! We arrived at the air strip early and waited. Small planes have it all over the big jobs, with their compulsory, tidy air strips, departure times, and luggage problems. There, you drive right out to the plane, throw your bags onto it, check to see if you're on the list.

Then you climb on board, take a seat, and bumpity, bump, off you go, waving at the occasional elephant or giraffe who is seeing you off. Landing is pretty similar, reversed of course: Luggage is pulled off and put on a cart; you already know it's there, as you probably put it on board. Then it is dumped out in front of you and off you go. Breakables need not apply.

WEDNESDAY, SEPTEMBER 4, 1996

Nairobi, the teaming, bustling city. There is something I don't like about it. I don't like the hotel. David won't be meeting me at the airport after all. Business first and then some confusion about the Jewish Holidays. All cleared up now. He could come up over the weekend, Friday or Saturday maybe. I have so much to do what with wanting to do all the photos and such. I will be busy no matter what. I could use some closeness with him, however. I have missed him. I told him that I had a few little treasures for him. He said I was the only treasure he wanted!! That did feel good. We have a semi plan. I will go to Florida the 26th of September and stay with him. He will come up to NY for a day or so during the week before. I look forward to his arrival. Went to the home of Karen Blixen. I was astonished to find her to be quite an accomplished artist.

Then went to the Giraffe Center where one can feed them. They have very long tongues which they unroll as they sloppily take the bits of food. Talk about close, we were cheek to tongue close. It was fabulous. Then as quickly as saying the end, my African adventure was winding down . . . but not the end by any stretch. I wanted more and I would have more and so this was really just the beginning. The end of one chapter and the beginning of my lifetime.

THE REINVENTION OF CAPTAIN MARVEL

I was sixty years young when I decided to move to Africa, alone. This was not decided on a whim, but rather a sort of well-thought-out plan that went like this: I wanted to go on shorter safaris, more frequently, so I thought if I moved to Africa, I could do that for a year or so. In actuality, a few years earlier, I stood at the top of Victoria Falls, in Zimbabwe, and asked the Falls for an answer. What should I do and how could I do it? Then one morning in late 2001, I woke up in a state of excitement with the answer—I would move there for a year. It was crazy, outrageous, more than a bit dangerous, and out of the question. I had no idea how I would accomplish this feat, and it was nothing short of a feat. I had a house and three dogs, a mortgage, bills to pay, and what I was suggesting bordered on the rantings of the madwoman of Madagascar. But as the days went by, it began to seem reasonable, workable, even by my unreasonable standards.

So, in the dead of winter 2002, I closed my house in East Hampton, lugged twenty-one boxes of things I had to have and couldn't live without into a waiting car, shipped my three dogs, and off I went. But wait, I am getting a bit ahead of myself.

First, I had to decide where the hell in Africa I was going to land, and then where would I have my base of operations. At first glance, it seemed as if there were a lot of choices, but closer examination quickly made that a fantasy. Wars and starvation eliminated countries like Uganda, Sudan, and Ethiopia, even though I had met some amazing Ethiopian people in Israel several years before. Thoughts of my previous safaris chimed in to eliminate many of the cities I had been to, like Arusha, Tanzania; Nairobi, Mombasa, Kenya; and Johannesburg.

They just couldn't offer me any of the amenities that I needed and desired in a home base, like great sushi and theaters that showed movies in English. Days turned into weeks, and I was no closer to a decision.

Then, as I was throwing my hands up in the air in frustration, a friend of mine mentioned that she and her husband had spent a week in Cape Town, South Africa, and that it was beautiful. Enough said, decision made, Cape Town it was. An hour on my computer was all that it took. Plenty of sushi, American movies in English, plentiful Asian cuisine, and English spoken there. OMG, eureka! So, I went back onto my computer to begin a search for my "not forever" home, but rather my "one year now or never" home.

The decision to move halfway around the world to a place I had never even been to brought with it a tremendous amount of stress, as one might imagine. Most people never move across the country, some never move out of their city or state, much less halfway around the world. What was I doing?

To make this even more challenging, I was living in a gorgeous home in the Hamptons at the time. I had no plans to rent my home, even though rentals during the summer bring a substantial price. I wanted my bathroom to remain pristine, with only my bottom warming the toilet seat and my body being washed in my shower, hence no renters. With that decision I basically kissed off about $40,000 or more.

I really knew next to nothing about Cape Town, but at that moment all I cared about was being closer to Nairobi, where I knew Hagai, my guide, could easily pick me up. Cape Town would serve the purpose, and they had sushi, first-run movie theaters, and, as a bonus, a mall with all of the designer fashions. What could possibly go wrong? So, I jumped off the cliff, no net in sight, and just went for it. I don't think I really know any other way to tackle challenges. Of course, there were the naysayers, plenty of those who wondered out loud if I had not only lost my senses, but why

I would be going into a jungle with lions, and tigers, and bears ... oh no. I assured all of them that not only was I of sound mind, but that there were no tigers and bears in Africa. I doubt that assuaged their overall fears.

After a bit of intense searching online I managed to find a four-bedroom, three-bath guest house in a place called Somerset West, a stone's throw from downtown Cape Town. The internet described this luxury bed & breakfast as being fifteen minutes from Cape Town center, a little gem hidden away in this lovely city.

The bed & breakfast was owned by a French guy, "Xavier," who was about fifty, give or take a few years. Some of my well-meaning friends decided this was a great sign. This could be my person, my soulmate, if you will. They reasoned that I was traveling halfway around the world to meet him, not to go on safari. I guess this made them feel a bit better about my move.

I would quickly find out that he was definitely *not* my person. Xavier liked them young, very young, like high school. In fact, I learned quickly that he had been dating a girl young enough to be his granddaughter. While my friends had been wrong about that person, it would turn out that they were on point about me traveling halfway around the world to meet **my** person, my soulmate. I, of course, was in the dark about all of this so it remained their little fantasy.

I arrived on March 1, 2002, along with twenty-one boxes of "stuff," an idyllic view of my future in Cape Town, and a fully paid for monthlong safari that had me leaving May 15. My three fur babies had yet to arrive and would be coming by Air Animal in a few short weeks. Their first-class delivery was paid for by the boyfriend du jour, someone very wealthy and powerful I had been seeing for several years.

Xavier picked me up at the airport, unceremoniously dropped me off at the house, handed me the keys, and promptly left for his dinner or playdate, depending upon your perception. Initially, I padded around the house feeling a bit lost and very nervous. I must have said to myself, "What the hell did I do?" a hundred times over the next few hours.

I methodically checked out each room, cringing at times over the choice of furnishings. There was no question that I was going to have to make "some" changes if I was going to live there for a year. The smell of recently smoked pot hung over each room like a cloud, and I quickly opened the windows to fumigate.

Fortunately, the warm winds blew gently through the house and made it feel almost like home. A bong was carelessly tossed on a low table in what was the TV room. A moment of panic set in, followed by confusion, followed by me nearly falling over from exhaustion. I went to bed and promptly fell asleep.

The boys were still in New York with their sitters and were scheduled to be shipped over in about a week or so, depending upon Customs and the laws in South Africa that day. The rules around bringing animals into the country changed by the minute, so we all had to roll with the punches.

The bed & breakfast came equipped with a housekeeper who ended up, two years later, as "mother of the bride." She and her daughter were living in a second cottage on the property. Elizabeth was a dignified and extremely wise Xhosa woman whose only education was life. She eventually became mother of the bride, my second mother, and was, no doubt, sent by God.

For the first few days I rented a car to get around, and that was a mission from day one. Learning to drive on the right side of the car, and the left side of the road proved to be challenging, but after a few nicks and scrapes, I managed to get the hang of it. It didn't take long to realize how costly renting a car was and so shortly after my arrival I ended up buying a pre-owned BMW. I never understood why you drive on the right side of the car, but the left side of the road. One head-on collision later and I finally got it, but still didn't really **get** it.

My first weekend alone in the house proved to be an eventful one. Elizabeth had the weekend off and had gone to her home. I woke up early and padded down the hallway to find a kitchen counter alive with ants having a feast of strawberry jelly without toast. The kitchen door was wide open, and the so-called protective electric gates were as well. It was obvious that Xavier had made himself at home, even though for the next year this was my home. How dare he invade my space? I paid for one year for the entire house, not for a house without the kitchen. True, his cottage had no kitchen, but that was not my problem. That night, I double-locked the kitchen door.

Bright and early the next morning I woke up, padded down the hallway once again, this time to find that he had forced the kitchen window open and unlocked the door. The kitchen had become a war-zone resplendent with ants, who had by now taken up residence on the counter.

Talking about challenges, I had a major one in front of me and had absolutely no idea what I was going to do about it. Since Elizabeth was off that weekend, there was no one to talk to and nothing that could be done until Monday, and even then, what could she really do?

Three mornings and three entry attempts later, and I knew it was not going to stop unless I came up with a solution. There was no way I was just going to give in and give up and let him hijack the kitchen. Here I was, halfway around the world, alone in a foreign country, no friends, no family, nothing except a temporary Visa and hope. Even my dogs were in limbo and had yet to arrive. What had I done and what was I going to do about it? I had the better part of sixty days to do something positive, because I was leaving for a month on safari on May 15 and that was not going to be changed. I was a rule breaker, a risk-taker, an adventurer, and someone who knew danger firsthand and still carried on.

I was awake night after night thinking about what to do. My fur babies arrived, severely impacted by their around-the-world plane rides, so I needed to attend to them before doing anything else. One morning, after about two weeks of hell, I woke up and wondered what it might cost to buy a home there. This was truly an "outside the box" thought. I dared not mention this madness to anyone, lest they decide I should be institutionalized.

I was already entangled in Elizabeth's life and watched her crying her eyes out day after day, all while her skin seemed to be turning gray.

"Don't cry, please, don't cry. I don't know how I am going to fix this, but I will fix it." Months later, I did.

The following week I called a broker regarding a home I had seen in the papers that day. It was a large, Spanish-style house in a suburb of Cape Town. Truthfully, I had no idea why I wanted to look at homes. I think I was just trying to find a solution to the problem before me. My house-hunting criteria was simple, with only one rule: if I had guests, I wanted to look for them. Thankfully, the broker got it.

The very first house I saw literally blew me away. It had been built by an Italian princess years earlier and was very grand, 8,500 square feet on an acre of grounds resplendent with high, ornate ceilings and oversized rooms. There were elegant iron gates surrounding the majestic two-story property. Inside were four large bedrooms, six bathrooms, two living rooms, two dining rooms, a gym, the must-have bar, family room, den, a gardener's toilet outside, and a lovely cottage that needed some work and which in my mind was for Elizabeth and her daughter.

It was to be a formidable task for sure, but it was too late, as I had already fallen in love with the house. I went to bed that night at what I now called the house of horrors in Somerset West, mentally decorating and redesigning my new home. The first step was to be new bathrooms.

By morning, I had rationalized the insanity of all of this and decided that my very first step would be to buy it! Shocking, insane in many ways, practical in others, totally crazy overall. The idea was, I suppose, a dollop of crazy, a scoop of total insanity, topped off with a shovel of madness. The perfect combination! To add a bit more foolishness, I had no idea how I would manage this nearly impossible feat financially.

To begin with, I couldn't buy anything, not even a dollhouse, without first selling my home in the Hamptons, which, unfortunately for me and my plans, was not for sale. But the truth was, a little issue like that had never stopped me from plunging right in, or jumping right off the proverbial cliff, so sanity went out the window. Two days later, with little thought about the how and more thought about the fact that I wanted this house, I met with the broker, made a full price offer, with contingencies, and returned to the house of horrors hyperventilating.

For starters, I wanted a longer closing date so that I could figure out how I was going to close at all. Time was ticking by as the safari date edged closer. Some might think, how fortunate I was when the sellers came back with a counteroffer that included renting the property back from me starting on the closing date. That was not something that I had in mind and clearly it didn't work. I have always believed that there is a solution to every problem, and now I had a problem to solve. I have always been a type A personality, sometimes on steroids. Like it or not, I have also always been an immediate gratification person, so I give you the money, you give me the keys, end of story.

It hardly mattered at all that we were halfway around the world in Cape Town, South Africa. A deal was a deal, and I just needed to have a better understanding of their needs.

There had to be a reason why they wanted to rent the house back for three months, so I needed to find out what that was. I discovered that several deals involving foreign buyers for the purchase of their home had fallen apart. So, they wanted assurance that this was a done deal, no exceptions, no changes, no backing out, so that they could buy another home. If I wanted this house, I had to make that happen. I had to create a miracle, from halfway around the world! No pressure!

I knew about focusing on what you want, manifesting it, if you will. I had done it before numerous times. The bottom line was that I wanted the house, and I was going to get the house, end of story. I relied on something that I have always believed in: that there *is* a solution for every problem. Sometimes one just has to look outside the box to find it. My solution was to look outside the box, find the solution, and get the house. That would be one hurdle, selling my house was another, and I was definitely putting the cart before the horse, so to speak.

At the end of March 2002, about a month after I arrived, I met with the seller's attorney and made a somewhat crazy suggestion.

I would put all the money for the purchase of the home into the lawyer's trust account by April 30, 2002. However, the sellers could not touch any part of it until closing, which would be either May 29 or June 29, their choice. At that point, they would get the money and I would get the keys. It all seemed pretty simple at least to me; however, this half-assed solution didn't address how I was going to put together the required amount of money for the lawyer's trust account in the first place. My house wasn't on the market.

I had absolutely no idea how I was going to accomplish the feat; however, I believed there was a solution to that problem too, I just had to find it and had roughly twenty-five days to do it.

A few things I knew for sure. I was sixty years young, alone in a totally strange country halfway around the world, and was leaving on safari in Kenya, Tanzania, and Zimbabwe for a month on May 15. I had also fallen in love with this home, put up a $25,000 deposit on it using my credit card, and was determined to make it mine, no matter what the challenges were. I think that was really representative of what my life had become. I never said that I couldn't do something, anything, no matter what it was. I always took things to the limit, until it was absolutely 100 percent certain that I could or couldn't do something. The caveat was that I usually ended up doing all of those "somethings."

I have always been of the mind that if you want something, you can have it, you just need to want it enough and focus. You are always in charge of your own destiny. At the end of the day I believed in myself, and that was my ticket to overcoming any challenges that might be thrown my way.

Sadly, most people are too fearful to follow their dreams or desires and just trudge along in a rather tedious way, day after agonizing day. They stay close to what they know, rarely venturing out of their comfort zone. They live with or right around the block from family and their friends date back as far as grade school. They work at the same job or company year after year, never risking, because it is safe and secure. Those are their watchwords because any other course puts them in jeopardy. Because of that it is a given that their lives end up tucked carefully into a very narrow, risk-free world. Fear is the word that hangs over many people's lives like a dark cloud.

On the other hand, I never let anything or anyone stop me from doing what I want. I have a rule that goes this way: If something is broken, and you can't fix it, NEXT! Just move on! That goes for relationships that are broken, marriages, and the like. If you can't fix it for whatever reason, NEXT, move on.

I was married and divorced three times and when things stopped working, I tried to fix it, and when that failed, I left. *Life is too short to stay if you're not getting what you need. I have always felt that if I was not happy, how could I make anyone else happy.*

One can always find an excuse to stay. There are a million of them: kids, money, religion, comfort. But not for me. Over the years of being married, I endured plenty of fighting and arguing and quickly learned there was no reward in that, only pain and sleepless nights. I had long since vowed that my next relationship, should there ever be one, would be a loving one infused with trust and appreciation. It would truly be a synergistic relationship, a "feel good" place filled with trust, admiration, and appreciation. By this time in my life, I had very few regrets at all and a rabid determination to ensure that my future would be filled with positive experiences.

As I sat in the Horror House that night, thinking about life and people, I recalled my relationship with David. He had been a dominant force in my life for years. He had been separated with a wife and small child when we met. From the very beginning of our relationship, there was tension between him and his wife, who pulled him back to her side frequently for the most frivolous reasons. They were back and forth, up and down, like a proverbial roller-coaster ride without an end. This back-and-forth, almost game-like relationship continued for years, and still continues today.

Over the years, the intimacy of our relationship ensured that we would keep in touch. The truth of it is that we maintain that close friendship born out of our feelings for each other that endured many challenges over the years. I often wondered if he and his wife would ever come to the realization that there were a boatload of issues in their relationship. I often wondered if the time would come when they would become tired of the emotional and physical distance that existed between them and long for a love that comes with a relationship of trust, love, and appreciation.

How long was it going to take them to realize that they deserved to have happiness, not anger and upset? Maybe never, I reasoned. This is what we as humans do when we fail to exercise our right to be happy, our right to be selfish, our right to live our lives, as our lives, and not as someone else's life. For sure, you get no points for suffering fools, and I wasn't going to be remembered for staying in a situation that made me miserable.

After careful thought and consideration, I reasoned that if I wanted to change things, any things, then I needed to just do it, jump off, jump over, jump around, but just JUMP, dammit. It didn't really matter what the situation was. I said to myself, just stop bitching and start doing, jump the hell off.

So, that was my thought process when I made the offer on this enormous home in Africa. I wanted it badly, but I had no idea how I was going to accomplish the purchase. I had no one to answer to in any manner; I didn't need an approval, except from the bank, and I didn't need anyone in my life to make me complete. I was already complete.

I took a cash advance of $25,000 from my credit card and promptly put it in the trust account at their lawyer's office. I was off and running, somewhere. There was no turning back at that point, and my downside, if it didn't work, was a bit of a challenge. Then I called my dear friend who was a real estate broker in the Hamptons and told him I wanted to put my house on the market.

Once that was done, I called my bank in the Hamptons and told the manager, who I knew, that I needed $100,000 quickly and short term. She authorized a drive-by on my home, and after the requisite amount of paperwork was completed, the bank wired the money to me for a period of six months. That relieved some of the pressure, but not all by a longshot.

The $100,000 transformed into 1,000,000 South African rand, which I put into my bank account in Cape Town. I had just bought myself a bit of time. I had to close the property in May or June, and thought that would be a "piece of cake." Sadly, it was anything but, however, that was the trick my mind played on me. The sellers accepted my new terms and chose June 20 as a closing date. There was only one other small hiccup, which was that I was leaving for a monthlong safari in Zimbabwe, Kenya, and Tanzania on May 15, returning June 16. Did I say small hiccup? In the middle of the madness, I had also made tentative plans to leave for New York on July 5, so I could pack up the house and ship my furniture to South Africa and my new home. One other little wrinkle was that as a type A personality I had to have everything done yesterday, so I began ordering materials for the renovation of my soon-to-be new home. Limestone flooring, toilets, sinks, granite, and other assorted design items to make my home truly mine. What could go wrong with this well-organized plan? Nothing and everything! You know what they say about the best laid plans? I think it says "The best laid plans of mice and men often go awry!"

I am sure that many people would be hyperventilating right about now or on the verge of a total breakdown, wondering how I could take on so much, with so little in the bag, but I was and still am of the mind that you just go forward, until you are stopped . . . if you are. You just keep on keeping on.

Never saying never . . . just move forward with your plan. This home was being renovated by an American princess following in the steps of an Italian one.

I willfully ignored the fact that I had miles to go before I could lay claim to my new home and one very long mile was selling my house in the Hamptons. Still, I focused on the end result of what I wanted: the house built by an Italian princess.

I had bathrooms to redo, cabinets to have built, walls to demolish, showers to install, a bathroom to completely rip apart and others to simply renovate (five of them), a cottage to rebuild, floors and walls to cover with granite and limestone, a stainless structure to go around the granite bar top I was designing, granite counters to design and have built, fireplaces to design and have built. There was also the matter of plumbers, electricians, alarm company, tile installations, and painters. I had one hell of a lot on my proverbial plate but plodded ahead, impervious to any outside interference, like the Reserve Bank.

This story wouldn't be complete without adding a little more insanity that is my life. In the midst of all this chaos, I decided to start a little business in Africa. I would teach the Xhosa women how to make beautiful, beaded cellphone bags. They were creative, talented, and needed the money, so what could go wrong with this plan? A hell of a lot. I started a workshop in Browns Farm, one of the townships, and within a very short time had dozens of girls working making beaded bags, most of which I still own. I don't live in fear, but the townships are very dangerous, and many young African men stroll around armed with AK-47s and think nothing of taking a life for a few rand. One day in particular I was taking cash for wages to the girls, which meant venturing into the township by myself, something I did regularly.

I had located a second workshop so I could add more girls and wanted to show some of them where it was located, so I picked up three of my best workers and drove a few short blocks to the space. I had already paid all the girls and so on my way back to the workshop I decided to drop them off across the street rather than drive up to the space. That decision turned out to be one of the best I have ever made. The following day the girls shared their story of fear with me. When they returned, several armed thugs were there waiting to take their wages then kidnap me and take my car. From that day forward, I never went inside the township without having one of the girls meet me outside. Eventually I provided work for nearly 150 young women and hopefully changed the lives of a number of people in the process. Now it seems the cellphones are far too big to fit in my beautiful beaded bags.

By April 25, my mom's birthday as it happened, were she still with us . . . I thought I had everything in place, but I was so wrong. Africa has something called exchange controls. They should have been eliminated after apartheid; however, they remain to this day. What this means is that you cannot take money out of the country, or bring it in, without the approval of the Reserve Bank. Bringing money in is a hell of a lot easier than taking it out, as I was to find out years later. When I made the offer, I contacted a local bank to loan me the money, but I had to get approval from the Reserve Bank. I was not a permanent resident then but nothing was said and the local ABSA bank moved ahead.

I was a neophyte about all of this, knowing nothing about moving money in or out of a country. I was, after all, an American and used to just taking my money when I wanted to and leaving the country on business or pleasure, or whatever. I didn't have to report anything to anyone, as long as it was less than $10,000.

Now, the idea of a Big Brother peering over my shoulder, telling me what I could or could not remove was totally alien to me. Imagine my shock when five days before the drop-dead date for the accepted offer, when all the money for the sale needed to be in the lawyer's trust account, the Reserve Bank announced they would only approve a 50 percent loan and not the 80 percent I was expecting. So sorry, they lamented, I was not a permanent resident and therefore they could not approve 80 percent. Why the hell they hadn't said something a month earlier was a mystery, but nonetheless there was nothing I could do but accept it and find a solution fast. I felt like I was free-falling from a failed sky dive. My wings had been clipped, and I was over the Atlantic Ocean. Initially, I spiraled out of control, asking questions of the Universe. I was wondering how in the world I would close the deal with only five days left and 30 percent short of money for either the house or the needed renovations. I crash landed into a wall over the following twenty-four hours before I picked myself up, brushed myself off, jumped off the cliff, and had an "outside the box" idea.

There is a solution to every problem, I mused, so I just needed to find one, quickly. The two constants in my corner were the bank and my love of the house.

So, I had some intelligent conversation with the bank, dazzled them with a bit of fancy footwork, and the bank agreed to an unusual but workable deal. They agreed to match every dollar that I had brought into the country since day one with loan money.

So literally every dollar that I had brought in since my arrival in March would be matched by the bank, including the $100,000 from my bank in the Hamptons.

Like I said many times before, there is a solution to every problem, one just needs to step back and find it. Think outside the box; it works every single time. On April 30, 2002, the entire amount needed for the purchase of my home landed in the lawyer's trust account. The deal was done, and I needed a big freaking drink.

So, it was on a high note that on May 15 I boarded a plane bound for Zimbabwe, for the first leg of my monthlong safari.

It would not be a fair representation of my time in Africa without discussing this safari experience. After all, I moved to South Africa to go on shorter safaris, more frequently. Even though I had finalized the deal for my new home, the bed & breakfast house of horrors was still a disaster. Here I was going away for a month, and I had to make absolutely certain that Xavier was not going to use the main house as his own personal party pad.

My three fur babies had arrived, and since Xavier was prone to leaving doors and electric gates open and having parties with very young people in attendance, how could I protect them? I couldn't and clearly needed someone to stay at the house while I was on safari, since Elizabeth would have no say at all after I left.

Sadly, the only person I could think of who didn't work was an ex-boyfriend, part-time gigolo, conman, and ex-con who I will call "Eric." Our relationship had been a rocky one at best and, for nearly a decade, slipped in and out of what I would now term emotionally abusive.

He was tall and good-looking, with great hair, but his shortcomings overwhelmed his good looks. He was permanently unemployed, on disability, and living in a small apartment in Florida that previously belonged to his parents and had been left to him when they passed.

He might have made a great gigolo were he not so demanding and manipulative, offering so little to any relationship. But for me, during that particular time and in the situation I was in, I reasoned, I could make this work. I thought that under the right set of circumstances, he would come to Cape Town, take care of my fur babies, and I would support him for a few months. In my mind, it was a vacation with pay to a place he had never been. I struggled for weeks with this dilemma, throwing out the options repeatedly to friends—Option One: safari and Eric coming complete with an overwhelming dose of drama, or Option Two: losing my $25,000 payment for the safari, but not having Eric and his drama in my space. For most of my knowledgeable friends, it wasn't a difficult choice. They were all leaning toward losing the $25,000 and the safari, rather than inviting this person back into my life again.

At the end of the day, for better or worse, I made my decision and placed a call to Eric in Florida. He was, as expected, pleased to hear from me because in his mind our relationship was for eternity and we were going to be together in wheelchairs.

He was wrong in his assessment, but I doubt he ever gave that idea up. I laid out my proposal, essentially a six-month paid holiday in South Africa, plus a small amount of money each month to pay his bills. A few more incidental negotiations and the deal was done. Several weeks later he arrived with only a modicum of expected drama. In truth, for me the real drama had just begun, but I didn't know it yet.

At that time, I had only one thought in my mind. I needed my dogs taken care of by someone I could at least trust. They were my family, and I loved them so much. I had to do whatever was necessary to ensure that Xavier would not come into the house and party with his teenage friends, putting my babies in jeopardy in the process. Their security was essential, and I was 100 percent certain that Eric would take care of things. He was an imposing figure and had a rough-and-tumble past with a stint in prison, so no one would challenge his presence. I felt safe and comfortable in my decision, at least in the beginning. As time went on, I questioned everything.

I embraced the situation with Eric on all levels, except emotionally. On that level, I held my ground and kept my feelings in check, or at least I tried to. I was not going to get emotionally caught up with this man ever again. It was far too dangerous for my health and well-being. I could be sexual with him but not intimate, as I knew that would be my downfall. I had already decided when I moved, I was not going to get involved with anyone in Africa, for a number of reasons, not the least of which were the emotions that normally accompany a sexually charged relationship.

So, both were out of bounds for me. I knew, however, that Eric could be my ticket to physical satisfaction, without any emotional entanglements. At least that was my intention. There's an old saying: "The road to hell is paved with good intentions," and I had placed myself on that road and was heading to hell, even though I didn't realize it at that moment. Getting Eric to Cape Town proved to be far easier than sending him home.

It was to be two years, two return trips, and a dramatic, Oscar-worthy exit from Panama before he was finally out of my life. Even then he made a few brief but memorable curtain calls, even after I married Paul.

On the positive side, however, the safari was actually fabulous, and I enjoyed every moment of it before returning home to the house of horrors, Eric, and the renovations. But once again, I am getting ahead of myself.

I was counting down the days before I could move out of the bed & breakfast and into my new and completely renovated home. I had my head in the clouds and was ill-prepared for the drama that lay before me.

CAPTAIN MARVEL STRIKES AGAIN

Safari day, May 15, arrived with a hug and a kiss as I unceremoniously left for my month in the bush, with Eric standing guard over the boys. I arrived in Zimbabwe with my soft safari luggage and a new shortwave radio complete with antennae, that I had purchased for Hagai's new vehicle. I was well aware of the problems in Zimbabwe under the ruthless rule of Robert Mugabe, but nothing could have prepared me for this trip. Over the years, I had seen various critical businesses disappear in Victoria Falls, which was a major tourist destination. Obviously, I found that very worrying, but on this trip, I was greeted at the airport by Zimbabwean police. They pummeled me with questions: Was I a journalist, a reporter? Why did I have this shortwave radio and antennae? What was I planning to do? They thought I had plans to broadcast the desperate conditions in Zimbabwe to the world, which of course was the furthest thing from my mind. I answered with honesty and candor, and their response was to seize my radio and antennae with the promise to return both upon my departure.

I argued vehemently, without reasonable results, until the manager of the private lodge where I was staying interceded and guided me to the car with words of caution. This was a dangerous situation I was in and yet, I had no idea how dangerous it really was. Over the next five days I was to discover just how strong Mugabe's hold was on the people and the direction the country was spiraling into, and it was not a good one.

Five days later, and ready to depart, I finally tracked down the shortwave radio and antennae. I boarded a flight headed for Harare and then on to Dar es Salaam in Tanzania and the beginning of what was to be yet another nightmare. I stayed overnight in a hotel in Harare, then took the morning flight to Dar es Salaam. My plans included an overnight stay in Dar es Salaam and an early-morning flight to Mount Kilimanjaro, where Hagai was to pick me up.

Our plans had been well thought out and structured without room for error or delays. Safari plans need to be handled that way, with one going from location to location on specific days. Then there are the lodges and private campsites to contend with. I had a private campsite, one of only a few in the Serengeti with a team and utility vehicle, so they could set everything up while I was enjoying several days in the Ngorongoro Crater. My only task was to show up on time at the right place in another country. No big deal, right? You know that old adage about "best laid plans."

I woke up at four in the morning to catch my 7:00 a.m. puddle jumper flight from Dar es Salaam to Kilimanjaro. I dressed quickly, checked out of the hotel, and made my way to the airport. Upon arrival I was informed that the flight was not going to be taking off until Saturday, two days later. My head nearly exploded with the news. My mind was bouncing around like a ball being smacked back and forth by two tennis pros. Being late was out of the question since every part of this trip was carefully planned. There was no margin for error, no delays, end of story. A solution was in order, and I needed to get outside the box and fast—however, whatever, I desperately needed an alternate plan.

I didn't even have Hagai's number with me, which presented a problem. I was already salivating about my planned dinner at Gibbs Farm in Tanzania that night, but there were no flights out to Mount Kilimanjaro until Saturday, and this was only Thursday morning. Frustrated, anguished, angry, and a bit pissed off, I climbed into a taxi and went back to the hotel that I had just checked out of.

I went to the manager and used the phone to call the house in Cape Town and guided Elizabeth, my trusted and loving housekeeper, confidante and mother in charge, about where to find Hagai's phone number.

I called him to say that I was delayed and would get back to him once I had a plan, which needed to be quick. There was no way I could fly out Saturday and still make my safari plans on time, and I had no intention of not making them. I took a deep breath and started thinking outside the box. It was then that I had another idea. A solution to my problem, if you will.

Since I couldn't fly and make it on time, I would drive to Arusha, actually be driven! I succeeded in getting the hotel manager to find a local car service that would drive me to Arusha, the capital of Tanzania. A few small negotiations later and I hired them for the princely sum of $500 USD, which of course I didn't really have in cash. Another challenge!

I phoned Hagai and told him to pick me up that evening around 6:00 p.m. It would take the better part of eleven hours to drive there from Dar es Salaam. That versus a short hop on the plane seemed like a crazy compromise, but at that point it was the **only** way to keep my trip on schedule. Within an hour, two African men arrived at the hotel to pick me up. The only problem was I didn't have $500 in cash, or any traveler's checks. The trip had already been completely paid for in advance, so I had no need to carry cash.

I had credit cards, but the company refused to accept one for payment. American Express was the only answer. Thank God, for some unknown reason, I had my checkbook with me, so I found an American Express office in town, wrote them a check for the $500 and, cash in hand, off we went.

Incredibly, looking back, I took off into the unknown, with two totally strange men, in a country that I barely knew, from a city that I had never been to, to meet Hagai eleven hours away for dinner. Today it sounds completely insane even to me, and one might ask, what was I thinking?

To that question, I would say this: I was thinking that I had paid $25,000 for this safari, and I was going to relish every single moment of it, regardless. The idea of being fearful and not fearless never occurred to me. I was going on this safari. It was up to me to figure out how I would do it, and this seemed like a good solution. In fact, it was the only one.

On some level, I reasoned that the hotel had arranged for the car service, and I trusted them to use a reputable company. The fearless side of me determined that I wouldn't be kidnapped and sold into white slavery or meet another unseemly end.

As it turned out, the drive was interesting but uneventful, which was a good thing. It was plagued by long bouts of silence and both men incessantly puffing cigarette smoke out the window. My two companions were relatively harmless, spoke little English, and we arrived at our destination around 8:00 p.m., some twelve hours later, in near total darkness. Gibbs Farm, and my dinner destination, was another two hours away over winding, treacherous roads, but I was adamant that I was going to dine there that night, regardless.

Hagai phoned ahead and said we were on our way and asked them to hold the kitchen open, and of course they complied. The meal, like most things in life, turned out to be better in my dreams than in reality and not worth all the effort to get there, especially at that hour. Another clear case of fantasy versus reality.

In hindsight, it would have been far better to have just eaten in Arusha and taken our time getting to Gibbs Farm. But it is what it is, and that is an experience. After dinner, I settled into my charming three little pigs thatched-roof cottage and went to sleep with a full stomach and a smile on my face. I had found a solution and I was on time for my adventure. Early the next morning we left our little pigs round accommodations and began our drive to the infamous Ngorongoro Crater in Tanzania.

The crater, which was formed when a large volcano erupted and collapsed upon itself, is quite an amazing place as it boasts all four seasons on its floor and hosts an incredible array of wildlife. Most species are represented there, save for the giraffe and crocodile, which mainly stay around the top of the crater. There are also a few hundred elephants that manage to make their way down to the floor of the crater.

Once I was safely at Gibbs Farm, I reflected on the fact that I had taken a situation that seemed hopeless and managed to get exactly what I wanted. I silently congratulated myself on a job well done. This was a major challenge and one with severe time constraints, and I jumped off, went outside the box, and made it work. I wondered why everyone didn't follow that thought pattern.

There was only one problem and that turned out to be the shortwave radio and antennae, which had failed to arrive with me at the airport in Dar es Salaam that morning, so we had no real communication. But Hagai, being a very inventive Maasai, used wire and managed in some strange way to contact his office while we were in the bush. It worked, and he was able to retrieve the radio and antennae after our safari was finished. Even with the bumps in the road and challenges to overcome, it was an incredible success. A month later, I returned to the drama of Cape Town, my beloved fur babies all intact, to Elizabeth, who had stopped crying, and to the nightmare of a relationship that had long since died and been buried but had since risen like a phoenix from the ashes. It was totally my doing and I silently accepted the blame. The boys were fine and Eric had served his purpose, so now I just needed to bite the bullet for another few months until he went back to Florida.

In my mind, there was no relationship; however, that was in my mind and not Eric's. He had already begun making plans that included Africa and me. Clearly, we were not in the same place, at the same time, and that would prove to be quite challenging, as there were five more grueling, drama-filled months left in our negotiated deal.

It was the evening of June 16, 2002, when I landed back in Cape Town, not quite ready to face the challenges that lay before me. The closing of my new home was nine days away, June 25, and on July 5, I was leaving for the states to pack up the as-yet-unsold Hamptons house, totally alone and without any assistance. That would be the last time I saw my beloved home from the inside. Exhausted and in need of a proper shower, my own lovely soaps, and a hairdresser, I arrived in Cape Town, taking one step at a time to meet my commitments and the upcoming drama.

Eric met me at the airport and, admittedly, it was nice to see a friendly and well-known face after a month in the bush. I quickly realized that I was going to need him for more than just a pet sitter and occasional sex partner. He was going to have to shepherd the slew of contractors that were about to converge at the new house. I was going to be gone for a month again to the Hamptons, and I didn't want the renovations to be at a standstill. Overwhelmed as I was with commitments and excitement, it hardly occurred to me that I had yet to sell my house in East Hampton.

Looking back, I don't suppose the seriousness of my situation really hit home because in my heart of hearts I "knew" that I had six months to repay the $100,000 to my bank in the Hamptons and that my house there would surely sell within that time. But then, what if it didn't? What the hell was I going to do then? Jump off, jump over, jump around, or just jump! It was a risky move at best!

My thoughts might have needed an overhaul because there they were in living color, but above all they were mine and I wasn't going to deny them.

And so it began, the renovations from hell, all while I was out of the country once again. Before I left, I was wise enough to demolish any walls that were on my list, write directions of what to do on others, have the replacement toilets, tubs, limestone, granite, glass doors, and other accoutrements sitting in the right rooms, which left little margin for error. I was, to say the least, prepared for most eventualities, and at the end of the day, the renovations were amazing and the house that luck built ended up looking incredible.

I returned from the Hamptons to Cape Town, August 7, 2002, after leaving almost all of my possessions on a truck that was bound for a ship that would be headed for Cape Town. On top of that I had left Eric in charge of renovations for my new home, which made him think our relationship was something that it wasn't. Once home I turned over a paint can, my seat of choice, and took over as commander in chief, Renovation Central. Eric, as always, struggled to stay in power, and so began the drama that would last until after I had met and married my fourth husband, Paul.

There was no doubt that Eric and I were in different, opposing places at the same time. I wanted to keep the relationship at arm's length, and he wanted to reel me back in so that I would continue to sponsor him, which in gigolo speak means support him.

There was a near daily struggle for control as Eric continued to marginalize and demean me. He used my age as a weapon of destruction, continuously noting that I was not eighteen any longer and couldn't do much of anything correctly, including squeezing orange juice to his liking.

I counted the days that were left in my "contract" with him, drank a bottle of wine each evening, and silently cried a lot. Men like Eric are nothing if not great manipulators, and he still managed to make me feel as if I had not really given 100 percent to him, even though he had "sacrificed" his life for me. There was even a time when I started to believe that he was right and that I was wrong, and "if only" I had approached this move of his differently, things might have worked out.

Nearly six months to the day, his clock ran out and he left for Florida. I was left guilt-ridden and wondering if he was right and that it was my fault that things didn't work out. My insane solution was to bring him back months later so that we could go to therapy and see what might be worked out! After the fact, two words came to mind: big mistake! Looking back, there are more words, like insane, stupid, ridiculous, and crazy, as well as abusive, violent, and manipulative.

Of course, therapy failed to resurrect our relationship, and Eric made an early departure, well before the additional six months we had discussed. I was relieved because the drama was weighing heavily on me. The next time I would see him was in Panama, in early February 2004, where I was taking a break with Greg, his girlfriend, and their baby, my grandson. Once again, I was the proverbial fool who thought we could mend some fences and at the very least be friends. That meeting and any mending was short-lived and proved to be the final nail in a coffin that should have been underground years before. It was during that trip to Panama that I reevaluated my life and decided that I was ready for a "real relationship with a grownup." The optimum word in my request to the Universe being grownup. I had entertained the antics of an immature, abusive person far too long.

Months later Eric repeatedly tried to reach out to me via email and social media. His errant behavior continued even after Paul and I met, and I had to constantly be on the "lookout" for him, hidden behind some nom de plume on Facebook as he tried in vain to make his way back into my life.

Looking back, my first mistake was thinking I could keep him at arm's length while he helped with my fur babies. Abusers know your vulnerabilities and they use them to manipulate and control you. Instinctively I knew that, but my desire to go on safari took precedent over my better judgment. For a time, the drama knew no boundaries, and I struggled to stay upright in the storm.

FROM OUT OF THE ASHES

The date was March 21, 2004. I had returned from Panama a few weeks earlier embraced by a wave of happiness after standing outside in the crisp air and declaring into the silence of the Universe, "I am ready for a real relationship with a grown up." Eric was **finally** gone, at least in theory, and I was feeling optimistic about life and the future in general. After all, I had been alone after my last divorce for more than twenty years. I have always believed that it is difficult, if not impossible, to declare something out loud that you don't truly believe or desire. There is something within us that stops us from lying out loud to the Universe. We can whisper but not make a declaration of intention.

Magically, almost one month to the day after I made my declaration in Panama, I met that grownup online in Cape Town, South Africa, and the rest was history, or at least history in the making. There are not many people who would have done what I did, move alone to a strange country where I knew no one, but I have always been nothing if not adventurous.

The idea of a life not lived to the fullest isn't a life lived, and so many people fail at living. Couples stay married or just stay together in the most unusual of relationships. Some don't even live together; others exist where one or both people have been having affairs. Sadly, they fail themselves and each other because they don't have the courage to say it's over, we must move on and make new lives for ourselves. It has become commonplace enough that it is ludicrous. I know many couples living the lie, and I have always been determined never to be one of them.

Consequently, moving, jumping off, jumping over, jumping around, living, and experiencing was always on the front burner for me. The relationship issue had always been a troubling one, although it might not seem the case, having been married and divorced three times. I always have been a very strong-willed, independent person, and my former husbands, while acknowledging my independence when we were dating, changed their tunes immediately once we married and wanted control. Clearly, that didn't work out very well, at least with the first three husbands. And the twenty-plus years after those divorces being on my own were honestly amazing years.

I had relationships and affairs that were emotional, and ones that were not, and I learned a lot about who I was and what I wanted in the process. It was truly an incredible growing experience that helped make me who I am today.

In the months leading up to my declaration to the Universe, I reached out to meet some men on the East Coast of the United States, with the idea that I was returning to the states in 2004. Originally when I made this move to South Africa, it was only for a year but clearly that changed, and I was now into year two and ready to return home. I had unearthed two potential men online but failed by choice to mention that I was living in Africa, for fear it would turn them off. I even had an imaginary conversation with how I might handle dating requests from either of them. It went something like this:

> *"Let's get together for drinks, tomorrow night."*
>
> *"Tomorrow isn't really good for me as I have a meeting."*
>
> *"How about next Saturday night for dinner?"*
>
> *"I'm going to be out of town for about two weeks, but once I get back that would be fantastic."*

I figured I could stall things for a little while anyway, but if they knew I was halfway around the world from the get-go, that would be an automatic NEXT.

I pondered on my telling the truth as well:

> "Let's get together for drinks tomorrow night."

> "Sorry, but it's a twenty-five-hour flight from Africa to the East Coast. How about a rain check?"

I knew that I couldn't make the move back to the states immediately, which brought me to the moment that changed my life. I had a number of couples as friends and a somewhat full social life on my own. With Eric out of the picture for good, I knew that I needed someone to round out my dinner parties. I made the decision to go online and find someone who was interesting and available as a friend. I chose Match.com, and after nearly wearing my fingers to the bone searching profiles, I found a guy who looked interesting. His online name was Butterfly Paul.

He was, to say the least, very good-looking, British, and was working in the townships with the Zulu tribal men. His camera skills bordered on nonexistent, as his picture was posted sideways, and he was shoulder-to-shoulder with a gorgeous blonde. Not the best way to attract women for sure. I was intrigued enough to reach out. The blonde mattered little to me, since I was only looking for a dinner partner and nothing more. I reached out with some imaginative wording like "Princess Searching For Her Prince Charming" and waited.

It wasn't long before he contacted me and, as it turned out, we had some things in common. I was also working in the Townships with the Xhosa women, and Paul was working in different townships with the Zulu tribal people. I was teaching them how to make beaded cellphone bags to sell in the open markets, and he had his team making beautiful, handcrafted butterflies and dragonflies. Over the next week or so we texted back and forth, then made a date to meet at a bookstore in downtown Cape Town.

When that night finally arrived, I was a bit nervous and a little skeptical, and as I was leaving home I told Elizabeth that I wouldn't be late. That turned out to be the biggest miscalculation of all time.

Paul arrived at the bookstore looking ruggedly handsome in a black leather jacket that hugged him like a glove. He was trim, in great shape, and movie star hot! I watched, salivating a bit over his sensuous body, as he made his way to where I was standing.

The bookstore coffee shop was filled with people, and he recommended heading upstairs to have some dinner. Our gazes never broke as we made our way up to the Italian restaurant that was tucked inside the local mall. We were glued together, as if we had known each other for decades. Dinner came and dissolved quickly into our mouths, and somehow, we completely lost track of time. The waiters began putting the chairs on top of the tables in an effort to get us up and out. We finally got the message as the lights flickered on and off. So much for being home early!

The next night I hosted a dinner party for a group of friends and was going on about my blind date from the previous evening when one of my friends announced, "I know him. I bought my business from his former business partner."

"Seriously? I can't believe it. So, come on, what's the story?" I queried.

"He's a good guy and I liked him. More than that I really don't know."

That morning Paul sent me a short email expressing how much he had enjoyed our date and that we should get together again soon. I couldn't remember having such a wonderful night and so I replied that I would love that.

I had already written two books on relationships, and I knew the rules about dating well enough to pass them on to others. Rule One: don't have anyone pick you up at your home until you know them.

That did not mean after the first date for sure. However, after my friend's testimonial, I decided that I could bend that rule a little.

The following day, I emailed Paul and told him we had mutual friends. It was then that we made a plan to get together with them the following weekend, a double date.

In what could be classified as very British he texted me.
Paul: Can I collect you?

In Brit speak this means, can I pick you up.

Me: Of course, that would be fine.

Right, wrong, or indifferent, the double date became a twosome when our friends canceled a few days later. I wasn't bothered at the time. The fact that my hairdresser knew him made me feel comfortable enough to bend my rules.

He "collected" me, but before we went out, I wanted to show him around my new home. I had even redone the cottage on the property for Elizabeth and her daughter. It was now resplendent with marble floors, a corner tub in the bathroom, and a lovely small entry hall with a leaded-glass window.

After showing Paul around the main house, our final stop on the tour was Elizabeth's cottage. Her mother Emma was visiting from the Eastern Cape. She had arrived the day before, after a grueling twenty-four-hour bus trip with chickens and goats joining the passengers. Emma didn't speak any English, she chewed tobacco, carried water on her head (until I got her a water tank), and bootlegged electricity. The cottage was one room and a bathroom but designed and renovated beautifully, as I had even added an entry hall onto the cottage. As we were stepping out into the courtyard ready to head to dinner, Paul turned to Emma and put his hand on her shoulder. "I want to thank you for showing me your home and I hope I didn't intrude."

I leaned back against the entry wall silently overcome with emotions. That was amazing! He treated her with such dignity and respect, a woman without education and one who didn't even speak a word of English. I was blown away, and that moment never left the forefront of my mind. I thought how sad it was that he didn't want a relationship. Fortunately for both of us, that turned out to be open for discussion. Today, Paul treats everyone with the same dignity and respect, and that amazing quality would cause me to rethink my return to the states.

That night at dinner, we closed another restaurant down, and it was starting to be a pattern. We were so engrossed in conversation that we failed to see customers leaving and waiters putting chairs onto the tables around us. As we crossed the street to the car, he took my hand, and it was magical and electrifying. Clearly, something was happening but neither of us knew what.

A true British gentleman, he brought me home, walked me to the bottom of the massive stone stairs that led up to the house, and kissed me on the cheek, again. At that moment I was still elated thinking that my future included returning to the states and finding that special relationship. It just goes to show you that what you want can be right in front of you, and unless you take a step back, it might be so close that you can't see it. I hadn't stepped back yet. A few weeks later I invited Paul over for a home-cooked meal.

I was having a few other guests and found him quite interesting and attractive. Elizabeth and I made scratch gnocchi, which blew the guests away. Once they had departed, Paul and I retired to the living room for what I thought would be interesting conversation. We soon found ourselves covered with my fur babies, Winston, Dakota, and Shakespeare, three Lhasa Apso boys.

They were energy personified and could barely contain their excitement that we were there waiting for them to pounce and play. Paul, consummate British gentleman that he was, had only kissed me on the cheek twice, and I don't know what I was expecting that night. I enjoyed his company and, clearly, he enjoyed mine. There was little doubt that we were sexually attracted to each other, and whenever we were on a date we were practically glued together. Now here we were on a couch alone, accompanied by a few glasses of wine, some music, and three fur babies.

He reached for me and gently pulled me toward him, kissing me with a fire and passion that I had not experienced for a very long time. We kissed gently, then passionately, with emotion that spilled over into a place I wondered if either of us had ever been to. Our passionate kissing lasted for more than an hour as he caressed my face and neck, but he continued being the respectful British gentleman that I had only just met. The depth of our passion exposed the feelings that were boiling just below the surface for both of us, but that we still failed to acknowledge for whatever reasons. A short time later, after more smoldering kisses, he left. His lips brushed against mine sweetly at the door, his fingers caressed my face, and he was gone. I was happy but truthfully surprised. I knew instinctively where this was headed and had no interest in pursuing that pathway, at least that was what I thought at that moment. I was headed back to the US and wasn't about to get emotionally entangled with anyone. The following morning, I received an email from him, that being the preferred method of communication, since he wasn't much for the telephone. He raved about my cooking and the amount of time that it had taken to make such an amazing dinner.

He was appreciative, grateful, and continued singing my praises for several paragraphs. Not once did he mention kissing my face off for more than an hour. He even told me about his eighty-six-year-old neighbor and how much of a mission she said making scratch gnocchi was. I hardly knew what to say about the passionate kissing that was a dominant force that night.

I struggled for a few minutes and then replied to his email: "Thank you for the compliments, and I'm not sleeping with you."

What followed was one of the most awkward silences I have ever experienced in my life. I waited and waited for a reply, but nothing came. I wondered if I had hit a hot button. I knew instinctively that once you spend an hour or so passionately kissing, the next step is bed, and that didn't really work for me. Yes, I found him incredibly attractive, very sexy, and he turned me on. But I had made up my mind years before that I was only going to stay in Africa for one year, which had already turned into two. I also had no intention of getting sexually involved with anyone because I didn't want the emotional hangover that comes with falling in love.

The whole, "OMG, I just had wild sex with someone that I was totally turned on by, got emotionally hooked in, but they are not," was not going to happen. That would be a disaster, and I was not going to allow it. I was moving back to the states and that was that. By the time I had finally finished my discussion with myself, Paul had replied.

"After I picked myself up off the floor, because that was never my intention, I realized that something was going on here, I don't know what it is, maybe it's love. If you're not afraid, we can see where this goes. At the very least, we could be friends."

There it was again. A struggle of conscience. What the hell was I going to do? I had plans. I had two men I was going to meet, one in New York and one in Chicago What was I going to do about that? This was not in my plans. But then one thing kept coming to the forefront of my mind. Paul had incredible qualities. He treated everyone with dignity and respect, and I knew that I could look forever and not find someone like that. That was an amazing and important character trait.

I struggled for a few days before finally coming to the decision that he was worth staying for. Yes, there was something going on here, and there was the chance that I could get hurt, and I had to be willing to risk it, if it meant my happiness. Finally, I responded. "Yes, there is something going on here and, yes, maybe it is love and I am willing to stay and see where it goes."

It meant that I could call him and say, "want to go to a movie?" and we could go to a dinner and a movie but not a movie and let me pin you against the wall.

One night, about a month into our "let's see where this is going" idea, my hairdresser friend decided to fix me up on a blind date with a wealthy guy he knew who owned a furniture store in Cape Town. Paul and I were still just dating, and so I accepted. It was to be another turning point in my life. It was a Sunday evening when he arrived, ear glued to his cellphone as he swept past my wonderful Elizabeth and into the living room, without so much as a hello. I entered the room to find him dressed to the "ones" in jeans and still on the phone. My three enthusiastic fur babies greeted him with lots of paws, but he angrily motioned them away. Strike one! We left for dinner, me dressed nicely, him in jeans and a T-shirt.

We got to the restaurant, and it became clear immediately that we were seated outside. Strike Two! I hate eating outside with the mosquitos and other flying creatures. Who knew, and I had left my jacket in the car. It was colder than a witch's tit outside, wind blowing, but he never even offered to go to the car and get my coat. He gave me his. Whoopee! Strike Three, he was out. The evening was a disaster, to say the least, and I vowed never to accept another blind date.

Over the next few months, Paul and I saw each other three or four times a week going to dinner and a movie, or just hanging out at the house watching television. We cuddled, we kissed, and one night I even lifted up my top and pressed my naked breasts against his naked chest. We held each other for a few minutes and then he went home.

The time we spent together was magical, and every moment we learned more and more about each other. The sexual chemistry was there, flashing brightly every moment we were together.

The attraction between us was undeniable. Our kisses were smoldering with passion, and we couldn't seem to get enough of each other. It was all we could do to keep from ripping each other's clothing off and making mad passionate love, but we held off for what seemed like an eternity as we learned more and more about who we were as people.

Then one night, we returned to the house after dinner and the sexual magnetism was too much. We ended up, clothing in a pile on the floor, naked, in bed, his hands running up and down my taut body, his lips caressing and kissing me from my neck to my inner thighs. We were in love with who we were as people, and this was the most magical way to show how much we loved each other. From that moment forward, our love was on display for all to see. Old-fashioned, yes, but magical, and it worked.

One night, a few months into our intimacy we were dining at a lovely Italian restaurant outside of Cape Town, and I took a sip of wine, looked at Paul, and said: "What about the paper?"

"You mean marriage?" he smiled lovingly.

"Yes."

"I married you when I moved in, but if you want the paper, then yes."

He took me in his arms, held me tightly and kissed my forehead, cheeks, and lips with such pent-up emotion.

"Georgene Summers, I love you," he whispered.

"I love you too, Paul Hunter."

With those words, we began to plan our wedding, a fairy tale that started with the words, "Once Upon a Time in a Land Far, Far, Away . . ." In my mind, this was going to be the wedding I had never had, that magical experience that is supposed to happen once in a lifetime, but often never happens.

In a perfect world, my parents would have been alive, and my father would have proudly given his blessings and walked me down the aisle, but that was not to be. My father had passed away in 1973 at the age of sixty-five, so that hope was long gone. My mother had followed him, although not for another twenty-plus years.

We planned our big day with the idea of including Greg and his small family, but they were to be an integral part of our wedding. I had hoped this could bridge the gap that hung like a storm cloud over our lives. The idea was inclusion rather than exclusion and of making them feel important.

No detail was too small, and I suppose we were prepared for everything except what ended up happening a few weeks before our wedding day, New Year's Eve, 2004. The weeks leading up to our impending wedding were uneventful except for the stress we both were experiencing. I had been married and divorced three times before, and there were always those nervous thoughts and feelings that invade your private moments of silence.

Was I doing the right thing? Should I just live with Paul and not get married again? Was he going to try to control me just as my other husbands had done?

Fleeting thoughts of what we were about to do and how our lives were intersecting mixed with concerns over any last-minute drama that might be created by my ex. As it turned out, he saved most of the drama for after the wedding.

The truth was, Greg arrived with enough drama for a hundred people, and looking back, he seemed determined to torpedo my big day for reasons known only to him. What I thought was a loving vision, bringing them to Africa for our special occasion, ended up as nothing more than a way for him to get more money out of his aging, wealthy grandmother. He planned it well and I fell for it! I bought right into the deception and the distraction and gave him precisely what he wanted. He always did have a flair for the dramatic, and this moment in time was no different.

After a dramatic, Oscar-worthy scene carried out in our swimming pool where Greg announced that the only person who ever really loved him was his grandmother, Vincent's mom, he demanded to go home. This was followed closely by a Greta Garbo–worthy exit, after which they flew on their "victim" wings directly to Beverly Hills and his grandmother. The Oscar-worthy performance continued unabated, and Greg got exactly what he wanted: money.

He told her that they had scrimped and saved for months to pay for their trip to South Africa for our wedding and we threw them out! Nothing could have been further from the truth. This was a total and complete fabrication, but one that resonated because he told it so well. Grandmother dearest rewarded these two conspirators with money and airline tickets back to Panama from Los Angeles. The truth was that my closest friend, my sister practically from another mother, Darleen, had paid for their trip as our wedding present. It was such a gift, and I was so appreciative of it.

In spite of the drama, our wedding plans moved along nicely, and six weeks before the big day, invitations had been sent to friends and family. They were hand-painted and conveyed the magic that we felt as soulmates, brought together in a Universe of chaos and confusion, halfway around the world in Africa. Our paths had crossed for a reason, and we were now destined to spend the rest of our lives together entwined in a love that had no boundaries.

Our invitations announced: **"Once Upon a Time, in a Land Far, Far Away, there lived a beautiful Princess and a handsome Hunter Prince."**

I had only been in South Africa for a few years but had made some inroads with regards to friends, so the invitations went to thirty people, plus some friends in the states that I hoped could or would come. In my previous three marriages, I had never had a real wedding, and so I was determined to make this the most incredible one ever, the first and the last one. The gardens in the back of my home were beautiful, with lots of greenery and brilliantly colored flowers, all part of the landscape.

An Olympic-size swimming pool stretched along the side of the house and massive stone steps led up to a used brick wall that sheltered my bunnies and chickens. Two of the chickens could fly, Henny Penny and her son, Pistachio, and fly they did. They spent many a day and night taunting the other chickens with their flying skills. Essentially, we had the setting and the entertainment all at our disposal because barring any unforeseen incidents, the chickens and bunnies could provide some moments of raw excitement. The basics were there, and now all I needed to do was embellish them to "over the top" for my fairy tale wedding. And so it began!

The wedding to my soulmate took place in Capetown, South Africa, on New Years Eve December 31, 2004 in the garden of my new home. It was a veritable fairy tale wedding with fifty guests, two that flew from California to be part of our magical day. It began with a rose petal handwashing ceremony at the foot of large stone steps that led to the garden. We stood by a beautiful Koi pond that was in the back of the house and then were joined in marriage under a traditional wedding canopy. The food was not traditional wedding fare but rather four courses of incredible Asian inspired cuisine created by a chef who had just returned from Vietnam. Our first dance was almost mystical as we melted into each other's' hearts and afterwards we cut the spectacular cake that was covered with white chocolate "cigars" and filled with three different layers of mouthwatering mousse and cake. It was an unforgettable day filled with magical moments that I shall never forget.

There was a cake made of three layers of magic and hundreds of white chocolate "cigars" that adorned each layer. Thin branches of white lifted to the sky above each with an offering of wedding Bugz Butterflies clinging on. The staff were to be dressed in sixteenth-century Mozart costumes, and one of them would be stationed at the foot of the massive stone steps that led up to the garden.

There, each guest would experience a "rose petal" handwashing ceremony before heading up the stairs, which were lit with old-fashioned lanterns. An enormous crystal chandelier was suspended over the swimming pool, in clear sight of the forty named bunnies and thirty-five named chickens who lived a stone's throw from the pool behind that four-foot brick wall in the backyard. Henny Penny and Pistachio, the South African ones, had a chicken's-eye view from their perch on top of the wall. The food was going to be prepared by a woman who had just returned from several months in Vietnam and, with her team would end up serving the most sumptuous courses of fish, chicken, duck, steak, and all of the trimmings, complete with an Asian twist, The lavish meal was topped off with a magnificent molten lava cake enveloped in freshly made whipped cream.

Hovering around the pool were several eight-foot-tall mirrors that greatly exaggerated your appearance as you passed by. The impact made you look like a character right out of *Alice in Wonderland* that had just fallen down the rabbit hole. Flowers of lilac and white cascaded over the tables like magical waterfalls.

Butterflies with glittering wings rose from the white-chocolate-cigar-covered cake and the beautifully decorated tables. Music filled the air with sounds of Michael Bolton, Rod Stewart and his American Songbook, and the classical strains of chamber music and Mozart and Chopin. The mood was one of elation and happiness.

My second mother, Elizabeth, looked like an African queen in a custom-made dress of bright yellow silk lined with a brilliant purple silk and an elegant hat of the same material.

She was the personification of elegance, and this was over the top. My wedding dress was handmade with layers of tulle and strings of Swarovski crystal beads that draped over the white corseted top. Dozens of tiny white buttons closed the corset at the back and a Parisian headpiece of crystals and feathers put the finishing touches on my elegant princess look.

I was Cinderella at the ball and Paul was my Prince Charming. Two very special friends flew in from California to complete our wedding party. One was my maid of honor, my dear friend and sister Darleen, and the other a fantastic gay friend, Justin, who gave me away. Less than a year later he sadly passed away, but Paul and I continue to celebrate his life and the magic that was him each and every day.

The only female rabbi in South Africa who would marry a Jew and a non-Jew presided over our wedding. She was amazing and invited our guests to be part of the occasion.

We stood surrounded by friends and family, Paul's daughter and son, and Elizabeth and her daughter, Patience, under a beautiful chuppah as we recited our vows. A dozen people stood and each one had magical words to say out loud about their wishes for us, which made the day even more special. Once the ceremony was over, the party began and we danced and ate amazing cuisine until long after midnight.

There are no words to express how magical our wedding was. It made up for the lack of celebration I experienced in my three other failed marriages. It was a day that I shall never forget, from the waiters in their sixteenth-century costumes, to the mouthwatering food and electrifying music. From the pungent rose petals that were thrown by well-wishers, to the mouthwatering white-chocolate-cigar-laden cake and the warmth from our friends, who were akin to family.

We awoke the next afternoon, as husband and wife, encased in a glow of captivating love and still a bit heady from the night before. The guests all gone other than our two amazing friends from California, and they were to remain with us for a few more days.

It was only after our celebration that I discovered my dear friend Justin was seriously ill and needed a surgery, one that he would not be able to get. He was a sixty-year-old gay man in desperate need of a kidney and sadly was not high on the list for donors. In keeping with who he always was, a fabulous friend, he didn't tell me of his illness in fear that it would ruin our wedding. So, he boarded a plane in Los Angeles and flew silently for twenty-five hours to South Africa, sick and in pain, to, as he said, "give me away." His friendship will remain forever in my heart.

The next time I saw him was in Los Angeles at the wedding of my dear friend Darleen, and he was in a wheelchair, still smiling, but unable to walk. He was still his irrepressible, devilish self. We were chatting away with several guests who had not met Justin, so I chimed in to introduce him.

"He gave me away at our wedding last December in Africa."

To which he quipped, "Yes, but you're back."

Always the comedian, always filled with a lot of levity and a smattering of sarcasm, always simply Justin. Months later he passed away leaving a legacy of love and creativity that will be remembered forever.

Life has its twists and turns and one never really knows how things are going to turn out, even though we think we do. We see our parents as invincible and our friends as trustworthy and loyal. We see ourselves as knowing far more than what we do and only realize how little we really know when it is too late to convey that to those that matter.

Only now do I realize how valuable the input of my parents was back then, and today, I wish I had listened more carefully to their words of wisdom. But like most kids, I was rebellious, stubborn, strong-willed, rude at times, hateful at times, deceptive, and I wrote the book on life, or thought I did.

In January 2012 my only son, Greg, passed away of complications from a failed bout with cancer. His death, unlike his life, was silenced by a lack of any sort of memorial service, either where he died, in Panama of all places, or where he had been born and lived most of his life, Los Angeles. His significant other chose not to have a service for whatever reason, and his death became anticlimactic in a world that was, for him, filled with drama, danger, and suspense. He lived for a time larger than life, challenging the world in his very own way.

He denied me the privilege of really knowing him, and sadly he denied himself the privilege of knowing me. As his mother, I was never able to really share with him the drama, danger, and excitement that I experienced, and that was both of our losses. I think had he allowed himself to, he would have really enjoyed knowing me. I am unsure who between us was the bigger loser.

My life today is a lot of things and none of them are routine or mundane. Paul and I don't fit into a particular mold, and for the most part, we are not welcomed by people who are our age.

We break too many stereotypes and smash too many molds of what we should be doing or looking like at our "age." It is fortunate that Paul and I met because we are both alike in so many ways. We would rather be zip-lining from one thousand feet above the jungle in the Eastern Cape, traveling at near breakneck speeds down eleven platforms, going from one to another until we reach the forest floor, than to be sitting around a table having brunch with a group of our "peers." We defy gravity and social norms in so many different ways.

Most of the people who are our peers and live near us act their age. They are graying, with some wrinkles, and their minds are on gardening, Zumba, or going on a cruise with three thousand other like-minded folks. They see us as aliens, and perhaps they are correct; after all, we met in Africa.

Most of them have never been outside the United States, much less to Africa, where to hear them tell it, there are lions and tigers and bears, oh no. I am constantly reminding people that there are no tigers or bears in Africa. As I age, I find that most people have a lot to say about places they have never been to and probably only read about in a travel article. While we don't fit in with most people our "age," we do fit in with people young enough to be our children or, scary as it sounds, our grandkids.

Our idea of having fun on a Sunday afternoon is going to a Drag Brunch in New London or New York, while our peers might be happy sitting around playing bridge or gardening. For that reason, we have a cache of young friends, and the only friends I have that are my age are my dearest "sisters" that I have known and loved for decades.

Looking back, I faced many challenges that would make most people cringe in fear, but ones that I turned into inspiration for myself and others. Did this begin when I walked on fire, or was it always underneath the surface of my being waiting to stand up and be counted? In this last quadrant of my life, it was inspirational that I stepped out of my comfort zone and declared I was a handbag designer, when I had no idea what I was doing. Inspiration was not allowing that foray into fashion to be sabotaged but rather to find a solution to the challenge at hand and still find a way for my nemesis to save face. There is inspiration to be seen from my Wall Street days as the only woman in the firm and one who hated the idea of cold-calling. But I did it. I rose to the challenge and reached my goal of making a lot of money. When I dipped my toe into the phone sex arena, it took courage and a dollop of insanity coupled with my desire to have freedom in my back pocket. It worked for twenty-plus years. I asked the Universe and a door opened and I stepped through, inspiring myself and others. That first safari in 1996 when circumstances sent me alone into the bush with just my guide, I ignored the cries of fearful friends about the dangers I was facing because I wanted something and I went for it. I didn't allow fear, theirs or mine, to control my life. I didn't allow myself to stay in the darkness that embraces fear and stops people from moving forward, preventing them from having experiences that will enhance and enrich their very existence. Moving alone to Africa was a mammoth step, but I never wavered and the Universe silently supported my decision and led me to the man who is my soulmate. Two whole people in a relationship that grows stronger each and every day.

Paul and I have now been married for seventeen years, and while this is the end of this story, it is really just the beginning of our lives together.

Today, I look back with feelings of great satisfaction knowing that I have done my best to inspire others to change their lives and have changed the lives of some very special people on the way. In

1996 on my very first safari, I met two young Maasai boys in a boma in the Maasai Mara. (A boma consists of cow dung huts, with openings in the walls to allow the sun to provide light and heat. It is surrounded by dried brush meant to keep the wildlife out.) Their father was a wizened man who told me he could no longer send his boys to school. I gave him the Kenyan shillings to pay for the boys schooling for that year after extracting the promise that he would do just that, send them to school. It turned out that I hadn't really thought this gesture out very well. The Maasai don't have bank accounts and one cannot send cash, so I had to figure out how to get the money into the right hands. Like I always say, there is a solution to every problem, just step outside the box and find one.

The following years I sent the school tuition money each year to a safari company in Nairobi who had helped with part of my initial safari and one of their guides made sure to pay the school for their books, uniforms, and tuition every year for the remainder of their school years.

I met Pilot when he was just a young boy, while in a boma in the Maasai Mara during my first safari in 1996. I sponsored his High School, and he found me twenty years ago on social media. He is now an amazing guide in the Maasai Mara and is married to the beautiful Selenia. They have two young boys and an incredible Foundation that is funded by donations from his safari visitors. They buy mattresses for schools, educate young Maasai girls and recently finished a project that placed two ten-thousand-liter water tanks in an area that serves two hundred villages, five thousand villagers. I am blessed to have them in my life as family.

ANGELS IN SIN

Then eighteen years ago one of the boys found me on Facebook. He is now an adult, married with two little boys and is a guide in the Maasai Mara.

He frequently calls me via FaceTime or WhatsApp in full Maasai garb, calling me "Mom" and Paul "Papa." Today he has his own safari company and takes gorgeous pictures of the wildlife in the surrounding areas and leads guests on amazing adventures. He and his wife pay it forward. They established a small foundation and they educate young Maasai girls.

They recently bought water tanks for a school and mattresses for the girls. We are currently working on a project to supply water to two hundred villages, five thousand people. I feel so proud of what they are doing and what part I was able to play in their lives. We are in communication several times a month and I love them like my own family. Another magical moment in my life happened in August 2020 when I was contacted with a friend request from a girl whose name was not familiar. She reached out and then immediately followed up with:

> Unknown girl: *Miss Georgene Summers, do you remember the Taita Discovery Center?*
>
> I was stunned for a moment as I had been there in 2002 while on another safari.
>
> Me: *Of course I remember.*
>
> Unknown girl: *You sponsored me in High School and now I am a teacher.*

My heart literally jumped from my chest and what followed have been some of the most loving, honest, and happiest communications of my life. Elizabeth has two little girls who are great posers and as cute as can be. Her husband passed away after a tragic road accident in 2017. We video chat, we Messenger, and we talk on the phone. She calls me "Mom" and Paul "Dad," and the girls call us Grandma and Grandpa, which I can't really wrap my head around. They are a blessing to us.

The part I played in her high school education was small in monetary terms, but monumental in how it changed her life and the lives of her girls.

A few months ago, I picked up one of my safari journals from the year 2002. I was leafing through the pages and found a paragraph that talked about sponsoring two children through high school after a written challenge I had posed at the school.

A blessing from my Nairobi safari in 2002 and the Taita Discovery Center. I met Elizabeth there and sponsored her High School. She found me on social media years later and has become my adopted daughter. Her two beautiful little girls, Rachel and Emily, are very special and growing up to be amazing young ladies. Paul and I got her mother running water and a two-thousand-liter water tank a few years ago, which was a first for her. Now mom can grow vegetables, drink nutritious water and not have to walk miles each day to collect the life-sustaining liquid. They are our family and our blessing.

Met Elizabeth and sponsored her High School, and now she is a teacher!

The winners were Elizabeth and a young man named Emerson. I cried tears of happiness as I read about meeting her mom Rachael at Taita in 2002. Today, I am happy to say that I am a part of their loving family, and that over the last few months we have provided running water to her mother and eleven other families that live close by. The water will provide Rachael with the ability to grow her own vegetables and sell them, giving her a small income.

In August 2021 our water project began with Elizabeth's brothers excavating the lengthy area that would house the pipes. The investment in this incredible project was small compared to the joy it brought upon completion. Now Rachael has running water and is also the source of water for her dozen neighbors who also have needed to walk miles each day to collect water and carry it back on their heads. We recently managed to install a two-thousand-liter water tank for Rachael so that in the drought, she will have rainwater to draw. The photos of her turning on the water for the very first time made my heart swell with pride and my feelings of joy went through the roof. I laugh inside when thinking that now Rachael is a bit of a businesswoman, charging a small fee to her neighbors for running water.

It is my hope that a part of my legacy is helping better the lives of other people, and I do it with great joy and happiness. My tears are tears of delight and pride. It makes my heart swell to know that I have done something to change the lives of a few special young people in another country, a world away.

Over my life I have traveled around the world alone and met many fascinating and interesting people. From bullfights in Mexico City to scuba diving in Acapulco, from the terra-cotta warriors in Xian China to the Taj Mahal in India, from landing in a bush plane on a strip of dirt with a greeting party of elephants and giraffes, to seeing hundreds of people sleeping on the top of cars as I landed in Delhi, India, from cradling a baby monkey in my arms in an open market in Bangkok, to eating a roasted pig in the Philippines, from holding a six-week-old baby Serval in my hands, to walking with two wild Cheetah at a wildlife rescue in Africa.

From watching a sex show in the red-light district of the Pat Pong in Thailand, to eating Korean barbeque in South Korea, from being Queen of the Night in my nightclub in Manhattan, to attempting to deliver a box of Cuban cigars to the Jordanian ambassador during my solo trip to Egypt.

I have lived, I have risked my life over and over with only a healthy fear at times, and I have reveled in every experience. While visiting the pyramids in Egypt, I photographed a "pyramid" of small children who were gathered around me. I rode on a camel, and it was brilliant. Later, I visited twenty-five mosques in Cairo by myself, my head and body respectfully covered at each one. I dined in a castle in England and climbed a mountain in Machu Picchu in my sleek Joan & David shoes (all that I had on my feet at the time). I swam underwater with a giant moray eel in Acapulco. I traveled around Sicily, entertained by princes and princesses for eleven days, and was entertained in the castle of a Rothschild. I rode on an elephant in Zambia twice and landed a plane in Rhode Island. I helicoptered over the Zambezi River in Zimbabwe two times and fed a giraffe in Nairobi. I drove a team of eight sled dogs in Calgary by myself and moved alone to Italy, where I lived for months in the Cassia and in Florence. I climbed the Great Wall of China and was fanned by two Mongolian women as I sat there exhausted.

I was privileged to be invited into the home of a Maasai family in a boma in the Maasai Mara, where they lived without electricity or running water. Their home was crafted from cow dung, with windows mere openings in the structure and a small open area in the front for the protection of their livestock at night.

Through my travels, I have learned that we are not an isolated country and should be tolerant and embrace other people, philosophies, religions, and cultures. I embrace them and make each visit important by making sure to know a few essential phrases in the language of that country. Over the years I have been lucky enough to get language lessons as a passenger in a variety of taxi cabs in New York City. Just another unseen benefit of living in the city.

Over the years, I have enjoyed other cultures and immersed myself in their way of life, going to their mosques and churches in various parts of the world, and even attending services now and again. I moved to Africa alone and met my husband, my soulmate, there. I am delighted to say that besides my two little families in Kenya, I have my second mother, whose name is also Elizabeth, a Xhosa woman who still lives in South Africa and is very much a part of our lives. She is amazing, my other mother, mother of the bride, and I adore and miss her.

Over the years my life has taken many twists and turns, but my regrets are few and my experiences rich, colorful, and immeasurable. I have learned many lessons over these years: There is a solution to every problem. One just has to look outside the box to find it. You can do anything you set your mind to so I never say "no, I can't do that." I don't know whether I can or not until I jump in with both feet. When one door closes another opens; I just have to be smart enough to walk through. Without risk there is no reward, so I take a lot of risks and have reaped the rewards. What I focus on expands, so I just focus on what I want, not what I don't have. I have made my life one of amazing memories and incredible encounters, ones that no amount of money can replace. I have lived, I have loved, I have been hurt, devastated, sad, happy, and introspective, but most of all I have endured, experienced, and enjoyed rich moments in time, all around the world.

Whether it was facing down a lion that was confidently perched on the hood of Hagai's car, ready to make short work of me, to crashing a wedding in Thailand. Whether it was climbing the Eiffel Tower or sitting in a tea house in Beijing, watching the dazzling art of face changing, where multilayered masks are changed at lightning speed by performers. Whether it was crashing my motorbike in Florence, a feat that landed me in the hospital, or moving to Italy alone into an apartment a block from where Aldo Moro was kidnapped. Whether it was climbing the Leaning Tower of Pisa or zip-lining in the Eastern Cape, I have lived!

Today I am at a rest stop in the eastern part of the states, where I have hung my hat for the past ten years, but it is only that, a rest stop and nothing more.

Tomorrow is another day, filled with amazing moments to experience, and I intend to do just that with Paul by my side. We are a team, and we are above all soulmates who found each other in a most unusual manner. If I look at my life, past and present, it is easy to see that the "apple didn't fall far from the tree" after all. I am like my mother.

She was for her time an adventurer, a risk-taker, a traveler experiencing life to the fullest. I just wish that I had "known" her then. This memoir is at the end, but my life with Paul is just beginning. There are many more adventures to experience. There are emotions to endure, sadness, joy, wonder, awe, amazement, gratitude, and hope all waiting to fill me with more life, and more love. So the end is my beginning, and I welcome it with open arms, regretting little, embracing life and love and all they have to offer, and knowing that there is much more out there for us to experience. And so, I say . . . *bring it on!*

www.ingramcontent.com/pod-product-compliance
Lightning Source LLC
Chambersburg PA
CBHW071853290426
44110CB00013B/1130